HUNTER

ROY BRAYBROOK

HUNTER

A personal view of the ultimate Hawker fighter

OSPREY

Published in 1987 by Osprey Publishing Limited
27A Floral Street, London WC2E 9DP
Member company of the George Philip Group

Sole distributors for the USA

Motorbooks International
Publishers & Wholesalers Inc
Osceola, Wisconsin 54020, USA

British Library Cataloguing in Publication Data

Braybrook, Roy
    Hunter: a personal view of the ultimate Hawker.
    1. Hunter (Turbojet fighter planes)
    I. Title   II. Baldry, Dennis
    623.74′64   UG1242.F5

    ISBN 0-85045-751-3

    Editor Dennis Baldry
    Art Direction Martin Richards
    Designed by Gwyn Lewis
    Filmset in Great Britain and printed through
    Bookbuilders Limited, Hong Kong

Title page In the 1960s manufacturers competed to produce photographs of stores that their aircraft had carried, or might conceivably carry somewhere in the future, and HAL was no exception. The Hunter is shown here with gunpack and a full load of 30 mm, the usual range of bombs, 68 mm, 80 mm and five-inch (127 mm) rockets, Firestreak and Fireflash (HAL)

Contents

Acknowledgements

The author is pleased to acknowledge the
invaluable assistance provided by the following
in the preparation of this book.
A W ('Bill') Bedford OBE, AFC
Air Vice-Marshal H Bird-Wilson CBE, DSO, DFC,
AFC
Roy Chaplin OBE
'Bob' Coles
Evelyn Covington and the staff of BAe-HQ
Library
John Godden
Alec Harvey-Bailey
Brian Isles
Gordon Isles
Trevor Jordan
the late Stefan Karwowski
Sir Robert Lickley CBE
R B ('Bob') Marsh
Peter Martin DFC
John Parker AFC
Air Cdre H A Probert MBE, MA and the staff of
the Air Historical Branch
Gp Cpt David Pugh
Duncan Simpson OBE
Vivian Stanbury
A E ('Bert') Tagg
Harold Tuffen
Ewald Wedin of Volvo Flygmotor
Barry Wheeler
Geoffrey Wilde of Rolls-Royce
R S ('Ron') Williams
former officers of the Rhodesian Air Force, and
the staff of the Public Record Office

This book is dedicated to the late John Dudley Stanbury, who, as chief draughtsman of Martinsyde, used his influence to have a young aviation enthusiast named Sydney Camm promoted from the company's works to a position in the drawing office. In so doing he initiated the career of a man who was to become for many years the technical head of Hawker Aircraft, and, taking in combination the number and quality of his products, probably the greatest fighter designer of all time.

Preface

Perhaps once in a generation a fighter design team produces an aeroplane that makes everything that their contemporaries are doing look like garbage. For one generation it was the Spitfire. For my generation it was the Hunter.

The Hunter was the last of the fighter line from the Hawker Aircraft stable. Since the second decade of this century outstanding high performance combat aircraft have been designed, developed and manufactured at Kingston-on-Thames in Surrey. This activity began under the name of Sopwith Aviation. It stopped very briefly after WWI, then restarted with a company that was destined to become the most famous of all British fighter manufacturers, Hawker Aircraft Ltd (HAL). More recently such activity has continued under the less glamorous designations of Hawker Siddeley Aviation and (ultimately) British Aerospace (BAe).

Strangely, some of the most successful aircraft developed at Kingston have attained their full potential in roles very different from those originally intended. Going back to WWI, the Sopwith Tabloid had been designed as a civil racing aircraft, but is best remembered for carrying out on 8 October 1914 the first-ever air raid on Germany. Two aircraft of the Royal Naval Air Service, each armed with a pair of 20 lb (9 kg) bombs, attacked the Zeppelin sheds at Düsseldorf and the railway station at Cologne.

Likewise, today's Hawk has achieved its greatest success in being selected to form the basis for the US Navy's T-45 carrier-capable advanced flying training aircraft, although it was originally intended simply to meet a Royal Air Force requirement (ASR.397) for a basic trainer to replace the Jet Provost. Similarly, the first generation of V/STOL Harriers, aimed at fulfilling an RAF demand for a Hunter replacement in the ground attack role, is to be seen in its most advanced form as the Sea Harrier air defence fighter for the Royal Navy.

This almost traditional change in roles was also true for the ultimate Hawker fighter, the Hunter. Though designed in the late-40s to pulverize a high-flying Tu-16 bomber, using the devastating firepower of four 30 mm Aden revolver cannon, the Hunter was destined to reach its peak many years later as a ground attack aircraft, though retaining a secondary air-air capability.

As the last true Hawker fighter, it was fitting that the Hunter should be one of the best-looking combat aircraft ever built. It handled very well in most respects, and it also inspired an unusual degree of affection in those concerned with its design, development, manufacture and operation.

My own love affair with the Hunter goes back to about 1950, when I went to my first real air display, at the Rolls-Royce test airfield at Hucknall near Nottingham. The first aircraft I ever saw that could be described as a jet fighter was the Hawker P.1052, a swept-wing research aircraft based on the P.1040/Sea Hawk, flown by chief test pilot (CTP) 'Wimpey' Wade. Compared to this relatively fast and quite attractive aircraft, the Gloster Meteors and de Havilland Vampires that followed in the show were distinctly pedestrian, and I came away feeling that Hawker Aircraft might be a good organization for which to work.

In September 1952, two years before I was to graduate, I went to Kingston for a preliminary interview and a look at the Hawker works. I still remember the vile smell of the tannery that used to be in the centre of the town, the rows of Sea Hawks in final assembly looking like metal sculptures of sea gulls, and at the far end of the production shop a mockup of what was referred to simply as the Sapphire-Hunter. Contrasting with the Sea Hawk's elongated teardrop shape, the Hunter, with its huge cylindrical fuselage and four massive channels for the new 30 mm cannon, looked a very lethal aeroplane.

Just a few days previously, I had been to Farnborough for my first SBAC Show. Westland showed the Wyvern TF4 turboprop strike fighter, which entered service with the RN in the following year. The swept-wing de Havilland D.H.110 fluttered to pieces before our eyes with tragic consequences. The Supermarine Swift was (wisely) restricted to demonstrating its high roll rate, but the undoubted star of the show was the Hawker Hunter WB195 (the second prototype) with the company's new CTP Neville Duke at the controls.

By the time the next SBAC Show came around (September 1953) the competition between the Hunter and Swift was hotting up, and the Supermarine aircraft was about to depart for Castel Idris in Libya, where its world speed record attempts would benefit from the higher ambient temperatures raising the speed of sound. Coordinated flying displays by two fighters of the same type had then become the fashion at Farnborough, one aircraft manoeuvring within sight of the crowd while the other attempted supersonic dives, barrel-rolling between sonic booms.

'Dave' Morgan and 'Mike' Lithgow flew the afterburning Swifts, while 'Bill' Bedford displayed the Sapphire-Hunter and CTP Neville Duke the blood-red record-breaking Hunter F.3 with afterburning Avon. For my money it was no contest: the Swift was an unlovely bulbous object, though its fuel capacity was doubtless necessary in an afterburning aircraft. For me the Hunter was (as the adverts claimed) 'The Finest Fighter Aircraft In The World'. My mind was made up: I wanted to design for Hawker Aircraft.

From 1954 to '56 I served a postgraduate apprenticeship with the Hawker company. I machined parts for Hunters. I did heat treatment on the bent spar-booms that were a feature of its wing design. I worked in the toolroom on the jigs and fixtures needed for its manufacture. I toiled in the deafening rivet-gun environment of the wing production line. I moved on to aircraft assembly at Richmond Road and the old airfield at Langley, where Sea Furies had been test-flown. Eventually I progressed to the flight sheds and servicing school at Dunsfold airfield, where I learned to give the Hunter its daily inspections and to correct systems faults. Finally, I returned to the design department at Canbury Park Road, to work in the production drawing office, the stress office, and the installations department, before gravitating to the project office. There I pushed my slide-rule on performance prediction and stability and control problems, before I was dragged off into the RAF for national service.

The project office was a special security area. It was also the department on which the company's future depended, and therefore Sir Sydney Camm (HAL's technical head) took a personal interest in it. I cannot say that I recall my first encounter with Sir Sydney, though one early meeting sticks in my mind. In those days it was a six-man office, and on this occasion I was standing in for the head of stability and control, who was on leave. A problem arose because my estimate of the maximum tailplane load for the P.1103 interceptor was several times higher than the preliminary estimate given to the stress office. Nobody placed much faith in the calculations of an apprentice, but nobody had time to check my figures. At this point Sir Sydney walked into the office and asked what the problem was. He then asked what was the weight of the aircraft, the tail arm, and the wing chord. With barely a moment's hesitation, he said that my estimate sounded sensible enough to him, and walked out. The great man, who had more experience than the rest of us put together (and was highly skilled in mental arithmetic) had spoken, and the problem no longer existed.

The other incident that sticks in my mind from that period was attempting to produce a better artificial feel system for the longitudinal controls of the Hunter. After a lot of thought I came up with a very complicated mechanism that kept the stick force per G within AP.970 limits. Then Neville Duke produced his own proposal for an infinitely simpler two-gradient spring feel unit that gave virtually the same results!

In 1958 I returned from the RAF to the Hawker project office, to work on Hunter developments and future projects. I well remember Sir Sydney some time later promising me fame and fortune if I could think of anything to do with the used Hunters that were flooding back to Dunsfold. I master-minded proposals to turn the Hunter into a four-seat liaison aircraft, a launch platform for the Bendix Penny target, and a rival to the U-2 high altitude reconnaissance aircraft. None of us could conceive at that stage that what overseas air forces wanted was simply a reasonably-priced refurbished ground attack aircraft that would last for many years.

In 1959 one of my great ambitions was realized when I flew in the Hunter Two-Seater. The weather was perfect, we reached Mach 1.05 in a dive, we clipped through the tops of clouds, and I had a personal aerobatic demonstration by Duncan Simpson, who was later to become CTP at Dunsfold. It was one of those idyllic days that you never forget.

It is very easy to become enamoured of a good-looking high performance aeroplane when you are young and fascinated by things aeronautical. For someone working for Hawker Aircraft, it would then have been equally easy to become disillusioned with the Hunter programme. In those days aircraft manufacturers kept their problems out of the public gaze more successfully than is the case today, but everyone at Kingston in the mid-1950s knew that the Hunter was encountering a new catastrophe almost every month.

Probably as a result of that experience, it was to become an unwritten rule in the Hawker project office, not to combine a new airframe with a new engine. This rule was clearly broken in the late 1950s with Ralph Hooper's P.1127 and its BE.53 engine, which led to the Harrier/Pegasus combination. The Hunter itself was even more of a problem, since virtually everything about it was new and untested.

Its first flight in 1951 came only 10 years after the maiden flight of the Gloster E.28/39 Pioneer, the first British aircraft to fly with jet propulsion. At the end of the war turbojet engines with centrifugal-flow compressors were just maturing, but British axial-flow compressors were barely out of the conceptual stage. Hawker Aircraft had enjoyed a long and fruitful relationship with Rolls-Royce, and when the axial-flow Avon ran into serious trouble it was rather as though someone had been completely let down by his oldest and most trusted friend.

In operational terms, the viability of the Hunter concept also rested on the immense power projected by its four 30 mm Aden cannon. If the aircraft was to succeed in its task, it had to achieve a quick, positive kill against a Tu-16, using a single short burst of fire. Unfortunately, associated with this high rate of explosive delivery were recoil loads and a gas generation rate completely outside Hawker's experience. The nose dipped, the nose gear stuck up, the structure surrounding the guns rapidly disintegrated, the engine flamed out, propellant gases exploded inside the nose, and discarded shell cases and links battered the airframe. Not all these problems occurred simultaneously, but the Aden installation in the Hunter certainly provided some unpleasant surprises. The P.1127 and V/STOL were a breeze compared with the Hunter.

In certain respects it can be argued that Hawker Aircraft was unlucky, for example, in regard to the airbrake problem that delayed the Hunter's introduction into RAF service. However, it is also arguable that part of the explanation for the aircraft's catastrophic beginnings was the company's lack of experience in dealing with the development of a jet fighter, a product that was far more complex than the piston-engined fighters on which it had built its reputation. When the company's first jet fighter, the P.1040 (a straight-wing aircraft with a centrifugal-flow R-R Nene) was ordered into production as the Sea Hawk for the RN, Hawker built 35, then dumped the aircraft and its many problems on its associate Armstrong Whitworth. This left Kingston free to continue with the next challenge (the Hunter), but it also deprived the Hawker team of invaluable experience in down-to-earth problem-solving for a comparatively modern fighter.

The Hunter's problems continued for year after bitter year. Like struggling with some multi-headed monster, it seemed that just when one problem had been solved, two more appeared, twice as bad as their predecessor. What made it all the more infuriating was that the Hunter was clearly only an interim aircraft: North American had the F-100 Super Sabre flying less than two years later, an aircraft capable of genuine transonic performance in level flight at altitude. If the RAF had been willing to switch to one of Hawker's supersonic proposals, there is no doubt that the company would have been delighted to drop the Hunter like the hot potato it had undoubtedly become.

However, in spite of all its problems, there was something about the Hunter that throughout the difficult years continued to inspire those concerned with its development in the belief that it would eventually be a success. Perhaps above all, it looked right. Simply to regard its beautiful lines was to realize that this was destined to be yet another success story for the Kingston design team, and for the company that had been in continuous production with its own fighters for longer than any other organization in the world. The rival Swift had been wrong from the outset; it was obviously doomed to failure. The Hunter was going to be right, though (with hindsight) it was to take far longer than anyone imagined at the outset.

And then suddenly all the major problems were in the past. The Hunter still had some faults, but it was also on the way to becoming one of the greatest combat aircraft of all time. The USAF tested it against the F-86 Sabre, then America paid big money to have it built in Belgium and the Netherlands. After one of the most detailed comparisons ever made, it was chosen for the Swiss Air Force in preference to a wide range of Western and Soviet competitors. The RAF told Hawker not to bother submitting the Hunter for evaluation as a Venom replacement in the Middle East, since it stood no chance of being selected, and yet it won.

Smaller air forces began to pay large sums (far more than we thought the market would stand) for extensively reworked pre-used Hunters. Test pilots began to refer to the Hunter as a datum against which to judge the handling characteristics of other aircraft. Other fighters of its vintage fatigued to pieces, were easily overstressed, and suffered from pilot-induced oscillations (PIOs) at high airspeeds. The Hunter just steamed on regardless, like some beautiful battleship.

One day, decades hence, the last Hunter will be taken out of service and buried in some museum. When that eventually happens, perhaps its best epitaph will be 'Bill' Bedford's words: *It looked good, it flew well, and people bought it*'.

Roy Braybrook
Ashtead,
Surrey
October 1986

Introduction

The Hunter is an important aircraft in not just one, but several respects. In regard to its early days with the Royal Air Force, it was that service's first British-built production fighter of any consequence to have an axial-flow turbojet engine, the first to have a swept wing, and the first to use four of the new 30 mm Aden cannon. It thus represented a massive advance over the Gloster Meteor that it superseded.

Viewed in an aerospace business context, it was the most successful of post-war British fighters, with 1,972 new-built and 574 rebuilt to meet later market demands. The Hunter is also remarkable for its longevity. Unlike contemporaries such as the F-84F Thunderstreak, F-86 Sabre and Dassault Mystère, the Hunter still remains in service with some very serious air forces, more than 30 years after attaining initial operational capability.

The Hunter furthermore has a special significance, in being the last of the fighters designed by Britain's premier combat aircraft team. It was the product of men who had joined Hawker Aircraft in the 1920s and 1930s, and had been with the company throughout WW2. They were men who had designed fighters to meet the real demands of a shooting war, and had then gone on to make that difficult transition from piston- to turbine-engined fighters.

The P.1127/Harrier that came along later was (in preliminary design and general appearance terms) the product of a different generation. These younger men had more in the way of academic qualifications, but were often lacking in the aesthetic appreciation that Sir Sydney Camm and his team had for what he termed a 'glamorous' aeroplane. In fairness, it has to be added that it is extremely difficult to design a good-looking V/STOL fighter around a single vectored-thrust engine, but the P.1127, Kestrel and P.1154 certainly revealed no new horizons in artistic achievement. As it happened, by the early 1960s Kingston was operating under the name of Hawker Siddeley Aviation, so the Hunter can quite accurately be described as the ultimate fighter from the Hawker Aircraft stable.

Whether the Hunter also qualifies for the title of the finest post-war British fighter depends on how the English Electric Lightning is viewed. Those who were concerned with its development doubtless feel that it had a useful rate of climb and service ceiling, and that it handled quite well (some pilots said 'like a large Hunter', which was praise indeed). At Kingston the Lightning tended to be regarded as an experimental aeroplane with a bizarre engine arrangement, an aircraft that had been given a weapons system and ordered into production as a low-cost substitute for the Fairey project that was the technical winner of the OR.329 contest for an all-weather interceptor.

However, our criticism of the Lightning was muted, since it had been designed under the direction of 'poor old Freddie Page', formerly of the Hawker project office. Most people were 'poor old . . .' in Sir Sydney's book, especially if they had forsaken that heaven-sent opportunity to design fighters for Hawker Aircraft. It may be added that the Fairey FD.2 record-breaker and the winner of the OR.329 contest had been designed under the direction of 'poor old Bob Lickley', another 'refugee' from that same office.

Viewed in historical perspective, the real manifestation of the gulf between the Hunter and the Lightning was that one aircraft was accepted on an international scale and the other was not. The Hunter was operated by the air arms of 21 nations in Europe, the Middle East, Africa, Latin America and the Far East. The Lightning was exported only to Kuwait and Saudi Arabia and only to the tune of 54 aircraft. In the export market the real successor to the Hunter was the Dassault-Breguet Mirage series, which continued the theme of combining high performance in both air-air and air-ground roles with relative simplicity and affordability.

Whereas the Meteor and Vampire had been exported while France was still on her knees and before the US saw the need to arm the entire non-Communist world, the Hunter was sold not only much later but also in a tougher environment. Aside from keeping thousands in work, and providing the money that funded HSA's flashy new offices and the private venture work on the P.1121 and P.1127, the Hunter programme could have taught us everything we needed to know about the export market. In addition to generating world-wide contacts and a fund of goodwill (which undoubtedly did eventuate), the Hunter experience should have taught HSA and our rivals at BAC that the general export market demand was for a high-performance affordable multi-role aircraft. Instead of understanding the Hunter lesson, we in Britain tried with comparatively little success to sell the Harrier, Lightning, and Tornado.

To summarize, the Hunter was the ultimate Hawker fighter and technically a big step forward for its day, combining a swept wing, an axial-flow engine and powerful new cannon. Its outstanding combination of qualities produced for Hawker a commercial success that few companies have equalled in the field of combat aircraft. Before describing the aircraft's development and applications, the following discussion looks first at the background to Hawker's use of the swept wing and Rolls-Royce's use of the axial-flow turbojet, the two features that were to provide the springboard for a quantum leap in performance by Britain's second jet fighter generation.

Chapter 1

The Company

To understand how Hawker Aircraft came to design the Hunter, it is worthwhile to appreciate something of the company's background and design philosophy. Its reputation was first established in the late 1920s and in the '30s with a succession of good-looking biplanes. The RAF invariably had a Hawker aircraft in front-line service, and Hawker aircraft always exported well.

To detail some of Kingston's big-number products, the Horsley sold 136, the Hart 1,031, its Osprey naval counterpart 138, the Fury 262, the Demon 306, the Hind 582, and the Audax 719. Turning to piston-engined monoplanes, the Hurricane had a production run of 14,027, the Typhoon 3,276 and the Tempest 1,402. The post-war Fury and Sea Fury accounted for a further 940 airframes. Together with the lesser successes, a total of 23,535 piston-engined Kingston-designed aircraft were built under the Hawker name, increasing to 41,727 if Sopwith aircraft are included. The only British manufacturer to surpass this figure was de Havilland with 43,134 (including considerable numbers of civil aircraft), although both Avro and Vickers each produced more than 30,000 aircraft.

It may have been an inevitable result of being in the fighter business for a long time, that the company became fundamentally conservative in its outlook. It was certainly a shock to this writer, on joining the Hawker project office in the mid-1950s, to find how difficult it was to get the company to gamble on any kind of technological advance. It would have been futile for any of us to draw a fighter with the tail-first layout that led (for example) to the Saab Viggen. The idea of combining half a dozen advanced technology ideas in a single new project (as General Dynamics did with the F-16) would have been seen as the height of irresponsibility.

A Hawker aeroplane was essentially something that looked good, handled well, met RAF requirements, did not kill its pilots, was easy to maintain, and (a point that is not always appreciated) was fundamentally flexible in its operation. It might not be the fastest in-service aeroplane in the world (though this had been true on occasion), but it was a good, honest aeroplane. It is very easy to scoff at this conservative approach, especially now, when astronomic R&D costs oblige manufacturers to achieve a massive advance to justify any new project. However, Hawker Aircraft had come to this philosophy after a great deal of experience, some of which had been painful.

The fact that the rear fuselage of the early Typhoon had been prone to flutter at high speeds was still remembered long afterwards as a blot on the company's record, and on the dependability of the stress office. This was somewhat unfair, as the fault was so obscure that the problems could not have been forseen. The elevator mass balance weight happened to be positioned so that fuselage bending induced destabilizing control inputs.

On this conservative theme, in the post-war years some British companies were quick to adopt a new family of aluminium alloys that promised a small weight saving. Camm preferred to wait and see, and it turned out that his attitude had been correct: these new alloys proved to be much more prone to fatigue failures. Hawker Aircraft might not be the first to employ new ideas, but nor did its aeroplanes come unglued in mid-air.

This conservative approach was undoubtedly one factor in Gloster and de Havilland taking the lead in jet fighter development during the war years. The other principal factor was that Hawker Aircraft was largely occupied throughout the war with a highly successful piston-engined fighter series that was the subject of continuous development. The Hurricane, which had first flown on 6 November 1935 and entered service in December 1937, was the basis for several major derivative designs. The Typhoon first flew on 24

February 1940 and was the subject of constant refinement to stay abreast of the Focke-Wulf Fw 190 series at low level. The thin-wing Tempest flew on 2 September 1942, and in due course accounted for 638 of the 1,771 V-1 flying bombs destroyed by the RAF. The Tempest II had its maiden flight on 28 June 1943 and required a major development effort from the company, but arrived too late to see action. The Sea Fury flew on 21 February 1945, and entered service with the RN in 1947.

To have diverted experienced design effort to jet fighters during the war would have had an adverse effect on the qualitative balance between British and German piston-engined fighters, probably without any significant improvement in the jet fighter situation. The gas turbine engine was simply not a war-winning development, since it was running on too late a timescale.

The Meteor I that saw very limited service with the RAF just before the end of the war was certainly a poor combat aircraft, and it is doubtful whether even the Hawker team could have achieved anything substantially better with the engines then available. From a commercial aspect, once Gloster and de Havilland had produced the first British jet fighter generation, there was no great point in Hawker switching its development effort to jet-powered aircraft until a new

Top left One of the world's leading advocates of single-engined fighters, Sir Sydney Camm was chief designer of Hawker Aircraft for approximately 40 years. He was responsible for 52 different types of aircraft, of which around 26,000 examples were built (BAe)

Above The Gloster E.28/39 'Pioneer' in flight It first left the ground on 15 May 1941 at RAF Cranwell, with Flt Lt P E G Sayer at the controls. It was powered by a Whittle W.1 turbojet of 860 lb (390 kg) thrust

generation of turbojets became available, and new requirements arose for naval jet fighters and a second jet fighter generation for the RAF.

The fact that there was no call for a Hawker jet fighter to enter service before the early 1950s does not mean that jet-propelled aircraft were not studied until after the war, although the design staff was working under great pressure and in unusual conditions. Shortly after the first bomb had fallen on Kingston, the experimental drawing office (headed by Frank Cross), the stress office and various technical offices were moved to Claremont House in Esher for the duration. Roy Chaplin, who was later to become chief designer when Camm was made chief engineer, was left in charge of design work that remained at Canbury Park Road. With the move 'Bob' Lickley (who had formerly worked in the stress office) became head of the project office with a staff of four: Vivian Stanbury (who in 1946 succeeded Lickley), 'Freddie' Page, Alan Lipfriend (who subsequently became a high court judge), and 'Charlie' Dunn (who became a university lecturer).

Claremont House had been built by Clive of India, and at different times had housed many members of various royal families. At the outbreak of war it was a Christian Science boarding school for girls. The school was evacuated to the West Country to escape the bombing of the London area, though the *Luftwaffe* then switched targets and pounded the West Country. In some respects this elegant house and its attractive grounds provided a significant improvement over the company's old offices in Canbury Park Road. As recalled today by Harold Tuffen (who was to play a key role in the design of the Hunter), the house had a swimming pool and several grass tennis courts, and the Hawker team created a small golf course on the grass area fronting the house. The possibility of the house being bombed was quite real, although the entire building was covered in camouflage netting. Camm and his wife spent the nights in the basement accommodation.

While the Kingston production drawing office under Chaplin continued to work on series-built aircraft, the Claremont team was busy with a

The Gloster E.28/39 was the first British aircraft to be powered by a jet engine. Although intended purely as a technology demonstrator, its basic layout was completely representative of future jet fighters

whole series of proposals, many of which never saw the light of day. With the establishment of a project office under Lickley, a new series of designations was introduced, beginning with the P.1000. This series was continued post-war at Canbury Park Road and then Richmond Road, until revised in the early 1960s to provide uniformity within HSA. This change was brought in by redesignating the P.1163 V/STOL project as the HS.1170.

The P.1000 was to have been a fighter with a large cannon in the nose and a Napier Sabre piston engine in the centre fuselage, driving two wing-mounted propellers by means of shafts and bevel gears. The P.1004 was a high altitude fighter to F.4/40, a specification that led to the Westland Welkin. The P.1005 was a light bomber to B.11/41, powered by two Sabre engines, and essentially a 'Super Mosquito', the requirements for which was later abandoned.

In common with other British fighter manufacturers, Hawker received information on the early gas turbines being developed by Frank Whittle's

Power Jets. The first Hawker jet project was based on the P.1105, using Whittle engines in place of Sabres. However, other British companies were already flying hardware. The first British jet-powered aircraft was the Whittle-engined Gloster E.28/39, which first flew on 15 May 1941. The Gloster Meteor was designed to F.9/40 and had its maiden flight on 5 March 1943. It was initially powered by two 1,500 lb (680 kg) de Havilland Halford engines, though other Meteor prototypes were employed as testbeds for the Metrovicks F.2, Power Jets W.2, Rolls-Royce W.2B/23 and Rover W.2B. Deliveries of the Meteor with the 1,700 lb (770 kg) W.2B/23 Welland began in July 1944. The twin-boom de Havilland Vampire was designed to specification E.6/41 and flew on 20 September 1943 with a 2,700 lb (1,225 kg) D.H. Goblin I. Initially named Spider Crab, the Vampire narrowly missed entering service before the end of the war.

Today, Stanbury recalls that Camm's attitude to jet engines was *enthusiastic but cautious*. As noted earlier, design effort was heavily committed in regard to the F.2/43 Fury (originally known as the

The first production British jet fighter was the Gloster Meteor F.I, powered by Rolls-Royce Welland I engines. Deliveries to No 616 Sqn began in July 1944 with EE221/G (above), the 12th F.I and the first operational Meteor (Gloster Aircraft)

Tempest Lightweight Fighter Development) and the N.22/43 Sea Fury, in the development of which Hawker had been assisted by Boulton-Paul and others. Stanbury also recalls drawing a Sea Fury with a turbojet literally in place of the Centaurus piston engine, an approach similar to that followed by Yakovlev in the development of the Yak-15 from the Yak-3U.

On the subject of wartime studies, Sir Robert Lickley writes that 'from 1942 onwards the small Hawker design office was heavily overloaded. Hurricane variants, Typhoon developments, Tempest I, II, and V, and the start of project work on the Sea Fury took up all the time, plus the B.11/41 . . . gave little time for further development'. He also notes that 'Until the Nene, the performance available from a single-engine jet from Hawker would not exceed by much the hoped-for Tempest I development'.

The first Hawker project designed from the outset around a turbojet engine is believed to have been the P.1035 of 1943, based on the Rolls-Royce B.41 (Nene). Unlike the Sea Fury modifica-

tion, this had the engine in the centre fuselage, with the pilot ahead in what was to become a conventional jet fighter layout. Having a double-sided centrifugal compressor, it seemed natural to Stanbury that the engine should be fed with air from either side, rather than from directly ahead (ie, from a nose intake). The project was therefore given intakes in the wing leading edge roots, feeding air through ducts with 90-degree bends to the engine. In order to minimize thrust loss in the jetpipe and heating problems in the rear fuselage, while maximizing fuel volume, Hawker schemed a bifurcated (ie, split) jetpipe with two nozzles in the wing trailing edge roots. Perhaps surprisingly, the company succeeded in patenting this form of jetpipe.

Various refinements led to the project being redesignated P.1040. This proposal appeared to be so promising that limited detail design work was begun on a private venture basis. However, by 1946 the RAF's Meteor had improved considerably (having begun life slower than the contemporary Tempest V), and Air Ministry interest in the P.1040

The D.H. Goblin-powered de Havilland Vampire is illustrated here by an English Electric-built, clipped-wing FB.5. The twin-boom layout gave a short jetpipe, helping to make possible an unusually light weight (de Havilland)

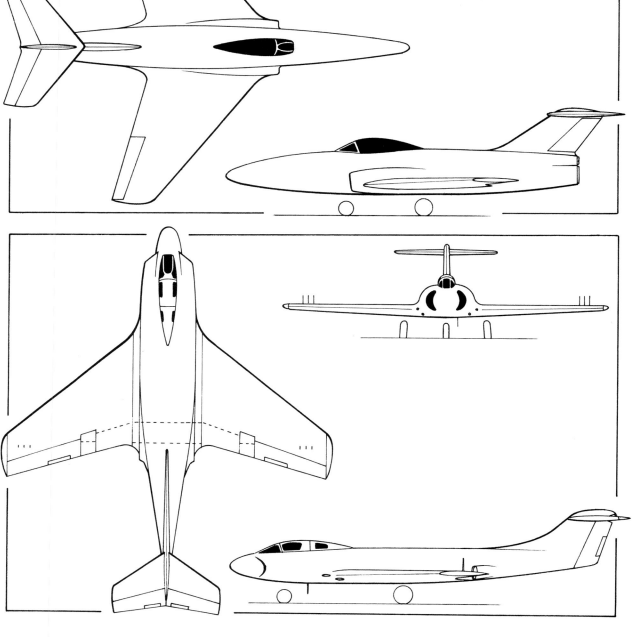

An early Hawker project study to specification F.43/46 for a single-seat day fighter. Most such projects were based on two Rolls-Royce AJ.65 Avons, but some (like this one) had a single AJ.65 and a liquid-fuel rocket motor
(Mike Badrocke)

Air Ministry specification F.44/46 called for a two-seat day/night all weather fighter with two engines. This Hawker study is mainly noteworthy for the use of intakes in the sides of the nose
(Mike Badrocke)

waned. On the other hand, the Royal Navy had yet to commission a jet fighter, hence the P.1040 proceeded under specification N.7/46, which led to an order for three prototypes and eventual production as the Sea Hawk. It may be added that Meteor improvements also killed off Gloster's own single-engined GA.2 Ace which was designed to E.1/44 and first flew on 9 March 1948.

Shortly after the end of the war, the Air Ministry appears to have made a policy decision in favour of twin-engined fighters, at least for the short-term. This was presumably based on the idea that the threat of the nuclear bomber demanded a high climb rate, and that this could be achieved more easily with two engines rather than one. The immediate outcome was two specifications for twin-engined fighters: F.43/46 for a single-seat day fighter, and F.44/46 for a two-seat day/night all-weather fighter. In the event, the latter was fulfilled by the Meteor NF.11, but the former provided the basis for F.3/48, the specification associated with the P.1067 Hunter.

A long-term advocate of single-engined figh-

ters, Sir Sydney Camm went to Bentley Priory (Fighter Command HQ) and argued against F.43/46, though this did not stop the project office carrying out a number of design studies to both specifications. His advocacy of a single, reliable engine was (like the company's generally conservative approach) the result of many years of experience. In Sir Sydney's view, the fastest fighters had always been single-engined, and this had also proved to be the correct design philosophy for safety. Propeller-driven twin-engined fighters such as the Mosquito and Hornet had been a handful in single-engined approaches, and many pilots were to be killed in Meteors while practising engine-out landings.

The preference for a single engine undoubtedly served Hawker Aircraft well for decades. However, it can also be argued that on a later timescale, once the need had gone for the engines to be set well out from the centreline (to keep the propellers clear of the fuselage) the company's bias against twin engines was misleading, as it eliminated the possibility of designing heavy multi-role fighters in

The prototype P.1040, devoid of hood and rudder trim tab, at Langley, with a Tempest V and Sea Furies in the background. Note the double-curvature windscreen, and the square-cut heat shields, which were quickly replaced by pen-nib fairings
(BAe)

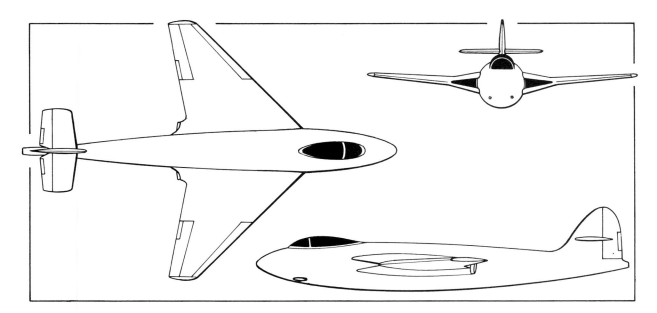

the class of the McDonnell Douglas F-4 Phantom II.

Despite this opposition in principle to twin-engined fighters, the project office carried out a large number of studies around F.43/46 and F.44/46, mostly based on the use of two Rolls-Royce AJ.65 engines. The AJ.65 designation was the manufacturer's shorthand for 'axial-flow jet engine of about 6,500 lb (2,950 kg) static thrust'. Around 1948 this designation was changed to the name 'Avon'. As an alternative to two AJ.65s, some of the Hawker projects of this series had a single AJ.65 and either one or two liquid-fuel rocket motors, each of 2,000 lb (907 kg) thrust. Some of the projects drawn had straight wings, while others had wings of moderate sweep.

The first-ever swept-wing Hawker project was probably the P.1047/1, which appears to have been drawn in August 1944 by Stanbury and approved by Lickley. Described as a 'Hawker Fighter: Interceptor Type', it was clearly derived from the P.1040, but the single B.41 (Nene) engine was supplemented by a liquid rocket in the extreme rear fuselage. Relative to the Sea Hawk, the armament was halved from four to two 20 mm Hispano cannon, and the spans of the wing and tailplane were considerably reduced. Interestingly, leading edge slats were proposed, a feature used on several wartime German swept-wing projects,

and later on the North American F-86 Sabre series, although this complexity was to be avoided by Hawker.

Some indication of the very limited knowledge of swept wing design then prevalent in the UK was that Stanbury's drawing retained the dihedral angle of the straight-wing P.1040. It was soon learned that sweepback produces its own dihedral effect, hence this physical upsweep would have given an excessive rolling moment in sideslip, probably evidenced by Dutch Roll at low airspeeds.

Discussing the German-inspired advent of wing sweep in an interview with this writer, Stanbury commented that 'sweepback was news to us', and that 'it looked terrible'. It is interesting also, that in talking of the preliminary design work that led to the Hunter, Stanbury talks in terms of two quite distinct phases: 'the German P.1067', and 'the Hawker P.1067'. He frankly accepts that the first P.1067 drawings were inspired by German swept-wing projects, featuring nose intakes and high-set tails.

In the light of Stanbury's comments, it may be worthwhile to digress at this point to summarize the reasoning behind the move to swept wings, and the line taken by German jet fighter developments toward the end of the war.

The P.1046/1 is believed to have been the first Hawker project with a swept wing. It appears to have been simply a P.1040 with the straight wing replaced by a wing of moderate sweep and high taper. Armament seems to have been changed from four 20 mm to two 30 mm cannon
(Mike Badrocke)

Chapter 2

The Sound Barrier and the Swept Wing

Until the 1940s the speed of sound and the associated compressibility characteristics of the atmosphere were of little concern to aircraft designers. For all practical purposes an aircraft's profile drag coefficient (ie, that at zero lift, governed by its shape and surface roughness) was a fixed quantity, producing a drag force that increased in proportion to air density and the square of aircraft speed. Doubling speed at a given altitude thus quadrupled profile drag. Lift-induced drag admittedly decreased as speed increased, but in the region of the aircraft's maximum speed this was a minor effect in comparison with the rise in profile drag. A one per cent improvement in maximum speed demanded two per cent more thrust and three per cent more power, hence progress in fighter speeds was basically a matter of steadily increasing the output from aero-engines.

But when high performance fighters such as the P-51 Mustang were dived from altitude, it was found that, instead of accelerating steadily, they encountered a sudden increase in drag, combined with severe buffeting and a loss of control effectiveness. As such aircraft approached the speed of sound, the local airflow was reaching supersonic speeds, first over the revolving propeller blades and later over the airframe. Unfortunately, in decelerating back to subsonic speed, the airflow tends to produce a shock wave, and in passing through this shock the air loses energy. These losses resulted in a drop in propeller thrust and a steep increase in airframe drag.

From a modern viewpoint, people were trying to push comparatively blunt objects to speeds for which they were completely unsuited. At the time the problem was viewed quite differently, and the idea got around (especially in the UK) that even with a more suitable form of propulsion a conventional manned aircraft would never penetrate 'the sound barrier'. It was clear that the speed of sound had been exceeded for many years by solid objects such as bullets and shells, but it was feared that lightly-built airframes with wings large enough for normal airfield operation would not be able to endure the severe buffeting produced as a result of supersonic flow.

This gut-feeling that the 'sound barrier' would prove to be not only impenetrable but also highly dangerous may have been the reason for cancellation of Britain's M.52 supersonic research project in February 1952. Designed by Miles Aircraft to specification E.24/43, the M.52 was to be powered by a Power Jets W.2/700 afterburning

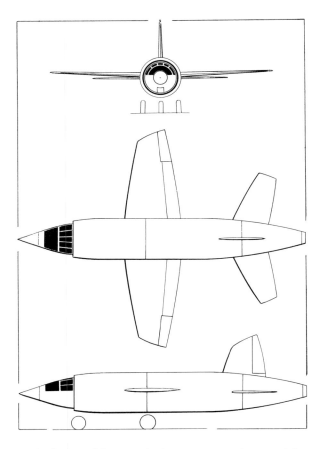

turbofan, and featured a biconvex-section straight wing tapering from 7.5 per cent at the root to 4.9 per cent at the tip. The pilot was in a semi-supine position in a jettisonable capsule that acted as the shock-cone for an annular intake. The M.52 had fully-powered flying controls and an all-moving tailplane. It was designed to reach a speed of Mach 1.5 at 36,080 ft (11,000 m).

At the time of the cancellation, Sir Ben Lockspeiser, Controller of Research and Development, stated that *The impression that supersonic aircraft are just around the corner is quite erroneous, but the difficulties will be tackled by the use of rocket-driven models. We have not the heart to ask pilots to fly the high-speed models, so we shall make them radio-controlled.'* However, it has also been suggested that the real reason for the cancellation was that those responsible for the government's research establishments were embarrassed by their failure to have appreciated the value of wing sweep in delaying compressibility effects to high subsonic speeds, and that the M.52 was abandoned purely because it had a straight wing.

Whatever the background to the M.52

cancellation, the US went ahead with its own supersonic research programme, initially with the straight-wing Bell X-1. The rocket-powered, air-launched X-1 first flew on 9 December 1946, and on 14 October 1947 it first reached supersonic speed, attaining Mach 1.06 at 70,140 ft (21,385 m). The pilot on this and many of the X-1's subsequent flights was a USAF officer named 'Chuck' Yeager, who went on to become a general, and was probably the most famous test pilot of all time.

In a recent conversation Brig Gen Yeager told this writer that 'The great thing about the X-1 programme was that it showed the need for a flying tail. We had a nitrogen system for tailplane trim, and also for cockpit pressurization. You lost the elevators at Mach 0.92, and flew it on tailplane trim. North American heeded the advice. The F-86A had an electric tail, and the F-86E had the first real hydraulic flying tail, whereas the MiG-15 had a ''welded'' tail.'

America obtained a vast amount of data from its manned supersonic experiments. Britain's model trials ('Operation Neptune') produced little information, though one of these Vickers models did reach Mach 1.38 on 9 October 1948. It is relevant to note that in March 1957 Aubrey Jones, then Minister for Supply, stated that *'In so far as we are behind in the field of fighter aircraft, it is because we were more reluctant than the Americans to hazard men and lives in experimenting in supersonic flight'*.

Sonic Challenge

To return to the discussion of aerodynamic principles, the fundamental problem was that in passing over (for instance) a wing, the air acquired a 'supervelocity' due to the aerofoil's thickness and the lift on that wing. While free stream air might be moving at only Mach 0.8 relative to the wing, the local airflow over the surface could easily reach Mach 1.2. As the flow then slowed to match free stream conditions at the trailing edge, a shock wave was often produced. Energy losses in the shock wave manifested themselves as an increase in drag on the aircraft. However, the sudden increase in pressure across the shock would also slow the boundary layer air. If this layer actually reversed direction and started moving forwards, the main flow would separate from the wing surface, giving more drag, buffeting, and a loss of effectiveness in the trailing edge controls.

To design an aircraft capable of high subsonic

The Miles M.52 was a supersonic research project, powered by an afterburning turbofan. It was cancelled in February 1952, officially to eliminate the risk to the pilot's life. It may also have been felt that its straight wing bore no relation to forthcoming operational designs (Pilot Press)

speeds in level flight, it was therefore necessary, in addition to giving it a great deal of thrust, to minimize these local supervelocities. This would delay the formation of shock waves to higher flight speeds, and also keep the shock waves as weak as possible.

The aircraft could be given a long, slender fuselage, and the canopy could be faired gently into the upper fuselage lines, although this spoiled rearward view. In regard to the wing and tail surfaces, the obvious move was to continue the trend toward lower thickness/chord ratios. However, there were increasing practical problems as the wing became more slender. For one thing, weight increased rapidly. In very simple terms, as wing depth decreased, skin thickness had to increase to give the same bending strength, and wing weight went up with skin thickness. To some extent this problem was to be alleviated later by the development of new forms of wing construction (eg, machined skins with integral stiffeners), but in the 1940s the idea of building a really thin wing for an acceptable weight was a very serious challenge. Thin wings also promised to be more complex, since they might well require slats to prevent flow separations from the leading edge at high angles of attack (AOA). Designers of that period needed an alternative way of

increasing speed, rather than gradually moving toward a solid-built, wafer-thin, razor-edged straight wing.

The Swept Wing

The idea of sweeping a wing in order to delay the drag rise caused by the formation of shock waves had been postulated by Busemann at the 1936 Yalta Conference. However, for most practising designers in Britain the concept of a swept wing remained unknown virtually until the end of the war. Germany was then much further advanced in terms of aerodynamic research, though the practical application of swept wing theory was extremely limited.

Three German jet-powered aircraft types had entered service during the second half of 1944. Of these, the Arado Ar 234 light bomber had a straight wing, the Me 262 fighter had a very limited sweepback, reportedly to counter a CG shift during design (as in the case of the earlier DC-3), and the Me 163B probably used sweepback only to make its tailless layout more practical. German designers were undoubtedly aware of the potential benefits of wing sweep in terms of delaying the drag rise, but they also knew the potential problems, and were evidently happy to

The Me 262 was technically the most significant jet fighter of the WW2 period, combining axial-flow engines, swept wings with leading edge slats, and an armament of four 30 mm revolver cannon. It out-performed the Meteor I by a large margin

leave the swept wing for a second jet fighter generation.

On the Allied side, the promise and the problems of the swept wing were not really appreciated until German research reports and details of German fighter projects became available at the end of the war. Immediately after VE-Day, a series of British teams combining experts from industry and the Ministry of Aircraft Production were sent to Germany to establish how far aviation development had progressed.

Although not directly related to the swept wing story, it is of interest that Hawker's Roy Chaplin went out with one of these teams, his unit being flown by RAF Dakota to Frankfurt, to investigate work done by Dornier at Friedrichshafen. This was in the French Zone, so the industry representatives were kitted out in RAF uniforms to eliminate any doubt over their nationality. Chaplin was able to examine the Dornier works and the experimental shop hidden in nearby woods. The latter facility housed the twin-engined Do 335 fighter-bomber, the fastest production propeller-driven aircraft in the world. The type first flew on 26 October 1943, and more than 40 were built before the end of the war. Maximum speed was approximately 480 mph (770 km/hr). The Do 335 had a slightly swept wing, but this particular investigation does not appear to have thrown any new light on German swept-wing research.

The German Lead

It is clear that if a designer takes a wing of a given thickness, and gradually sweeps it aft, the thickness/chord ratio measured in line of flight reduces, since its physical thickness is unchanged and the stream-wise chord lengthens. However, German wind tunnel tests showed that the actual improvement in the speed at which the drag rise occurred was much better than this simple approach would suggest.

In order to provide a rough estimate of the actual value of wing sweep, it was initially taken that a shock wave would form when the component of local airflow velocity at 90° to the quarter-chord line reached Mach 1.0. We now know that shock-free flow is possible on a properly-designed straight wing with local airflow moving at up to at least Mach 1.3, so this basic assumption was highly conservative. Nonetheless, the idea of resolving local flow velocity into two components (along and across the wing) was a useful one.

In trying to establish how early tunnel tests compared with this simple criterion, the writer examined boxes of old reports still held at Kingston. The main sources of swept wing research data available in the UK in 1945/46 appear to have been reports from Völkenrode, the *Aerodynamische Versuchsanstalt* at Göttingen, and the *Gesellschaft für Luftfahrtforschung* in Berlin. In addition, there were records of interrogations of technical experts such as Dr Alexander Lippisch of Messerschmitt and Professor Kurt Tank of Focke-Wulf.

All this information indicated that sweep increased critical Mach No (ie, the speed at which profile drag coefficient suddenly increased) and reduced drag. On the other hand, the German experts pointed out that sweepback gave a lower maximum lift coefficient and aggravated tip-stall. This led to what they termed 'an abrupt variation in pitching moment', and what we would now call 'pitch-up'. Strangely, Kurt Tank thought that tip stall becomes less severe at sweep angles beyond 18°. Lippisch commented that tip-stall could be cured by the use of wingtip leading edge slats. The Germans also said that the increase in critical Mach No is in practice not as high as indicated by the 'cosine rule' (ie, by taking velocity components). This fall-short was ascribed to root and tip effects, reducing the local sweep of isobars and thus promoting the growth of shock waves.

German tunnel tests indicated that sweeping a 12 per cent wing (NACA 0012-64) back from zero to 30° (reducing streamwise thickness/chord ratio to 10.4 per cent) increased critical Mach No from 0.73 to 0.84. At altitude this would correspond to a speed increase of 63 knots (117 km/hr). Other tests indicated that the speed increase might be closer to Mach 0.08, but the improvement was still worthwhile. Taking the same wing to a sweep of 45° reduced thickness/chord ratio to 8.5 per cent, and took the critical Mach No to more than 0.90. German research also suggested that the speed improvement (as measured on isolated wings) would not be spoiled by the addition of a suitable fuselage, provided that this body was 'arranged symmetrically in the centre of a swept-back wing', but that the effect is often decreased by the presence of engine nacelles.

A summary of first-generation German projects was provided by Nonweiler's RAE Report Aero 2070, *'German High-Speed Aircraft and Guided Weapons'*. According to this study, the *Luftwaffe's* plan had been to terminate production of the Me

The Me 163 was a rocket-powered tailless swept-wing interceptor that flew its first operational missions against B-17s in August 1944. Its wheeled undercarriage was jettisoned after take-off, and it landed on a skid on grass, causing a number of spinal injuries

109 and Fw 190/Ta 152 series, and to purchase limited numbers of advanced piston-engined aircraft as an interim measure, pending availability of jet fighters. The interim use of new piston-engined fighters was based on the twin-engined Do 335 and the high-altitude Blohm und Voss Bv 155, derived from the Me 109. In addition to bridging the timescale gap, the Bv 155 was seen as an insurance policy against the failure of the new jets to perform well at altitude.

As the next phase of this plan, jet-powered combat aircraft were then to be introduced in three categories: A single-engined fighter exemplified by the Heinkel He 162 *Volksjäger*, a twin-engined aircraft with a crew of two or three (such as the Me 262 or Ar 234), and a multi-engined heavy bomber, instanced by the four-engined Junkers Ju 287. This last aircraft was the only one of the named examples to have a significant amount of wing sweep (25° forward sweep), but this was used primarily to take the wing structure aft of the bomb bay.

As stated earlier, the practical application of swept wings in wartime German aircraft was extremely limited, although wind tunnel testing of swept wings was far in advance of anything being done in Britain or the US. The Me 262 had only 12° of sweep, and a thickness/chord ratio of 10.9 per cent. The tailless Me 163B had 23° of sweep and a thickness/chord ratio tapering from 14.4 per cent at the root to 8.7 per cent at the tip.

Both the Me 262 and Me 163B were found to run into the drag rise at Mach 0.75. In the case of the Ju

287 it came earlier, but the rate of drag increase was less steep. The Me 262 succeeded in reaching Mach 0.86 in a dive, though this was associated with violent buffeting, increasingly nose-heavy trim, and extremely heavy ailerons. The Me 163B was flown to Mach 0.82 in a dive, but there it encountered a very strong nose-down pitch.

In discussing German wartime fighter projects of conventional layout (ie, ignoring the many tailless designs), perhaps the most interesting example in the Nonweiler report was the Focke-Wulf Ta 183, which was to be powered by a single Heinkel/Hirth turbojet of 2,860 lb (1,300 kg) static thrust.

The wing of the Ta 183 was to have an area of 244 sq ft (22.45 m²), a 40° sweep on the quarter-chord line, and a thickness/chord ratio of 11 per cent. All-up weight was given as 11,200 lb (5,080 kg), making it comparable to the MiG-15, a lightweight fighter by modern standards. Maximum level speed was estimated at Mach 0.70 at sea level, increasing to Mach 0.86 at 36,080 ft (11,000 m). Sea level rate of climb was put at 5,750 ft/min (29 m/sec). The Ta 183 was to be armed with either two or four 30 mm cannon, and it was planned that the wing would be skinned in wood, although the fuselage would be of conventional metal construction. Perhaps the most unusual feature of the design philosophy was that, if the elevators became ineffective, the ailerons could take over longitudinal control.

Additional material on wartime German studies is now available through the Public Record Office (PRO). For example, in September 1945 Dr Waldemar Voigt wrote a report on Messerschmitt's project investigations into single-engined jet fighters, comparing the relatively conventional P.1101, P.1106, and P.1110 with the tailless P.1111 and P.1112. Final conclusions had not been drawn at the end of the war, but wind tunnel data had indicated that a level speed of 540 knots (1,000 km/hr) could be achieved, corresponding to Mach 0.92 at altitude. The two tailless projects were found to give the best combination of maximum level speed and landing speed, but these designs were felt to be potentially dangerous at high speeds due to pitching moments (presumably the result of shock-induced flow separations). Voigt concluded that it should be possible to provide the same performance with less technical risk, using conventional (ie, tailed) designs.

Another useful document is a once-secret, top-

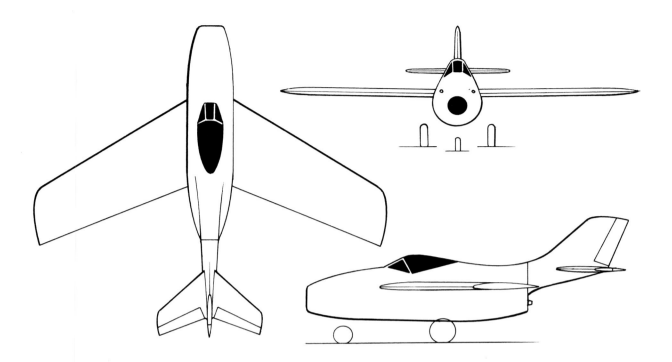

level (*Geheime Kommandosache*) assessment of single-engined fighter designs ('*Entwürfe für 1-TL-Jäger*') that had been submitted by Focke-Wulf, Messerschmitt, Heinkel, Junkers, and Blohm und Voss at the request of the chief development commission (*Entwicklungshauptkommission*) of the technical air equipment (*Technische Luft Rüstungs*) branch. These designs had evidently been presented very early in 1945, and were to be discussed at a meeting on 27/28 February with a view to reaching a decision on which designs warranted development. Four relatively conventional designs, the Focke-Wulf I and II, and the Messerschmitt P.1101 and P.1110, were compared with five tailless designs, viz, the latter company's P.1111, and the Heinkel P.1078, the Junkers EF. 128 and the Bv 212.

To summarize the swept-wing state of the art in 1945 as illustrated by these documents, Germany had carried out far more wind tunnel research than the Allies, but had not had time to exploit this knowledge in terms of production aircraft. The only operational fighter with an aerodynamically significant amount of sweepback was the Me 163B, which had probably used sweep to achieve better stability and control characteristics in a tailless layout, rather than to delay compressibility effects.

The best guidance for Allied designers contemplating the first post-war fighter generation was nonetheless to be gleaned from German experts and their project studies. If tailless configurations are discounted, the layout generally adopted had a quarter-chord sweep of 40° and a t/c of around 10 per cent. An axial-flow turbojet was usually set low in the fuselage, fed by a circular nose inlet, and exhausting through a short jetpipe, the fuselage extending aft over the nozzle. The horizontal tail was mounted either on this slender rear fuselage, or high on a swept vertical tail.

The tailed designs are of interest in showing exactly where German fighter technology stood at the end of the war. The Focke-Wulf I project had a wing of 40° sweep and 10 per cent thickness/chord (t/c) ratio, while the F-W II had a sweep of 32° and the same t/c. The P.1101 and P.1110 had a common wing design, with 40° sweep and a t/c tapering from 12 to 8 per cent.

All four projects were comparatively light, weighing roughly the same as a Gnat trainer. The main difference between the two companies' proposals was that the Meeserschmitt projects

had wing loadings over 30 per cent higher than those from Focke-Wulf. As a result, the former company's designs were rather faster, the P.1110 offering Mach 0.89 at 23,000 ft (7,000 m), while the latter company's projects landed slower, the Focke-Wulf I at 88.6 knots (164 km/hr).

Designed by Prof Kurt Tank, the Focke-Wulf Ta 183 was typical of WW2 German thinking on swept-wing fighter development. Note the moderate sweep angle, sawn-off jetpipe, and pod-and-boom fuselage configuration. It was also very light by post-war standards
(Mike Badrocke)

The Messerschmitt P.1101 was probably the closest that the Germans came to a fighter with significant sweep by the end of WW2. The prototype was found by an American intelligence team, and formed the basis for the Bell X-5 variable-sweep research aircraft
(Mike Badrocke)

In some respects the Messerschmitt P.1110 project was closer to the general line of post-war fighter development than the P.1101 and Ta 183. The engine was set well back in the fuselage, with a jetpipe that extended to the tail, and it had lateral intakes (actually flush NACA-type)
(Mike Badrocke)

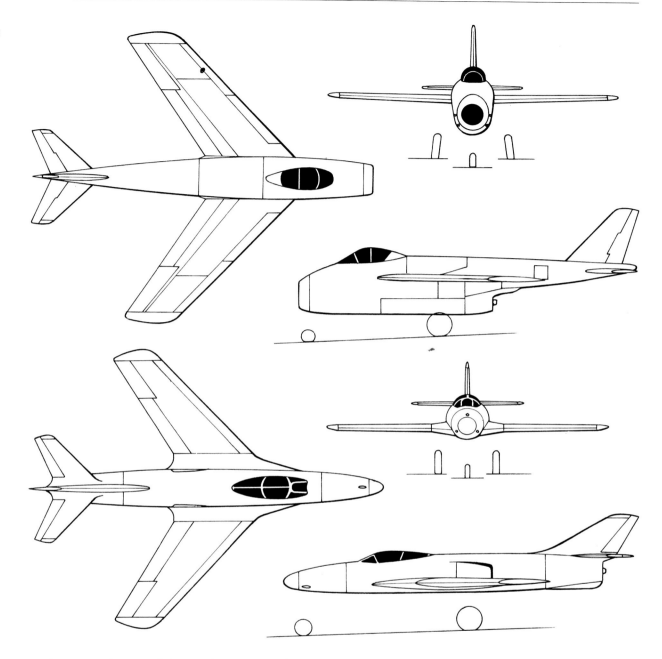

As one future fighter that was almost completed at the end of the war, the P.1101 is worth considering in more detail. The prototype was discovered on 29 April 1945 at Oberammergau by the US Army, and (along with Dr Voigt's team) taken back to Wright Field by a Combined Advanced Field Team led by Robert J Woods, chief designer of the Bell Aircraft Corporation.

The P.1101 had an empty equipped weight of 5,719 lb (2,595 kg), internal fuel of 2,756 lb (1,250 kg) and an all-up weight of 8,961 lb (4,065 kg). The wing had an area of 170.6 sq ft (15.7 m²), and was

equipped with plain flaps and leading edge slats. It was expected to reach Mach 0.72 at sea level and 0.87 at 23,000 ft (7,000 m). Landing speed was put at 93 knots (172 km/hr). Initial climb rate was estimated at 4,380 ft/min (22.25 m/sec). It was to be armed with two or four 30 mm MK 108 Rheinmetall cannon. The *Luftwaffe* assessment from which these figures are taken is vague on the subject of powerplants, but it is believed that the project comparisons were made on the basis of each design having a single Heinkel/Hirth HeS-111 turbojet of 3,000 lb (1,360 kg) static thrust.

Chapter 3

The Jet Engine

Viewed in the light of previous British fighter developments, the second novel feature of the Hunter (after the swept wing) was its use of an axial-flow turbojet engine. Since there is some confusion in most published works regarding the genesis of the aircraft gas turbine, it may be worthwhile to summarize the early history of this class of powerplant, leading up to the Rolls-Royce AJ.65 Avon that was to equip the Hunter.

Jet propulsion occurs in nature, and has for centuries been the basis for various toys and for rockets used for both peaceful and military purposes. The basic idea of jet propulsion has thus never been a patentable invention, although some of the devices proposed to achieve jet propulsion were. Only in the last few decades has this form of propulsion been relevant to manned vehicles, as the need has arisen for a powerplant with a thrust that (unlike that of a propeller) does not decrease as speed increases.

France's Joseph Montgolfier is said to have postulated the use of jet propulsion for hot air balloons in 1783, using lateral openings to produce bursts of gas and thus encourage 'translational' movement. In 1908, only five years after the first flights by a powered aeroplane, another Frenchman, René Lorin, took out French patent No 390256 on the concept of a reciprocating engine from which no power was extracted at the shaft, but in which the consequently increased energy of the exhaust gases gave propulsive thrust. In essence the expansion stroke would take just enough energy to power the compression stroke, leaving the gases that escaped through the outlet valves at a high pressure and temperature for a second stage of expansion through an exhaust nozzle. Although the modern gas turbine is mechanically quite different, and provides a large-scale continuous supply of gases, the thermodynamic principle is basically identical to that of the Lorin concept.

In the same way that high-powered reciprocating steam engines were replaced by steam turbines, the internal combustion engine of the 1908 Lorin patent was in due course superseded by various types of gas turbine. It is believed that the first public showing of a gas turbine (presumably for electricity generation) occurred at the Chicago World Exhibition of 1904, but by the late 1930s there were numerous gas turbines in existence, notably in Switzerland and Hungary. The possibility of applying such powerplants to driving an aircraft propeller was recognized, but gas turbines were then larger and heavier than comparable piston engines.

If the gas turbine was to become competitive in aircraft applications, it needed improvements in compressor and turbine efficiency, and new materials to make possible very high turbine entry temperatures (TETs). The potential and the needs of the gas turbine in aircraft applications were detailed in a paper presented by Maurice Roy in the *Bulletin de l'Association Technique Maritime et Aéronautique* in 1928, which also emphasized the value of jet propulsion at speeds too high for conventional propellers. However, even before Roy's paper, a number of patents had been published concerning the use of gas turbines for jet propulsion, the earliest of significance being that of Guillaume (French patent 534801) in 1921, based on an axial-flow multi-stage compressor.

Although France undoubtedly led the way in forseeing the basic concepts of gas turbines for jet propulsion, it was the Germans and the British who first put these ideas into practice. One of the first to become seriously interested in such lines of

development was a young physics student named Hans Joachim Pabst von Ohain, then attending Göttingen University. In 1934 he carried out the preliminary design of a gas turbine with a radial-flow compressor and turbine mounted back-to-back, basing his performance calculations on the relatively modest pressure ratio of 3:1.

While planning to take out patents and sell the idea to an engine manufacturer, von Ohain very wisely decided that his chances would be improved if he could demonstrate a working model. This he had constructed by the local garage, where he had been parking his car. Unfortunately, the working model suffered combustion system problems, with burning continuing through the turbine and jetpipe. The scale of development effort needed to rectify matters was clearly outside his financial means. However, his physics tutor, Professor Pohl, introduced him to Heinkel. The latter appears to have been seriously interested in jet propulsion (the liquid rocket-powered He 176 was to fly in June 1939), and hired von Ohain to develop a turbojet engine for use in

The first flight by an aircraft powered only by a gas turbine engine was made on 27 August 1939 by this He 178, a technology demonstrator for the HeS-3B powerplant

aircraft propulsion. In order to have a demonstrator working quickly, gaseous hydrogen was used as fuel, and von Ohain had the HeS-1 running with a thrust of 250 lb (115 kg) by April 1937.

This early success encouraged Heinkel to proceed with gas turbine development, although from a competitive viewpoint his decision had the disadvantage that the German Air Ministry (RLM = Reichluftministerium) then persuaded Junkers and BMW to begin work in this field. Both of these companies chose to develop axial-flow engines, and at the end of the war were (at least temporarily) in the lead as far as German turbojets were concerned.

Heinkel's HeS-1 feasibility demonstrator was soon followed by the HeS-3A, which produced a static thrust of 992 lb (450 kg), and in the spring of 1939 was flight-tested under an He 118. The HeS-3B had the same thrust, but incorporated various design changes. The idea of a back-to-back radial-flow compressor-turbine unit was retained, but the engine also had a single-stage axial-flow impeller, and a reverse-flow annular combustion chamber. On 27 August 1939 the HeS-3B made its first flight in the He 178 from the airfield at Marienehe, with Heinkel test pilot Erich Warsitz at the controls. It was the world's first flight by an aircraft powered solely by a gas turbine engine.

The He 178 had been designed specifically as a technology demonstrator for the HeS-3B. It was a shoulder-wing aeroplane with a span of 26 ft 3 in (8.0 m) and an overall length of 24 ft 6½ in (7.48 m). Wing area was 85 sq ft (7.9 m²). Take-off weight was a modest 4,410 lb (2,000 kg), but the maximum speed achieved by the He 178 was a remarkable 345 knots (640 km/hr). If this figure is correct, this aircraft was faster than all of the operational piston-engined fighters then current.

The next stage of Heinkel development was the He 280, which first flew on 2 April 1941, and is generally regarded as the world's first turbojet-powered fighter. It was also the first with an ejection seat. The He 280 was powered by two HeS-8 engines, each producing 1,300 lb (590 kg) thrust, and designed specifically for reduced diameter, so that there would be room for the nacelles under a low wing.

This aircraft was not ordered into production, as it was inferior in performance to the Me 262, which had its maiden flight with Junkers Jumo 004 engines on 18 July 1942. However, the technical success of the He 280 gave Heinkel grounds for

acquiring the Hirth engine company. This provided very useful additional facilities for the development and production of the company's next powerplant, the HeS-011 of 3,000 lb (1,360 kg) thrust. Large-scale production was planned for the second half of 1945, and this would have become the standard engine for Germany's swept-wing single-engined fighters.

Metrovicks were the British pioneers in axial-flow engines, instanced by this F.2/4 Beryl turbojet, mounted for preliminary flight tests in the rear fuselage of a Lancaster, LL735/G

British Developments

In the UK, serious work on gas turbines for jet propulsion began around 1936. Engines with axial-flow compressors were designed by a group at RAE Farnborough, led by Dr A A Griffith and Hayne Constant, while centrifugal-flow engines were developed by a Power Jets team led by Flt Lt (later Air Commodore Sir) Frank Whittle. Early RAE designs were built by Metropolitan-Vickers Electrical ('Metrovicks') and Whittle engines first by British Thomson-Houston (BTH) and then by Rover, who were finally succeeded by Rolls-Royce (R-R).

Looking first at British axial-flow developments, the Air Ministry formally authorized RAE to start work on the problem of the gas turbine in 1937. Some accounts of this line of work say that the first public mention of British work on turbojets for aircraft occurred in January 1944, but in fact the existence of the first Metrovicks contract was published in January 1938. The RAE was aiming to produce a turboprop engine, and various components had been built and tested (though no complete engine had run) when war broke out in 1939.

From this point onwards Air Ministry wanted quick results, and RAE therefore proposed a simple turbojet engine, merely deleting the power turbine and propeller transmission of the earlier project. The preliminary design details of this F.1 engine were handed over to Metrovicks in July 1940. It was then further developed under the direction of Dr D M Smith, leading to the 1,800 lb (815 kg) F.2, which first ran on the testbed in December 1941.

The Metrovicks F.2 had its first flight in the rear fuselage of a Lancaster testbed on 29 June 1943. Two F.2s took to the air in the Gloster F.9/40 on 13 November 1943, this being the first flight in the UK by a jet-propelled aircraft with axial-flow engines. Further development produced the F.2/4 Beryl, which by November 1945 was producing a thrust of 3,250 lb (1,475 kg). Dr Smith's team went on to develop the F.9 Sapphire.

Some accounts of that period say that Air Ministry then asked Metrovicks to withdraw from the aero-engine field. However, this writer's recollection from conversations with Dr Smith was that Metrovicks had no wish to remain in the roller-coaster world of aviation once the war was over. At the end of 1947 an agreement was therefore reached with Armstrong-Siddeley whereby the latter company would take over further development and production of the Sapphire. The contribution of Dr Smith and the Metrovicks team has received very little publicity, but it is almost certainly true to say that at the time of the Sapphire hand-over that company was the British leader in advanced turbojet technology.

Turning to British centrifugal-flow turbojet developments, Whittle had first been attracted to the idea of using gas turbines for jet propulsion while a flight cadet at the RAF College at Cranwell in 1928. As mentioned earlier in this account, at that time gas turbines had often been discussed in the context of fixed installations (ie, for power stations), but were regarded as still some way in

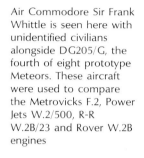

Air Commodore Sir Frank Whittle is seen here with unidentified civilians alongside DG205/G, the fourth of eight prototype Meteors. These aircraft were used to compare the Metrovicks F.2, Power Jets W.2/500, R-R W.2B/23 and Rover W.2B engines

the future, because of the large improvements that would be needed in compressor and turbine efficiencies, and the very high turbine temperatures required for efficient operation, temperatures that precluded the long life needed for ground applications.

Whittle recognized that aircraft applications could accept much shorter lives, and that low air temperatures at high altitude would permit an increased temperature rise for a given blade material. In addition, some of the work of compression could be done very efficiently by the ram effect of forward speed, and in a jet engine turbine losses affect only part of the expansion process. Since the combination of piston engine and propeller had a very limited potential for high speeds, there appeared to Whittle to be a clear case for developing gas turbines for jet propulsion.

On the other hand, Air Ministry felt that the practical difficulties were too great. In consequence, nothing much happened until 1935, by which stage Whittle was an engineering officer, and studying for his MA at Cambridge. With the help of two ex-RAF officers and a firm of investment bankers, a company named Power Jets Ltd was formed in March 1936, Whittle's allocation of shares being held in trust for the Air Ministry.

In June 1936 Power Jets placed an order with BTH for the manufacture of its first engine, less the combustion chamber, which was contracted separately. The basic engine configuration was a double-sided centrifugal-flow compressor, a reverse-flow combustion chamber, and a single-stage axial turbine. Testing began on 12 April 1937, the main problem then being with the combustion system, although later there were turbine blade failures. In addition, the centrifugal blower, which had been designed to give a pressure ratio of 4:1, was performing well below expectations.

In the early days of the company, Air Ministry had regarded Whittle's work as long-term research. However, by the summer of 1939 it had been decided that Power Jets had the basis for a practical aircraft engine. A contract was therefore placed for the first flight engine, the 800 lb (325 kg) W.1, and Gloster Aircraft was contracted to design and build an appropriate aircraft, to specification E.28/39. The first flight of aircraft W4041 took place at RAF Cranwell on 14 May 1941, the pilot being Flt Lt 'Gerry' Sayer. The aircraft was officially named 'Pioneer' and unofficially 'The Squirt'.

In the meantime, early in 1940 the Air Ministry had already ordered the development of the more powerful 1,600 lb (725 kg) W.2 engine. By mid-1940 Gloster was authorized to proceed with the design of a twin-engined fighter to specification F.9/40, to exploit the performance potential of the W.2. By this stage other British manufacturers were becoming involved in turbojet development, and the first flight of the F.9/40 (serial DG206) was made with two 1,500 lb (680 kg) de Havilland Halford H.1 engines on 5 March 1943, with Michael Daunt as pilot.

The Halford series also used a centrifugal compressor, but it was single-sided, whereas all Whittle's designs had double-sided impellers. The 2,500 lb (1,135 kg) de Havilland Goblin flew in the E.6/41 Vampire on 20 September 1943, and was the most powerful British jet engine in full production before the end of the war.

The last of the Whittle series was the W.2B, which was initially manufactured by Rover, and was destined to become the basis for the R-R Welland and the General Electric (GE) I-series. The Gloster E.28/39 was seen in April 1941 by General 'Hap' Arnold, USAAF, who subsequently asked GE to duplicate the Whittle engine, this company being chosen for its experience with high-temperature turbines for piston-engine superchargers. Bell Aircraft was selected to develop a suitable twin-engined airframe to take the GE engines, this selection being partly based on the proximity of Bell's plant at Buffalo, NY to GE's facility at Lynn, Massachusetts.

By arrangement between the British and US Governments, Power Jets sent one W.1X engine and a full set of engineering drawings of the W.2B to GE, this material arriving on 2 October 1941. The first of a batch of 15 engines of the W.2B type, designated 'I-A' ran on the testbed at a thrust of 1,250 lb (565 kg) on 18 March 1942. The first of three prototype Bell Model 27s or XP-59As, serial 42-108784, had its official first flight at Muroc Army Air Base on 2 October 1942, although there had been several 'high taxies' two days earlier. This was the first flight in the US by a turbojet-powered aircraft. The pilot was Bell's Robert Stanley.

The XP-59A with two 1,400 lb (635 kg) GE I-A engines had a maximum speed of 350 knots (650 km/hr) at 25,000 ft (7,600 m). The production aircraft, the P-59A/B with 2,000 lb (907 kg) J31s reached 359 knots (665 km/hr) at 30,000 ft (9,150 m). A total of 50 were built, but they were used mainly as a lead-in to the Lockheed P-80 Shooting Star. One was exchanged for a Meteor, and given the RAF serial RJ362/'G'.

The final outcome of the Bell jet fighter programme was the Model 40 XP-83 long-range escort fighter, powered by two J33-GE-5s of 3,750 lb (1,700 kg) thrust each. The aircraft was capable of 543 knots (1,006 km/hr) at 15,660 ft (4,750 m). Although mediocre as a fighter, it was of some historical interest, in being armed with six examples of the ill-fated T17E3 0.60-inch (15.24 mm) machine gun. The first of six prototypes had its maiden flight on 27 February 1945, but no production order was forthcoming. The XP-83 was, in fact, the last conventional fixed-wing aircraft made by Bell.

To complete the history of early British-inspired US turbojet development work, GE went on to design the 4,000 lb (1,815 kg) I-40, which first flew on 10 June 1945 in the Lockheed XP-80A. The company also produced the TG-100 axial-flow turboprop, which ran in May 1945, and the TG-180 axial turbojet, which ran on 23 April 1945 and became the J35. Westinghouse developed the Type 19A and flew it as a boost engine on an FG-1 Corsair on 21 January 1944. Two Type 19Bs (which

The Bell XP-59A (Model 27) provided the first flight in America by a turbojet-powered aircraft. Equipped with General Electric-built W.2B engines, it first flew on 18 March 1942 (Bell Helicopter Textron)

later became J30s) flew in the McDonnell XFD-1 Phantom I on 26 January 1945.

To revert to British centrifugal-flow developments, in January 1943 Rolls-Royce took over the responsibility for the Whittle production series from Rover, acquiring the latter company's Barnoldswick facility in exchange for a tank factory at Nottingham. The initial series engine was the 1,600 lb (725 kg) W.2B/23 or Welland. Most of the flight testing was done with the engine in the rear fuselage of a Wellington bomber, beginning in late 1942. The engine first flew in the F.9/40 on 12 June 1943, at which stage it was rated at 1,400 lb (635 kg).

Over 100 Wellands were built, the delivery of the first Meteor I taking place to 616 Sqn on 12 July 1944. The Meteor I was never used in combat with German fighters, but it was employed briefly in destroying V-1 'flying bombs', the first being literally knocked down on 4 August 1944. The first production series of the Meteor had an extremely modest performance, reaching only 356 knots (660 km/hr) at 30,000 ft (9,150 m), a speed virtually

identical to that of the Bell P-59A/B. However, the Meteor III with the slightly modified B.37-1 (Derwent I) engine of 2,000 lb (907 kg) reached 428 knots (793 km/hr) at the same height.

Of this improved version 280 were built, a few serving with the RAF in the final advance into Germany. The post-war Meteor IV had the vastly superior 3,500 lb (1,590 kg) Derwent V, and first flew on 15 August 1945. In the following year a clipped-wing Mk IV established a world speed record of 616 mph (991 km/hr).

Though it retained the Derwent name, the Mk V engine was a scaled-down B.41 Nene. The Nene had first run on 27 October 1944 and by November 1945 had been type-tested to a thrust of 5,000 lb (2,265 kg). Due to the 49.5-inch (126 cm) diameter of the Nene, it was difficult to find a suitable flying testbed, and its maiden flight thus took place in a XP-80A (serial 44-83027) at Hucknall on 21 July 1945. A half-inch (12.7 mm) increase in the Nene impeller diameter produced the Tay, which was licence-built by Hispano-Suiza in France, and by Pratt & Whitney as the J48. The latter company made 4,000 J48s and over 1,100 Nenes. The Nene was used in the Hawker P.1040 Sea Hawk, which first flew on 2 September 1947.

Under an agreement arranged by the British Labour Government of the day, some 25 Nenes and 30 Derwents were sold in 1946 to the Soviet Union. Up to that time the most powerful engines available to the Russians were the BMW 003 of 1,760 lb (800 kg), which was copied as the RD-20 for the Lavochkin La-160, and the Junkers Jumo 004, which was produced as the 2,050 lb (930 kg) RD-10 for the Yakovlev Yak-15.

Aside from the fact that these were far less powerful engines then contemporary British products, it is worth noting Whittle's comments on the Germans' decision to accept the Jumo 004 for the Me 262: *They put this engine into production at a stage in its development history that would be considered far too early in this country, and it was technically a long way behind the British engines, being much heavier in proportion to its power, having a much bigger fuel consumption, and only a fraction of the life. Moreover, it had the serious disadvantage of being very sluggish in response to the throttle*'. Hayne Constant stated in discussing the Jumo 004 that Smith's F.2 engine was 25 per cent better in sfc (specific fuel consumption) terms, and five per cent better in thrust/weight ratio.

It is clear that the acquisition of the Nene in

particular was a major coup for the Soviets. The less powerful Derwent became the RD-500 of 3,527 lb (1,600 kg) thrust, and was manufactured for the Yak-23 and La-15. The Nene was first built as the 4,930 lb (2,235 kg) RD-45 and was later uprated to 5,940 lb (2,695 kg), roughly in line with the Tay. Redesignated Klimov VK-1, this engine was employed in the Mikoyan-Gurevich MiG-15 and Ilyushin Il-28. With afterburner it became the 7,450 lb (3,380 kg) VK-1A/1F in the MiG-17. There can be little doubt that without the British Nene the Soviets would have taken many years to catch up with the West in fighter performance, and would never have dared to have pitted their combat aircraft against the F-86 Sabre in Korea.

Rolls-Royce's centrifugal-flow engines were unquestionably one of the major technological successes of the mid-1940s, with almost 19,000 built, this total including licence-production in seven countries. Development had been centred at Barnoldswick, under chief engineer Dr (later Sir) Stanley Hooker. Notwithstanding the company's development of Whittle-originated centrifugal-flow engines, R-R also did some early work on axials. Dr Griffith moved from the RAE to R-R in 1939. He appears to have been hired specifically as a gas turbine expert, and had a staff of one (Donald Eyre), but reported directly to Lord Hives. The first result of this association was the CR1 experimental 14-stage contra-flow gas generator, which first ran in 1942. This was not successful, but there were subsequent project studies of the 2,500 lb (1,135 kg) AJ.25 and the 5,000 lb (2,265 kg) AJ.50 during the war years.

In a report dated 26 June 1945 Griffith proposed an axial turbojet of 5,200 lb (2,360 kg), giving roughly the same thrust as the Nene, but with 60 per cent less frontal area and 20 per cent lower fuel consumption. On consideration, R-R decided to adopt the engine configuration proposed by Dr Griffith, ie, a 12-stage axial-flow compressor driven by a single-stage turbine, but to aim for a higher thrust category. On 5 July 1945 preliminary design work began on the AJ.65, ie, an axial-flow jet engine of approximately 6,500 lb (2,950 kg) static thrust. Detail design began three months later. The AJ.65 was a fairly ambitious project for its day, aiming at a pressure ratio of 7:1 (later revised down to 6.3:1) in combination with a compressor efficiency of 85 per cent, compared to the 4:1 pressure ratio with 80 per cent efficiency achieved by Whittle.

Like Whittle, Hooker had excelled in the

development of centrifugal-flow compressors, and the experience of the Derwent V had shown that R-R could develop a new engine of this type in as little as seven months. However, when the company took on the full-scale development of a large axial-flow engine, it was a whole new world. In Hooker's words, '*We leaped off at the deep end, and landed in so much trouble that it took about seven years before the AJ.65 could be given a clean bill of health*'. Some at Kingston would regard that period as an underestimate.

The following account of the engine's early development is based largely on notes kindly provided by Geoffrey Wilde of Rolls-Royce.

In planning electrically-powered rig tests of the Avon compressor, the company decided to test the first four and the last eight stages separately, prior to testing the 12 stages combined. The initial rig test on the front four stages was carried out towards the end of 1946. These trials indicated that at lower and intermediate speeds the complete compressor would be incapable of stable operation. Indeed, the engine would probably be

unable to accelerate from idling to full speed!

The following is the author's attempt to explain axial-flow compressor surge in simple terms. The compressor duct and blading are designed so that at full speed the air has a constant axial velocity component throughout the assembly. As the air moves through the compressor, its pressure is increased and its density rises, hence the duct cross-section has to be tapered to hold the axial velocity constant. However, at lower rpm the pressure ratio is reduced, as is the need for duct taper. The mass flow through the duct is dictated by exit conditions, hence at low rpm the duct cross section at the forward end is too large and the axial flow velocity is consequently much smaller than the blading is designed to expect. The angle of attack on the blades is thus increased, giving a tendency to blade stalling and engine surge. This tendency may be countered by swivelling the blades to match engine speed, or by bleeding air from part-way along the compressor, to increase axial flow velocity upstream.

Returning to Wilde's account, rig tests on the

The Lockheed P-80 Shooting Star was the first jet fighter to become operational with the USAAF. Its development began in June 1943, when the company was asked to design a fighter around the de Havilland H-1 (Goblin) turbojet (Lockheed-California)

complete 12-stage compressor began at the turn of the year. As predicted, these tests showed that the first four stages were badly stalled below 60 per cent rpm, and that the compressor delivery characteristics did not match those of the turbine. In addition, at the design speed (7,720 rpm), the engine had no surge margin, ie, the operating line and the surge line coincided. A further cause for concern was the low efficiency of the single-stage turbine, which required a higher TET than planned, if the engine was to achieve the design thrust. This low turbine efficiency also contributed to the compressor-turbine mismatch.

The complete AJ.65 first ran on the testbed at Barnoldswick on 25 March 1947, and immediately confirmed the expectations arising from the compressor rig tests. The engine was difficult to start, would not accelerate, broke some first-stage blades, and it was found that in coaxing it to 5,000 lb (2,265 kg) thrust the turbine overheated. In Wilde's words, 'A state of malfunction existed; our worst fears had materialized, and there was now a crisis'.

The crisis called for sweeping measures, and R-R took them. In the second half of 1948 the AJ.65 was transferred by Lord Hives from Hooker's team at Barnoldswick to Derby, where A C (Cyril) Lovesey was put in charge of the programme.

In order to allow the engine to run in some form, the first four stages of compressor were removed, although this reduced the pressure ratio to 4:1. It also gave a very uneconomical sfc, and a very low mass flow and thrust. Next, the third and fourth stages were reinstated, producing a 10-stage compressor with a pressure ratio of 5:1. Then the compressor capacity was reduced by increasing the diameter of the hub, a step that resulted in the RA.2. This was first flown on 15 August 1947 in a Lancastrian, while further development work on components continued on the ground throughout 1947 and '48.

Again quoting from Wilde, 'The rate of working on the compressor and turbine rig tests for the AJ.65 were unparalleled, and have never been matched since'. At least six new compressor designs were evaluated in the space of two years, and in one case a completely new 12-stage design was created in only three months!

The long-awaited breakthrough came with the discovery that stable matching with an adequate surge margin could be achieved by swivelling the inlet whirl vanes and the blades of the first four stator stages. This was done as a function of engine speed, to reduce the AOA on the rotor blades at the front of the engine, and thus the tendency to stall. Unfortunately, engineering management at R-R was reluctant to grasp this particular nettle, although this complexity was later adopted by both GE and P&W in overcoming similar problems.

The alternative means to alleviate stalling of the front compressor stages was to use interstage bleeding. In the course of rig tests early in 1949 the combination of variable inlet whirl and progressive bleed was explored, and found to be highly effective in providing an adequate surge margin.

Typical of first generation British turbojet engines, the Rolls-Royce Derwent had a double-sided centrifugal compressor, which led to a comparatively fat nacelle, limiting the maximum speed that could be achieved. The Derwent I powered the Meteor III, the most advanced British jet fighter to serve in WW2
(Rolls-Royce)

Although R-R had been loath to adopt variable incidence compressor stators, Lovesey accepted variable inlet whirl and an interstage bleed system programmed as a function of compressor speed. These features were incorporated in subsequent engines of the series.

While the front end of the engine was being substantially revised, the company's turbine group had designed and tested a two-stage turbine to replace the inefficient single-stage unit employed up to this point. The new design was at least 10 per cent more efficient, smaller in diameter, and somewhat lighter. It also reduced jetpipe losses.

Equipped with a rebladed 12-stage compressor, variable inlet whirl, interstage bleed, and the new two-stage turbine, the engine became the RA.3 Avon Mk 1. It weighed 2,225 lb (1,010 kg), compared to the 2,400 lb (1,090 kg) of the initial engine. Design started in July 1948, and the RA.3 first ran on the testbed on 4 April 1949, achieving the design thrust of 6,500 lb (2,950 kg). It first flew in October 1949, and deliveries began in July 1950 for the Canberra bomber, which was to enter

service in 1951. This formed the basis for the engine that was also to power the Hunter, Comet and Lightning.

The second production series was designated RA.7, and had modified compressor blading to increase mass flow and a high TET to give a rating of 7,500 lb (3,400 kg) for both the Canberra and Hunter. Design started in March 1949, and the engine was running on the testbed by August 1950. The powerplant for Britain's first swept-wing fighter generation had taken five years from preliminary design to run in something approximating to a usable form, and its troubles were far from over.

To end this chapter on a happier note, by 1947 von Ohain was chief scientist at the USAF Aerospace Laboratories, and by 1975 he was chief scientist to the USAF Propulsion Laboratory at Wright-Patterson AFB. Whittle received a well-deserved knighthood, and £100,000 in lieu of patent royalties, which in those days was a great deal of money.

The Rolls-Royce Nene and its J48/Tay derivative provided the power for many of the first post-war fighter generation, including the Hawker Sea Hawk and the MiG-15 (Rolls-Royce)

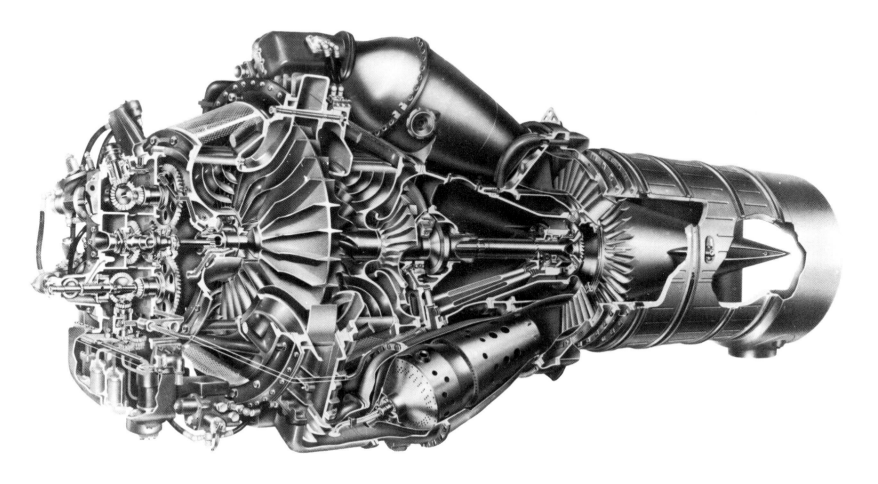

Chapter 4

Projects and Specifications

To recapitulate on the fighter requirements situation in the UK just after the end of the war, the Air Ministry had issued two specifications: F.43/46 for a twin-engined single-seat day fighter, and F.44/46 for a twin-engined two-seat all-weather fighter. Sydney Camm was trying to win RAF support for the idea of a single-engined single-seat day fighter, while as insurance the Hawker project office carried out studies on the basis of the two official specifications. These designs were generally designed around a powerplant consisting of two AJ.65 engines, though some used one AJ.65 plus rocket boost. A mass of information on German swept-wing research and fighter proposals had been brought back to the UK by technical intelligence teams, and had filtered through to fighter designers via RAE.

Manufacturers in the US had received much the same information, but were more prepared to gamble on the swept wing. On 1 October 1947, one of the most significant dates in fighter history, the swept-wing North American XP-86 flew for the first time. Deliveries of the resulting F-86A Sabre to the USAF began in February 1949. Less than five years after the advent of the first jet fighter in the UK, Britain's lead among the Allies had been wiped out in a single blow.

At this stage Hawker production facilities were committed to the piston-engined Sea Fury, which entered service with the RN in 1947, while the experimental drawing office had just completed work on the straight-wing P.1040 with the centrifugal-flow R-R Nene engine. However, it was clear that the naval market was too small to provide continuity for a company the size of Hawker. The future depended on winning the order for the next RAF fighter generation. To prepare the ground for that win, Kingston had to get hands-on experience of swept wings and rocket boost motors, if that was the way that the fighter business was moving.

From the mid-1940s to the mid-1950s, Hawker appears to have lagged more than a year behind Supermarine in terms of a whole series of new developments. For example, Kingston flew the straight-wing P.1040 (VP401) on 2 September 1947, but Supermarine's comparable Type 392 (TS409) had flown on 27 July 1946. Likewise, the navalized Sea Hawk prototype (VP413) had its maiden flight on 3 September 1948, but the navalized Type 398 Attacker (TS413) had flown on 17 June 1947. The Attacker entered service with the RN in August 1951, while the Sea Hawk's entry was delayed to

March 1953. Each was powered by a single Nene engine, and the only consolation was that the Kingston aircraft was credited with 547 knots (1,014 km/hr) and the Attacker only 512 knots (949 km/hr).

In order to carry out full-scale research into sweepback, Hawker then put a 35° swept 10 per cent wing on the P.1040, producing the P.1052 to specification E.38/46. The first of two prototypes (VX272) had its maiden flight on 19 November 1948, the second flew on 13 April 1949.

Despite the modest thrust of its Nene engine and the fact that the tail surfaces were still unswept, the P.1052 could exceed 520 knots (965 km/hr) at sea level, and (according to Neville Duke, who should know) could reach Mach 0.90 at altitude. At low speeds its general handling appears to have been good, and its Dutch Roll characteristics quite gentle. The P.1052's ailerons were good throughout the speed range, but in mock combats with a Meteor F.4 at medium level, it was found that the elevators were somewhat ineffective and stick loads excessive.

It should perhaps be explained that sweepback produces a dihedral effect (ie, rolling moment due to sideslip) which increases with AOA. At low speeds swept-wing aircraft tend to have too much dihedral effect and insufficient weathercock stability (yawing moment due to sideslip). This combination manifests itself as a combined rolling and yawing oscillation known as Dutch Roll, the motion of the aircraft being analogous to that of an ice-skater.

Speed records and racing have always provided useful publicity for aircraft, and Hawker appears to have decided by 1949 to get some PR mileage out of the P.1040 and P.1052. However, the company was not yet in a position to go after the world speed record. The Meteor record set by Gp Capt 'Teddy' Donaldson in September 1945 had been lost to the US in the following year, and for some time it was going to be a story of Americans competing with Americans. On 19 June 1946 a highly modified Lockheed P-80R reached 623.8 mph (1,004.2 km/hr), and on 25 August 1947 the Douglas D-558 Skyrocket research aircraft took

One of the greatest fighters ever built, the North American Sabre is shown here in the form of an F-86A-5 (serial 49-1137). Deliveries of the -5 began in 1949, after production of 221 F-86A-1s (USAF via Robert F Dorr)

Hawker's first jet aircraft, the prototype P.1040, probably photographed at Boscombe just before its first flight on 2 September 1947. The high-tech attitude indicator on the nose was presumably to show the pilot where a Centaurus would be (Cyril Peckham, HAL, via Brian Isles)

The Hawker flight test team, presumably at Boscombe in 1947. The line-up includes 'Bob' Marsh (third from right), who later became head of the project office and then assistant chief engineer at Kingston (BAe via Brian Isles)

the record to 650.796 mph (1,046.6 km/hr). Perhaps more significantly, on 15 September 1948 a perfectly standard F-86A-1 produced a speed of 670.981 mph (1,080.1 km/hr), a very commendable figure, considering that the J47-GE-1 axial jet produced a static thrust of only 5,200 lb (2,358 kg), ie, roughly the same as the Nene.

The world speed record was beyond Hawker's grasp for the time being, but there were other records and events closer to home in which the speed of the P.1040 and P.1052 could be demonstrated to good effect. On 13 May 1949 'Wimpy' Wade set a new record from London to Paris, covering 221 statute miles (355.6 km) in 21 min 27.6 sec. This gave an average speed of 617.9 mph (994.2 km/hr), and knocked 6 min 9.7 sec off the time set by Sqn Ldr 'Bill' Waterton of Gloster Aircraft in a Meteor T.7 in the previous December.

In August 1949 the first post-war UK national air races were held at Elmdon, Birmingham airport. In the SBAC Trophy Race, Wade came first in the P.1040 at an average speed of 510 mph (821 km/hr), followed by John Derry of de Havilland in

the swept-wing tailless DH.108 at 488 mph (785.6 km/hr) and the same company's John Cunningham in a Vampire at 470 mph (756.6 km/hr). In the Kemsley Challenge Trophy Cunningham's speed in the Vampire was unchanged, but he crossed the line with Hawker aircraft both in front and behind. Duke won in the P.1040 at 508 mph (817.8 km/hr), and chief production test pilot 'Frank' Murphy came third in the Sea Fury at 340 mph (547.3 km/hr).

Returning to the technology struggle between Hawker and Supermarine, the latter company skipped the swept-wing-plus-straight-tail stage of the P.1052. Nonetheless, only one month after the maiden flight of the P.1052, Supermarine flew the 'all-swept' Type 510 (VV106) on 29 December 1948. Relative to the P.1052, the Type 510 had an additional 5° of wing sweep, giving 40° on the quarter-chord line.

It was not for another 18 months that Kingston reached the 'all-swept' stage, when Wade took the P.1081 (VX279) into the air for the first time, on 19 June 1950. The P.1081 had been produced by

The P.1040 illustrates how the intakes and bifurcated jetpipe produced a deep wing root and useful space in the rear fuselage. The wing-body blending was useful aerodynamically, reduced wing weight, and provided space for the mainwheels
(BAe via Brian Isles)

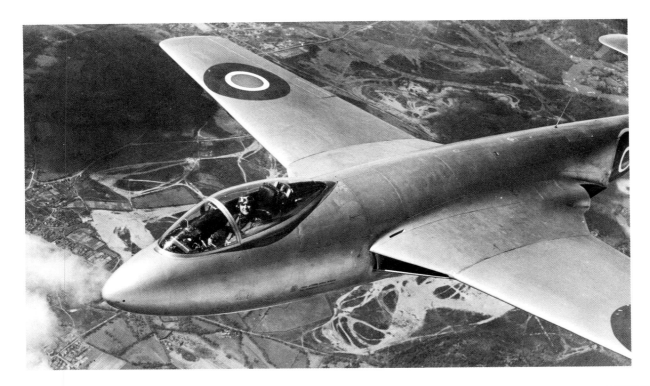

'Wimpy' Wade in the cockpit of VP401. In comparison with the later Hunter, the small size of the front fuselage is striking, the space ahead of the cockpit housing only the nosewheel (Cyril Peckham, HAL)

An early production Sea Hawk F.1/WF145, probably photographed during deck trials on HMS *Eagle* in 1952. Catapulting was assessed as straightforward, and deck-landing characteristics as excellent. Note the auxiliary inlets on the centre fuselage (BAe)

taking the second prototype P.1052 and giving it a new rear end with a straight-through jetpipe and a swept tail. It is debatable whether really accurate measurements were made of the performance of any of these interim types, but reports speak of the P.1081 reaching Mach 0.89 in level flight at altitude.

Earlier in 1950 there had been indications that in replacing the Meteor F.8 the Australian Government might be interested in a P.1081 with the uprated Tay engine in place of the Nene. Among other considerations, at that time Merlin production was running out in Australia, and there was a wish to continue the link with R-R. However, the development of the Tay was deferred, the aircraft went ahead on the basis of the Nene, and Australia lost interest.

At the time the abandoning of the P.1081 by the RAAF was viewed as evidence of anti-British sentiment, but the truth is probably that the RAAF wanted to be sure of a good swept-wing fighter for early use in Korea. Whatever the motiviation, by October 1950 the RAAF's choice had switched

from the P.1081 to a variant of the Sabre, and in the following year a licence was negotiated for the Commonwealth Aircraft Corporation in Melbourne to build the CA-27 Sabre with an Avon engine and two 30 mm Aden cannon.

On 3 April 1951 the P.1081 crashed near Lewes in Sussex, and 'Wimpy' Wade was killed. It will probably never be known for certain why the aircraft crashed. The theory inside the company was that Wade, who earlier that year had taken part in an exchange of civil test pilots between the UK and US, may have been trying to duplicate the transonic dives that he had made in the States in an F-86. However, he did not discuss such a plan with the project office, who would have warned against it. Whereas the F-86 has a hydraulically-powered flying tail, and the Hunter was to begin life with an electrically-trimmed tailplane, that of the P.1081 was fixed, pitch trim being effected by means of an elevator tab. The aircraft thus had no effective means of recovery from a transonic dive, in which the elevators would be rendered useless by shock-induced flow separations at the hinge-

The P.1052 was simply a P.1040 with a wing of 35 degrees sweep, the tail surfaces remaining unchanged. This first prototype, VX272, first flew on 19 November 1948
(BAe)

line. One can only conjecture that Wade may have been counting on the aircraft's dive recovery flaps, which Kingston had found effective on earlier models, but we now know to have been of little value on the company's swept wings.

The transonic dive theory is supported by accounts of a sonic bang at the time of the accident. Wade used his Malcolm ejection seat, but hit the ground still strapped to the seat, and was killed. Relieved of the weight of pilot and seat, and with the drag of the open cockpit, the P.1081 then levelled out and landed in a nearby field with comparatively little damage.

Wade was succeeded by his deputy, Neville Duke, who was officially appointed CTP in mid-April 1951. Later that year Hawker moved its flight test facility from Langley to Dunsfold, since the former site was too close to the main London airport at Heathrow. An important new member to join the team that year was A W ('Bill') Bedford, who had just left the RAF.

To complete the story of the Hawker technology demonstrators, the P.1072 was produced by installing an Armstrong-Siddeley Snarler liquid-fuel rocket motor in the rear fuselage of the P.1040

prototype (VP401). The first rocket-assisted flight took place on 20 November 1950, and in all Wade and Duke made three flights each. The rocket had fuel for only 2 min 45 sec, producing a 'terrific' climb performance and the prospect of reaching 50,000 ft (15,250 m) in $3\frac{1}{2}$ min from wheels-rolling. However, the aircraft was unpressurized and consequently limited to 40,000 ft (12,200 m), hence this climb performance figure could be produced only by extrapolation. Flight tests were terminated following a minor explosion in the rocket motor during relighting, on Duke's third flight.

Once again, Supermarine appeared to be in the lead. The Air Ministry shortly after the P.1072 trials decided to abandon the idea of rocket boost in favour of afterburning, which Supermarine had been testing on the Type 535 (VV119) since 23 August 1950. This aircraft also marked that company's switch (somewhat belatedly) to a tricycle undercarriage.

With hindsight, the first 10 years of the post-war period might be regarded almost as a 'phoney war' between the two rival companies, when very little seemed to be happening. Judged on the evidence

The P.1081, Hawker's first 'all-swept' aircraft, was produced by modifying the second prototype P.1052, VX279. The thick wing root, originally associated with the bifurcated jetpipe, led to a large trailing edge fillet (HSA via Brian Isles)

of first flight dates and aircraft entering service, Supermarine was consistently in the lead, while Hawker bumbled along somewhere in the rear. It is probably closer to the truth to say that (contrary to appearances) Hawker was laying the foundations for a stunning victory with a brand-new and vastly superior aeroplane, while Supermarine was digging a hole for itself with a series of changes to a fundamentally bad design.

It may be that the fundamental differences between the two companies stemmed from their histories and technical leadership. Kingston had a long tradition of designing fighters. If you worked there, you were taught that the only thing that really mattered was producing the best fighters in the world. Supermarine had no such tradition, having established its reputation with flying boats and racing seaplanes. In addition, Kingston had Sir Sydney Camm to lead its design team, a man with an unrivalled record of successful fighters. 'Joe' Smith of Supermarine had done an outstanding

job in refining Mitchell's early Spitfire into one of the world's great combat aircraft, but he was hardly an inspirational leader in the Camm mould.

In practical terms, it may be that the basic difference was that Supermarine chose to proceed directly from the Attacker to the Swift via a series of building-block changes, whereas Kingston was simply using the Sea Hawk to generate a series of technology demonstrators, which in turn would provide know-how for the design of a completely new aircraft, the P.1067 Hunter.

Project Studies

Following the end of the war, the design detachment at Claremont House had returned to Canbury Park Road in Kingston. Lickley, Page and Dunn departed for greener pastures, leaving Stanbury and Lipfriend as the senior project engineers, assisted by a draughtsman named J P ('Johnny') Kerr, who later went to Canadair. Most of the three-view project drawings of this period

In the early post-war period the Hawker project office studied a large number of different aircraft shapes. This tailless concept appears to have had a bicycle undercarriage, as later used for the P.1127/Harrier series (Mike Badrocke)

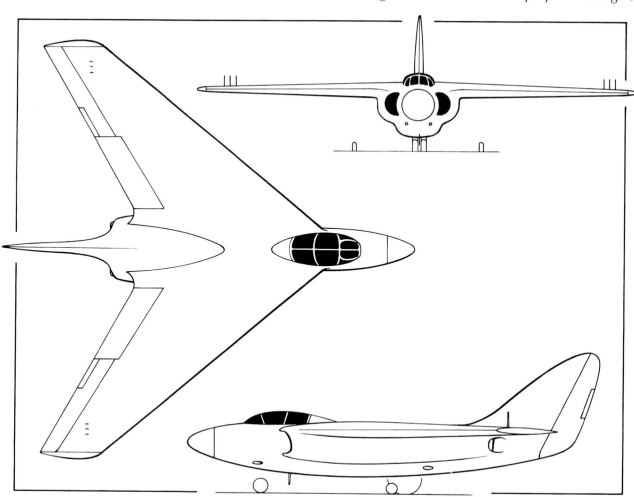

appear to have been done by Kerr and formally approved by Stanbury.

It is clear from the allocation of project numbers that Hawker was carrying out studies of the kind of fighter it wanted to build (ie, single-engined) in parallel with studies based on F.43/46 and F.44/46. Projects aimed at these specifications run from P.1048 to P.1065. Between these extremes the project office 'wallpaper book' includes a variety of single-engined designs, instanced by the P.1062. This might be regarded as a derivative of the P.1052, but with an RB.44 Tay engine and a selection of rear ends, including a straight-through jetpipe, evidently paving the way to the P.1081.

Of the two fighter specifications, the one mainly of interest at Kingston was F.43/46, relating to the design and construction of a prototype for a day interceptor fighter, to be suitable for the series manufacture of 600 aircraft at a maximum rate of 20 aircraft per month. This series of project studies shows very clearly the sudden swing from straight- to swept-wings early in 1946.

The company had begun with straight-wing configurations clearly inspired by the Me 262, although the vertical tail was pure Sea Fury. The P.1048 was suggested for the day fighter and the P.1056 for the two-seat all-weather fighter. It next seems to have struck the project office that asymmetric effects were not inevitable in the case of twin-jet fighters, so the engines were brought in to what we would now call a semi-conformal installation on the sides of the fuselage (as Bell had done with the P-59 series). However, the designers were still stuck with their piston-engine concepts when it came to balance considerations: the engines were still located well ahead of the CG, necessitating a very long rear fuselage.

One striking example was the P.1061, a straight-wing aircraft with two AJ.65s in the lower front fuselage, making it look like a scaled-up version of the Bell X-14 V/STOL research aircraft. Aimed at F.43/46, the P.1061 had provision for a fixed 20-inch (51 cm) radar dish in the nose. It also had a large recoilless gun situated between the wing spars, firing down a tube that emerged just below the radar, the propellant gases exhausting alongside the engine nozzles at the wing trailing edge roots.

Although presumably drawn earlier, the P.1057 to F.44/46 was an all-swept configuration with the engines set slightly further aft, though still well ahead of the aircraft CG. In a later development of this concept the engines were moved further aft, the wing was moved from a mid- to a low-setting, and the inlets were extended almost to the nose. This appears to have been the end of the line for Hawker night fighter studies, possibly because the word had passed that the Air Ministry would settle for a Meteor derivative (the NF.11, designed to F.24/48), pending the drafting of a new specification for a swept-wing twin-engined aircraft (the Javelin) at a later stage.

Studies of the F.43/46 day fighter continued with projects such as the P.1064, a low-wing aircraft with all-swept surfaces, semi-conformal AJ.65s, and a recoilless gun in the nose. However, the project office became concerned about fuselage frontal area, in this case 45 sq ft (4.2 m²). This led to something analogous to the Lightning engine layout, with one engine set high in the rear fuselage and the other low and much further forward. A similar arrangement was used in the Lavochkin La-200. This reduced frontal area to 32 sq ft (3.0 m²). The result looked rather like a deep-bodied Saab Lansen. It was still not a 'goer', but the study was moving in the right direction, and the wing was beginning to look interesting. In plan view, the project now looked like a half-way house to the Hunter.

Before leaving the subject of the F.43/46 studies, mention should be made of the P.1065, powered by a single AJ.65 and a boost motor of 2,000 or 4,000 lb (907 or 1,814 kg) thrust. It began life with a FOD-prone ventral inlet, then switched to semi-circular inlets in the wing leading edge roots. It was basically a much smaller aircraft than the twin-AJ.65 designs. It had a wing area of 340–370 sq ft (31.6–34.4 m²), whereas that of the twin turbojets had grown to 480 sq ft (44.6 m²). Fuselage frontal area was down to a modest 24.5 sq ft (2.3 m²).

To some extent the P.1065 was more like a 'Hawker aeroplane' than the big twin-jet designs. However, Sir Sydney would have been very conscious of its lack of operational flexibility (ie, that it was good for interception and nothing else) and of the adverse attitude that overseas air forces would take to the idea of using a liquid-fuel rocket motor. His attitude would almost certainly have been that, provided Rolls-Royce could coax a little more thrust out of the AJ.65, there was no reason why a good fighter could not be designed around a single engine. Moreover, it would be an aeroplane in the Hawker tradition, what Harold Tuffen describes as *the smallest possible airframe, the largest possible engine, and a reasonable military load*.

While studies proceeded on the basis of planned RAF requirements, a variety of designers at Kingston were drawing single-engined swept-wing fighters, first with the Nene, then with the Tay, and finally with the AJ.65 Avon, which at that stage was still expected to have a thrust of only 6,500 lb (2,950 kg). These proposals were discussed with the Ministry of Supply (MoS), and early in the following year Hawker was issued with specification F.3/48, dated 13 February 1948, and destined to provide the basis for the P.1067 Hunter.

The specification covered the design and construction of a prototype for a day interceptor fighter, although the design was also to be suitable for the economic production of a total of 800 aircraft. The design requirements placed primary importance on very rapid engine starting without external assistance, reaching idling in not more than 10 seconds, and preferably 5 seconds. Fuel or propellant for six successful starts was to be carried. A pressurized cabin was required, but the manufacturer was warned not to tap air from the

engine *superchargers* (!). One of several demands that Hawker never did meet was for inert gas purging of the drop tanks. The Ministry may have been slow to catch on to the absence of superchargers, but at least it was aware that tricycle undercarriages were being employed by some manufacturers. If the aircraft had a nosewheel (the specification warned), provision had to be made for easy replacement of the nose section, when damage due to the collapse of the nosewheel had occurred. The airframe was also to be designed for a load factor of 7.5G, and a diving speed of Mach 1.0, but the EAS (equivalent airspeed) limit need not exceed 620 knots (1,150 km/hr).

Appendix 'B' was the real meat of the matter. The Air Staff wanted a single-seat fighter landplane for day interceptor duties, capable of operating in any part of the world. Its primary role was to be destruction of high-speed, high altitude bombers in daylight, as soon as possible after the bomber was first detected on the radar warning system. Great importance was therefore attached to the

Wade alongside the Snarler nozzle of the P.1072, which was produced simply by installing the rocket in the rear fuselage of the prototype P.1040, VP401. The rocket was supplied with fuel for only 2.75 minutes of operation (BAe via Brian Isles)

need for immediate takeoff, the maximum possible acceleration, and the highest possible 'climbing speed'. It was visualized that the interceptor aircraft would be closely controlled by ground radar to within a mile (1.6 km) or so of the bomber, and that the interception would be completed visually.

One of the interesting points in the specification was that the Air Staff expressed the wish to have a maximum speed at 45,000 ft (13,700 m) of approximately 547 knots (1,104 km/hr), which corresponds to Mach 0.953. It is interesting firstly because even the Hunter with the 200-series Avon was incapable of this performance. The FGA.9 clean had a maximum of Mach 0.945 at 36,080 ft (11,000 m), and at the specification height was down to Mach 0.915. According to MoS Form 2110, the basically similar Hunter F.6 was good for 527 knots (976.5 km/hr) at that height, or Mach 0.92.

On the other hand, even the Hunter F.1 was faster than the contemporary Sabre. According to MoS Form 2110, the F.1 reached 524 knots (971 km/hr) or Mach 0.913 at 45,000 ft (13,700 m). The prototype XP-86 was incapable of reaching that attained height, but the F-86A-1 attained 502 knots (930 km/hr) or Mach 0.875 at that altitude. The later F-86E and -86F appear to have been slightly slower.

The speed demand is also interesting historically as a left-over from F.43/46. This earlier specification, dated 24 January 1947, went on to say that *'If, however, it is felt that this would delay production of the aircraft due to difficulties in the design of swept-back wings, then they would consider a more conventional design with a speed of about 500 knots (925 km/hr, or Mach 0.87) at that height, on the understanding that the wing design could be changed on later models to give the highest speed called for'.*

Reverting to the F.3/48 specification, perhaps the most important aspect of performance (since it ruled out the Sabre) was time-to-height. The demand was that *'from the time the pilot presses the first button to start the first engine to 45,000 ft (13,700 m) is not to be more than six minutes, excluding any time for taxying'.* Again referring to Form 2110, the Hunter F.1 had a climb time of 11.65 minutes to that height, and this figure was almost certainly given from wheels-rolling rather than finger-on-button. The corresponding figure for the F.6 was 7.1 minutes, which is the same as the manufacturer's brochure figure for the FGA.9,

The P.1072, probably at Bitteswell, where flight tests were carried out for proximity to the Armstrong Siddeley works. The aircraft had acquired the tail-bullet of later Sea Hawks, and an external rear-view mirror (BAe)

timed from wheels-rolling. The Hunter thus never came anywhere near the specified time-to-height figure.

In regard to operational ceiling, the specification stated that the rate of climb was not to be less than 1,000 ft/min (5.08 m/sec) at 50,000 ft (15,250 m). Form 2110 gives the corresponding operational ceiling of the F.1 as 45,900 ft (14,345 m) at clean take-off weight, this figure increasing to 47,500 ft (14,480 m) in the case of the F.6. It is noteworthy that the best of the production-series Hunters was (in this respect) the F.2, with an operational ceiling of 47,800 ft (14,575 m). Once again, the Hunter clearly failed to meet the performance specified.

Climb performance was of crucial importance in meeting the threat of the nuclear bomber, but MoS was (quite justifiably) afraid that these demands would be met by cutting back on internal fuel. It was therefore specified that *'an endurance of not less than one hour is required, to include a climb to 45,000 ft (13,700 m) and 10*

A rare shot of the Snarler in action. Only six flights were made, a minor explosion occurring in the rear fuselage during Duke's last test. Air Ministry chose to abandon rocket boost in favour of afterburning (BAe via Brian Isles)

minutes of combat at that height, and the remainder cruising at economical speed'. It was added that some increase in endurance was desirable, if it could be achieved without detriment to performance in other respects. The specification also asked for an investigation into the practicality of increasing range by means of drop tanks, for use in reinforcing overseas bases or in low altitude interception.

Form 2110 gives the F.1 a maximum endurance of 1.3 hr and a combat endurance of 0.55 hr, ie, 33 minutes. The initial production aircraft came

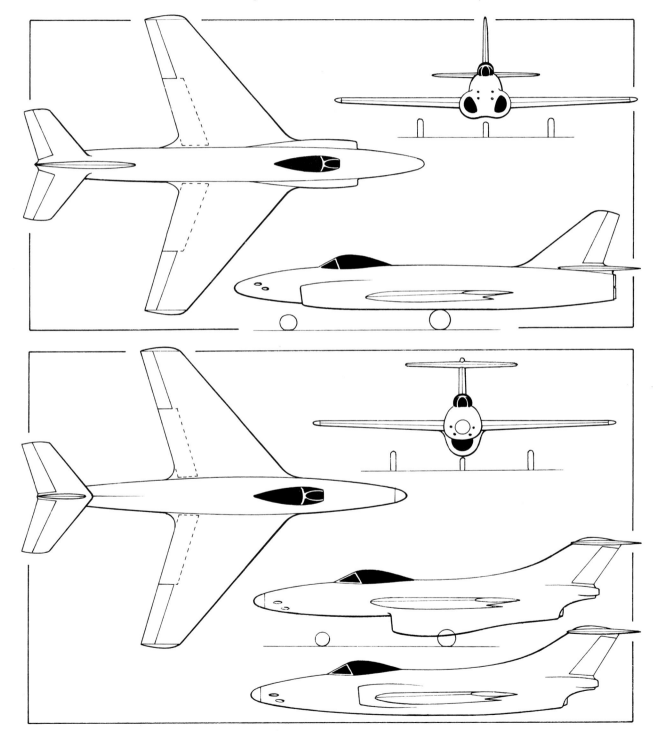

Project studies to F.43/46 included a variety of engine layouts. In this case the design appears to have been based on stacking the two engines one above the other to economize on frontal area. Note the awkwardly-positioned tailplane
(Mike Badrocke)

The P.1065/1 was yet another day fighter project, one of a series of preliminary designs studied to compare alternative powerplants arrangements. It had one turbojet engine and a rocket motor, and the air intakes were cut back, relative to earlier studies. The ventral inlet illustrated a lack of appreciation of water and debris ingestion problems
(Mike Badrocke)

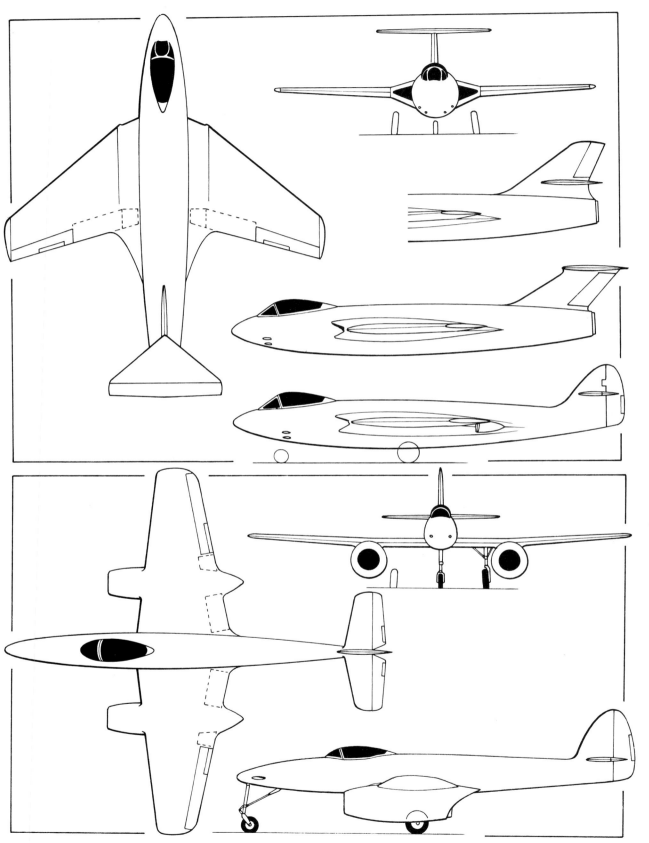

The P.1062 designation covered a series of studies relating to swept-wing derivatives of the P.1040. Note that dihedral was retained. A variety of tail shapes and alternative jetpipes are illustrated (Mike Badrocke)

The P.1048 was an early study of a possible twin-jet fighter layout, similar to that of the Me 262, but with a characteristic Hawker tail (Mike Badrocke)

nowhere near the specified endurance. Later models could exceed it handsomely, but at considerable cost in climb performance.

Airfield performance was specified under standard conditions, with the aircraft taking off in not more than 3,600 ft (1,100 m) to 50 ft (15 m) and landing in a similar distance over the same screen. The F.1 actually took off in 4,900 ft (1,495 m) according to Form 2110, and landed in 5,800 ft (1,770 m). Landing distance remained unchanged as the aircraft developed, but the F.6 had the much shorter takeoff distance of 3,900 ft (1,190 m). The manufacturer's figure for the FGA.9 is 3,200 ft (975 m), which is clearly at odds with MoS data, since the FGA.9 is 910 lb (413 kg) heavier than the F.6. All these distances relate to clearing a 50 ft (15 m) screen.

In view of the current emphasis on fighter turning performance, it is interesting that F.3/48 quoted no specific figures, simply stating that 'the best possible manoeuvrability consistent with the above qualities is required at high altitude'. It is doubtful whether the Ministry ever measured the aircraft's turning performance with kinetheodolites (which the Swiss regarded as standard practice), but Form 2110 gives the F.1 a turn radius of 8,150 yd (7,455 m) at 471 knots (873 km/hr) at 45,000 ft (13,700 m), corresponding to 1.29G. Equipped with the 'big' Avon, the F.6 improved these figures, with a radius of only 6,900 yd (6,300 m) at the same height, corresponding to 1.4G.

In view of the long delay in the Hunter's initial operational capability, it has to be noted that the specification stated that 'air brakes are an essential requirement'. However, there was no mention of pitching moments or change of trim on airbrake extension. It merely said that 'the application of the brakes must not cause the aircraft to vibrate so that the gunsight cannot be used'.

The armament demands are derived from the earlier F.43/46, which said that the aircraft should be designed to take either two 30 mm Aden with 200 rd/gun, or one recoilless 4.5-inch (11.4 cm) gun with six or (if possible) 10 rounds of ammunition. The guns were to be so placed that muzzle flash would not inconvenience the pilot at night.

At the time that F.3/48 was drafted, there was some doubt as to the future of the Aden gun, so the 20 mm Hispano was reintroduced into the specification. In revised form it said that the aircraft should take either four 20 mm Hispano Mk V with ammunition for 15 seconds, ie 200 rounds each, or two 30 mm with enough for 10 seconds, ie

200 rd/gun. Alternatively, the aircraft could be designed to take one recoilless (RCL) 4.5 inch (11.4 cm) gun with seven rounds. However, the project office copy of F.3/48 carries a handwritten note by Stanbury to the effect that the RCL gun need not be considered, presumably on the advice of the MoS. The specification also called for a GGS with radar ranging, requiring provisions to be made for a scanner.

In regard to 'accommodation', the specification called for the cabin to maintain a pressure equivalent to not more than 25,000 ft (7,600 m) when the aircraft was at 50,000 ft (15,250 m). In addition, 'either the cabin must be jettisonable', or the aircraft must be fitted with an ejection seat. Provisions were required for de-icing and demisting the windscreen, a further aspect on which the Hunter was to fall far short of intentions.

Perhaps surprisingly, there was no demand for armour plating and self-sealing tanks, although the Sea Hawk had self-sealing tanks. This may indicate that the OR Branch believed the Soviets would follow the British lead and develop unarmed bombers (like the Canberra) in order to achieve the greatest possible height. The specification simply reported that the Air Staff would like an appreciation of the effect on performance of fitting armour protection. If fitted, the armour, including a bulletproof windscreen, should afford protection for the pilot against 30 mm fragments (presumably from his own guns) at a range of 300 yd (275 m) from in front, and from 10° above, below, and on either side of that line. The fuel tanks need not be self-sealing, but they had to be compartmented so that one strike would not cause the loss of more than half the remaining fuel. Purging with inert gas was required. Strangely, the earlier F.43/46 had stated that bulletproof protection was not required, but the windscreen and pressure cabin had to be strong enough to prevent them being damaged by 'window' (chaff) released by the aircraft being attacked.

Night flying equipment, including cockpit instrument lighting was required, but not landing lights or resin lights. Equipment was to include a VHF multi-channel transceiver to ARI.5395 and IFF Mk III. In addition to a gyro-stabilized DR compass, a standby magnetic compass was required. This eventuated as an E.2A on the windscreen arch. Oxygen was to be sufficient for one hour at 25,000 ft (7,600 m). Finally, the specification stated that the design was to provide for simple and rapid servicing to facilitate a quick turnround.

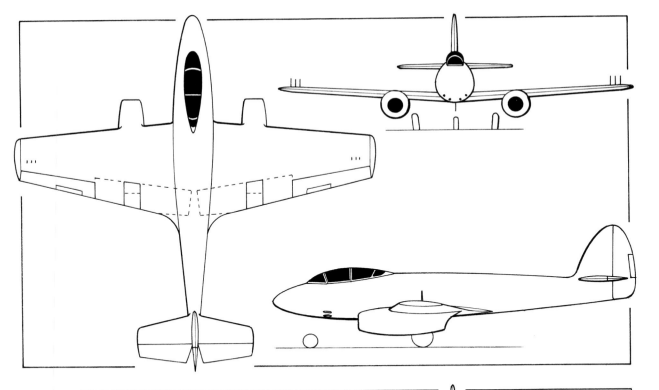

The P.1056 night fighter was proposed for specification F.44/46, powered by Avon turbojets
(Mike Badrocke)

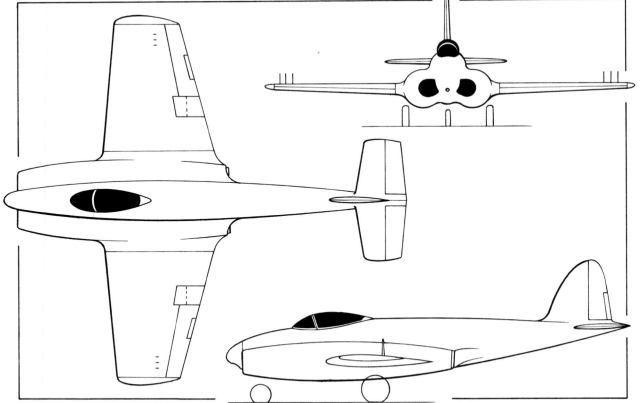

The garish P.1061, a very conservative approach to specification F.43/46 for a night fighter. The centre of gravity (CG) solution is indicative of a familarity with heavy piston-engines
(Mike Badrocke)

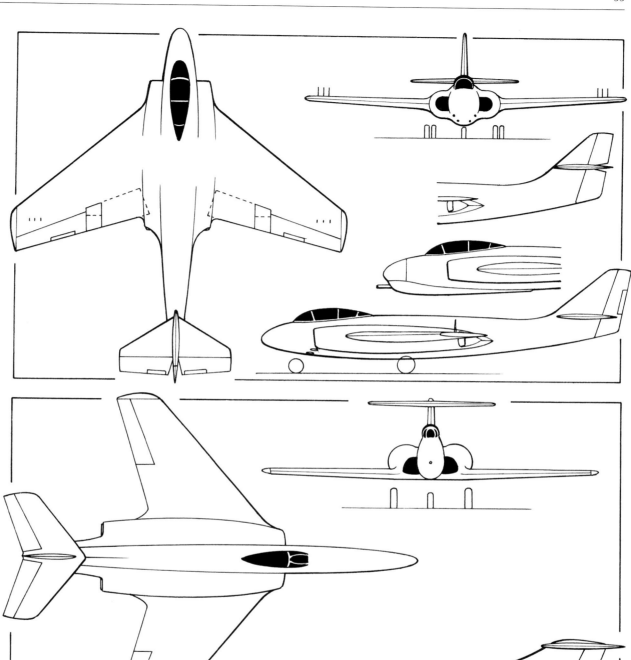

The P.1057/1 to
specification F.43/46 had
provision for a massive
RCL gun of 4.5 inch (11.4
cm) calibre
(Mike Badrocke)

The P.1064/1 to
specification F.43/46
(Mike Badrocke)

Chapter 5

Preliminary Design and the Operational Requirement

It is difficult to establish with confidence precisely how the Hunter design originated, not only because it happened a long time ago, but also because many people were involved over a period of several years. The general public may like to think of a chief designer sitting at his drawing board and producing one beautiful definitive design, but at Kingston in those days several project engineers would usually produce a number of possible designs to meet one requirement.

The company, acting on the advice of the chief designer, accepted one design to run with, and it was then transformed into a working product. In the course of this transformation its external shape often changed considerably. Because a three-view drawing that is of no particular significance one day may be transformed overnight into the basis for a multi-million programme, there are problems in researching decades afterwards how the design actually began.

In the case of the Hunter there are special difficulties, since the aircraft was regarded in the mid-1950s not only as an interim type, but as something the company looked forward to forgetting. In addition, Vivian Stanbury (head of the project office) left in 1956 to become chief designer of the car division of R-R, and was thus no longer concerned with aircraft. Most members of the project office dispersed for a variety of reasons.

Stanbury's recollection is that the P.1067 was one of a long line of single-engined projects. One early example was the P.1049 of January 1946, a single-seat interceptor with one AJ.65 and extreme sweepback, aimed at high subsonic performance. The company had received many German reports on swept wings, and was encouraged by RAE (especially Farren) to use sweepback. Stanbury recalls that 'We relied very much on RAE, not so much on their tunnel tests (we didn't believe them), but on advice and discussions. The key people were Miss Bradfield in the small tunnel and Perring in the larger ones. Also Handel-Davies and Morris in Aero Flight'.

The first outcome of the pressure for a swept wing was the P.1052 technology demonstrator. According to the MoS, the 'magic figure' for wing sweep was 35° on the quarter-chord line, and this angle was in fact used for most Hawker designs to F.43/46 and F.44/46. Stanbury believed this sweep angle to be worth an additional 30–40 mph (48–64 km/hr) in level flight.

The growing mass of swept wing tunnel data led to a generally-accepted graph showing the maximum usable aspect ratio as a function of sweep angle. High values for either parameter encouraged the tendency to tip-stall, hence a compromise was necessary. However, Stanbury says that the P.1067 wing was drawn simply to look right, and that the aspect ratio *'came out in the wash'*.

Since this series of single-engined projects began with the Nene and Tay engines, they originally featured lateral inlets in the P.1040 tradition, to feed air to both sides of the centrifugal compressor. Some had bifurcated exhausts emerging at the trailing edge root, which Stanbury felt (aside from increasing fuel volume) gave a nice thick root and thus helped structure weight.

The same line of reasoning led Stanbury to support the idea of a mid-set wing: *'Once you discard the idea of a straight-through wing, a circular-section fuselage goes with a mid-wing with a splayed-out root. It helps both the aerodynamics and the structure. Propellor-ground clearance is no longer a consideration, so the undercarriage can be short, the mainwheels going into the bulge created by the intakes and exhaust. You have a wing root that is thick structurally but thin aerodynamically'*. Stanbury would clearly approve of the F-16 with its mid-wing location and deepened root. Where Hawker went wrong later was with the P.1121, in taking a mid-set thin wing directly to fuselage ring-frames: the result was a record high in wing structure weight.

According to Harold Tuffen, who by then was second-in-command to Frank Cross in the Experimental DO, the single-engined project became serious in the second half of 1947, when the Air Staff at last abandoned the F.43/46. The first drawing in the project office 'wallpaper book' of what Stanbury refers to as *'the German P.1067'* appears to have been made by John Kerr and completed on 13 December 1948, to be formally approved by Alan Lipfriend. Since this was more than nine months after the specification had been received, it follows that a number of GA drawings were prepared before this one, quite possibly

The P.1052 first flew in November 1948, over a year after the North American XP-86 Sabre. Deliveries of the Sabre began only three months after the maiden flight of the Hawker aircraft (Cyril Peckham, HAL)

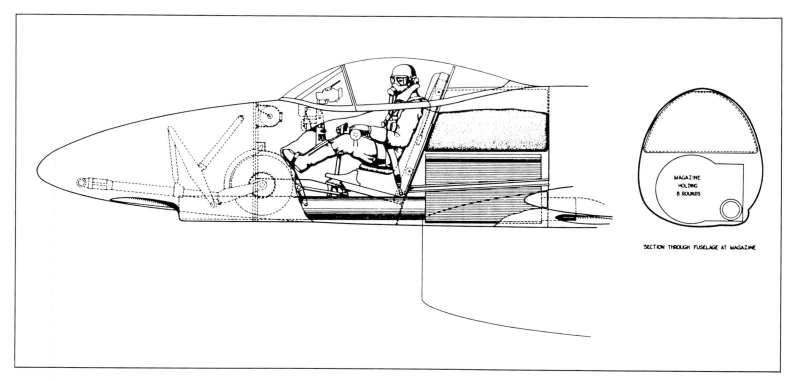

SECTION THROUGH FUSELAGE AT MAGAZINE

MAGAZINE
HOLDING
8 ROUNDS

without the originators bothering to have project numbers allocated.

Stanbury himself made the first sketch from which the series evolved. The original P.1067 was (Stanbury admits) virtually a copy of wartime German swept-wing single-jet projects, with a nose intake and high-set tailplane. As he says, 'an axial asks to have the intake in the nose' to provide a direct supply of air. The high tail gave a long arm and a short, lightweight jetpipe. The fuselage was basically an untapered cylindrical shape, to facilitate the installation of an afterburner, despite Camm's insistence on dispensing with reheat. Stanbury recalls Camm inviting Joe Smith of Supermarine to see the drawing, and Smith (taking his life in his hands) commenting 'I would put a bit of shape in it, Sydney'.

The P.1067 drawing of December 1948 features a wide elliptical-section front fuselage to take the bifurcated inlet ducts around the cockpit. The vertical tail is swept, but the horizontal tail is straight. Data on the drawing refers to an RA.2 engine of only 6,000 lb (2,720 kg), and an armament of four 20 mm Hispano cannon in the lower front fuselage.

A slightly later drawing by Kerr, designated P.1067/1 and dated 2 January 1949, shows some changes, including a circular-section fuselage and a cropped-delta tailplane. The engine is here referred to as the Avon RA.5 of 6,500 lb (2,950 kg) thrust. Two of the four Hispanos had been moved to the wing roots. The P.1067/1 had a span of 33.5 ft (10.2 m) a length of 41.5 ft (12.65 m), a wing area of 340 sq ft (42.5 m²), and a sweep angle of 42.5°. Fuel volume was 300 Imp gal (1,365 litres).

The most fundamental change in the course of P.1067 design development was the switch from a nose intake to lateral intakes broadly similar to those of the P.1040. In Stanbury's words, 'We could never reconcile the idea of all that wasted volume around the cockpit. Also, we had good experience with side inlets on the P.1040'.

Before leaving Stanbury's account, it is of historical interest that he visited RARDE at Fort Halstead in Kent to examine a mockup of the 4.5-inch (11.4 cm) recoilless gun referred to in the specifications. The massive barrel was fed with projectiles from a seven-chamber rotating drum, and Stanbury was appalled at the idea of this massive inertia thudding around inside the fuselage, and at the installation problems. None of the other visiting industry representatives liked the idea, and in due course the project was abandoned.

In researching this book, the author approached Fort Halstead for information on the gun, and learned from Gp Capt David Pugh that an extensive check of RARDE archives had

The massive 4.5 inch (11.4 cm) RCL gun housed in the alternative nose of the proposed Hawker P.1048/3 interceptor fighter, which featured AJ.65 Avon engines slung under the wings (HAL)

produced nothing more than the project calculation books, dealing with the pressures generated during firings, and the stress estimates for the various parts of the gun. Those who had worked on the project had by then retired, hence it may well remain something of a mystery.

The story now moves to Harold Tuffen, who was to transform the 'hole-in-the-nose' design into a handsome aeroplane in the great tradition of Hawker fighters. According to Tuffen's notes, following receipt of the specification in March 1948, the first Hawker proposal was made in the following month. A three-view drawing and data sheets were prepared by Lipfriend, supervised by Stanbury. Detail design began as a private venture, but it gradually became clear that the company had made a false start, although a mockup of the 'German P.1067' was largely complete and a replica of the nose intake had been sent to Derby for static tests with the engine (it gave very satisfactory results) before work was halted in February or March 1949.

One Saturday in May 1949 Tuffen rehashed the layout to show a 'solid' nose and wing-root intakes, and detail design work then recommenced. Various accounts have indicated that the switch to lateral intakes was made because of concern that a nose intake produced a cramped cockpit, or because of the need for a four-gun package, or because R-R preferred lateral intakes (which is nonsense). Tuffen insists that the switch was made because the company changed its approach to the fuel system.

The original plan had been for an internal capacity of 280 Imp gal (1,273 litres), consisting of a 40 Imp gal (182 litre) collector tank just behind the cockpit, and two 120 Imp gal (545 litre) integral tanks in the wings. Integral tanks were attractive technically, as they eliminated the weight of conventional bag tanks, but the concept was still new at the time. Such tanks had been used on various American transports, and on the Lockheed Hudson and Airspeed Ambassador. However, in the end Hawker took a typically conservative decision against integral tanks, on the grounds that they lacked the necessary

The 'Hawker P.1067/1' was proposed for specification F.3/48, powered by an Avon turbojet and armed with four 30 mm cannon (Mike Badrocke)

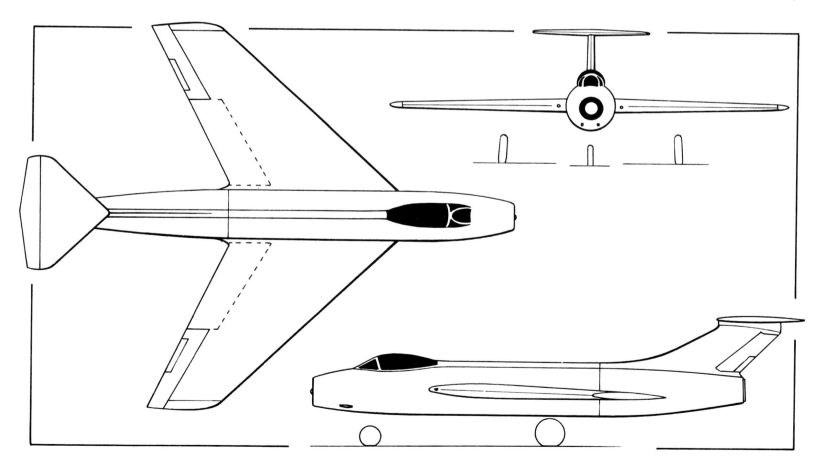

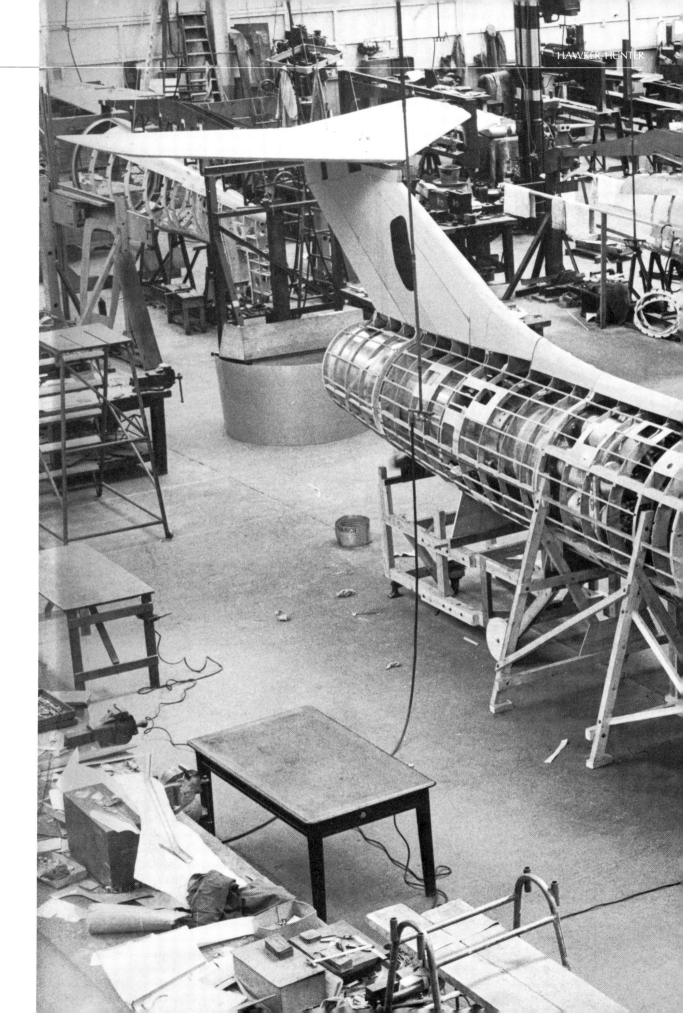

Mockup of the P.1067 at an intermediate stage of design development, the original nose intake having been abandoned, but the T-tail retained. Note the thickened wing root, associated with lateral intakes, and the nose-mounted radar ranging
(BAe)

background experience relevant to a 7.5G structure. There was also the fear that, when an integral tank leaked (as it inevitably would), the kerosene jet-fuel would just stay there, waiting for someone to come along with a match or cigarette, whereas avgas for piston engines evaporated. In the course of 1948 tests were run on a simple structure representing a wing integral tank, but the results were not encouraging. After discussions with MoS, integral tanks were therefore abandoned, and this is what caused design work to be halted in early 1949.

With hindsight, the decision to use bag tanks was probably a good one. By the time integral tanks were adopted for the P.1127/Harrier V/STOL aircraft (in which weight was of crucial importance) there was far more experience available, and potential leak paths could be minimized by integral-machined skins, but the tanks still leaked. There were initially fears that leaking fuel would run down the anhedral wing and ignite on the hot reaction control valves at the wingtips, but in fact this has not happened.

Once integral tanks had been rejected, the P.1067 wing was found to be a very inefficient fuel container (which remains true today), so, in Tuffen's words 'We just stuffed everything in a very long fuselage'. The possibility of a ventral intake (as on the P.1065) was considered briefly, and experts from RAE were consulted, notably Dr Seddon and Miss Bradfield. One of the most important influences on the design was an RAE paper by Dr Küchemann, indicating that wing root intakes could be used to increase the sweep of the inboard isobars and thus the critical Mach No of the wing.

The second stage was thus an aircraft with lateral intakes, though for some time it retained a high tail. Camm was not happy about this tail configuration, and demanded to see a proper structural investigation. A full-scale layout of the rear end was drawn by 'Digger' Fairey, but the DO didn't like it, and Camm clinched it with a decisive 'No!'. The project had begun life with afterburning (since this is what the RAF expected), but performance investigations led to the conclusion that it was unnecessary, and Camm had it deleted.

In the light of Camm's opposition to the T-tail, it was now drawn relatively low on the fin, as low as Stanbury felt it could go without it hitting the wing wake. Looking at the fuselage-mounted tailplane of the P.1127/Harrier, Stanbury later commented that the earlier tailplanes could evidently have

been set lower, even on the Sea Hawk, with bifurcated jetpipe, but in fact the Kingston V/STOL series has incurred a great deal of vibration and skin cracking through the proximity of the tailplane to the jets.

With the fuel tankage of the P.1067 completely revised, it now had 333 Imp gal (1,514 litres), all in the fuselage. Shortly afterwards, around a foot (30.5 cm) was added to the front fuselage just ahead of the front transport joint (at the leading edge root) to provide radio space. Another change was an increase in fuselage diameter from the 50 inches (127 cm) drawn in the project office to Tuffen's 52.5 inches (133.4 cm), so that it could take either the AJ.65 or the Sapphire.

Before leaving Tuffen's account of the preliminary design, it may be noted that his recollection of the armament development is that 'We never took the idea of four 20 mm very seriously; for a long time the aircraft had two 30 mm Aden in the lower front fuselage with fixed shell boxes, and two 20 mm short-barrel Hispanos (as fitted to the Typhoon and Tempest) in the wing roots with shell boxes in the fuselage'. At that stage the Aden was projected in both 30 mm and 20 mm forms. In due course the proposal changed to four Aden in the lower front fuselage, with shell boxes fixed in the upper fuselage. This was clearly inspired by the Sea Hawk's four-Hispano installation, which was one of the worst features of the aircraft, since shells tended to jam in the inaccessible chutes.

In a meeting with MoS representatives this proposal was criticized, partly on the grounds that men would be clambering over the aircraft with heavy ammunition. (The Hunter is a lot bigger than the Sea Hawk, and Aden ammunition much heavier than Hispano). However, a junior Ministry man suggested a removable gunpack, Camm liked the idea, and it went on to become one of the Hunter's best features. The gunpack design was done by Derek Campbell and Geoffrey Brassington of the experimental DO.

Returning to the basic shape of the airframe, the wing section was designed by John Dubbery, based on research by NPL. Like the preceding P.1040 and P.1081, the P.1067 began life with hydraulically-operated dive-recovery flaps, fitted on the under-surface of the inboard wing, immediately aft of the auxiliary inlets. These flaps proved to be of little value at the high speeds achieved with swept wings. Today the only evidence that the P.1067 ever had such flaps is a transverse channel in the lower surface of the forward pair of fuselage bag tanks, where the operating rods once ran. There seems to be some doubt whether these flaps were really intended as airbrakes or an emergency device, but the fact that the wing flaps were stressed for high-speed use supports the latter proposition.

It was later discovered that the Hunter's flaps were unsuited to use as airbrakes in high-speed formation flying, gun attacks, or transonic dives. This was undoubtedly a bad fault, and it led to a long delay in the aircraft reaching the squadrons. At the time this was a very serious matter, as the Hunter programme was proceeding on a 'super-priority' basis to meet the threat of 500 MiGs that the Soviets were said to have in Central Europe.

The other major fault in the basic design was the lack of a 'flying tail', ie a fully-powered tailplane. In a typically conservative move, Hawker had decided to progress slowly, and to use *power-assisted* controls in pitch and roll, with a 'manual' (ie, foot-operated) rudder. Power assistance resulted in the pilot experiencing a fraction of the

control surface loads, rather than merely overcoming a spring-feel unit. It also meant that in emergency (if hydraulic supplies failed completely) the pilot could fly the aircraft manually, although the control column loads would be very heavy at high speeds.

With so little background on powered flying controls, this decision was perfectly understandable, but opting for power-assistance had the disadvantage that pitch control had to be achieved via the elevators (ie, the hinged trailing edge portion of the horizontal tail). This in turn meant that pitch control at high subsonic speeds was heavy and ineffective, since elevator deflections would cause flow separations at the hinge line.

With the benefit of later knowledge, one would probably say today that placing the horizontal tail above the wing plane was asking for pitch-up. On the other hand, locating the tail part-way up the fin simplified the structure considerably. In the case of the P.1121 the tailplane was set low on the fuselage (following the lead of the F-100), which minimized

The first prototype P.1067, WB188, approaching completion in the experimental works at Richmond Road. The tailplane and fin have been mounted on the rear fuselage. Beyond a second rear fuselage, and a centre and front fuselage have been joined (BAe via Brian Isles)

the risk of pitch-up, but required a substantial ring-frame and a rigid cross-member to ensure that both tailplane halves moved together. This arrangement was undoubtedly far heavier and more expensive than that of the Hunter. Moreover, the Hunter's pitch-up problem turned out to be relatively minor, and easily tamed by a leading edge modification.

Having discussed the shortcomings of the basic design, it must be added that the P.1067 also had some very good points. Compared to the F-86, the Hunter was fundamentally a more cerebral product. As the Germans appreciated, swept wing benefits are restricted by the loss of isobar sweep at the root and tips, a limitation that North American failed to address. Since a weight penalty is paid for wing sweep, it is important to maximize the aerodynamic benefit by taking the aerofoil's peak thickness forward at the root and aft at the tips. The Hunter achieved this by virtue of the root intake and the 'streamwise tip'. One of the facts that was subsequently to impress the USAF evaluation team was that the Hunter could run away from a Sabre in a dive, and superior wing design was certainly a factor in this difference.

Lateral intakes also made possible a better design of front fuselage, with the minimum of wetted area, the maximum of useful volume, and excellent accessibility. Compared to the Swift, which also had lateral intakes, the Hunter had little intake depth at the fuselage side, hence there was less drag from the boundary layer diverters.

As discussed earlier, the lateral intakes gave deep wing roots, reducing the weight of the spar booms. These deep roots also made it possible to stow the mainwheels in the wing, whereas in the Sabre they were housed in the lower fuselage. This arrangement gave a much wider and more stable undercarriage track, the Hunter figure being 14.75 ft (4.5 m), 78 per cent more than the 8.3 ft (2.53 m) of the F-86. It also made possible a centreline stores position for the Hunter, although only Singapore has ever exploited this potential.

It can be argued that the Hunter's lateral intakes made it an inherently more flexible aircraft in terms of development for other roles. A five-camera nose was developed without any real problem, although the RAF turned out to be satisfied with three cameras, and it must be admitted that photo-reconnaissance versions of the Sabre (and MiG-17) were produced. However, the Hunter was basically more amenable to a large-scale rehash: it readily took the AI.20 radar in

the P.1109 version (in this writer's view, the most elegant of all Hunters), whereas the Sabre needed much more surgery to become the F-86D, and early MiGs were extremely limited in dish size.

Operational Requirement

While the design of the P.1067 progressed, the operational requirement (then classified 'Secret') continued to develop. It should perhaps be explained that the specification F.3/48 related to the P.1067 prototypes, while the associated operational requirement (OR.228) formed the legal basis for production orders. The early drafts of OR.228 (which first appeared in December 1946) actually related to the twin-engined F.43/46. Although this concept was abandoned, the RAF need for a day interceptor fighter to replace the Meteor survived, serving as a basis for both the F.3/48 Hunter and the F.105D Swift series.

As far as can be established from the records of the Air Historical Branch, the first issue of the requirement that related to F.3/48 (ie, OR.228/3) specified the powerplant as a single Avon or Sapphire, and stated that 'Provision shall be made in the design for the incorporation of exhaust re-heating on a scale to be agreed by DGTD(A)'. In OR.228/7, covering production of the earlier marks of Swift, it is specified that the Mks 1 and 2 should have the Avon Mk 10501 ECU without reheat, while the Mks 3 and 4 should have the Avon 10801 with reheat to 1,500°K.

In OR.228/8, for production of the Hunter F.1, approximately the first 50 aircraft were to have the Avon Mk 10701 ECU without reheat, and provisions for the Mk 10401 until the later engine was available. However, from about the 51st aircraft onwards, the Hunter (F.3) was to be fitted with the Mk 11001 ECU with reheat to 1,500°K. This document also called for intake anti-icing (which was never found to be necessary, due to the aircraft's speed, and rate of climb and descent), and for engine change within three hours. The corresponding issue for the Hunter F.2 (OR.228/9) called for the Sapphire Mk 1101, and stated that the 'design shall be such that reheat to 1,500°K can be introduced retrospectively'. Finally, OR.228/11 was associated with specification F.119D, dated 13 August 1952, and related to the fourth prototype P.1067 (ie, the P.1083) with 52° leading edge sweep, the RA.14 Avon with 1,500°K reheat, 330 Imp gal (1,500 litres) of fuel in the fuselage, and 130 Imp gal (680 litres) in the wings. In the event, afterburning was used only in the

In the mid-1950s Hawker Aircraft hoped to follow the Hunter with the P.1121 supersonic strike fighter. This photograph shows (beyond the Hunter sections) the front and centre fuselage of the P.1121 prototype, and the mockup (BAe)

Hunter F.3 prototype and the Swift F.3, F.4 and FR.5, of which only the FR.5 reached true operational status.

Turning to matters of armament, it may be recalled that when OR.228 originated in 1946 the demand was for two 30 mm Aden cannon or one 4.5-inch (11.4 cm) recoilless gun. The armament section of the OR went through several phases of development, as the recoilless gun faded into obscurity and the prospects for the Aden waxed and waned. The details of this development are more readily traced through OR.228 than through the various stages of F.3/48.

In OR.228/3 the wording was changed to say that *The aircraft is to be designed to take four 20/30 mm Aden guns with 7.5 seconds fire. If two of the guns are removed, at least 10 seconds fire is required from the remaining two. Alternatively, the design is required to take four 20 mm Hispano with 15 seconds fire, but this is not to prejudice the primary requirement for the Aden gun'.*

In OR.228/4 of October 1948, the normal load is laid down as two 20/30 mm Aden guns with 10 seconds fire (ie 200 rd/gun), and the overload case is two guns with 13 seconds fire (260 rd/gun) or four with 7.5 seconds (150 rd/gun). However, it was added that the aircraft had to be basically suitable for the incorporation of four 20/30 mm guns at a later date *'if this becomes necessary. The additional weight may be regarded as an overload, and is not to prejudice the performance of the design for the normal armament case'.*

Continuing this line of thinking, OR.228/7 of March 1951 referred to specification F.105P2 for the Swift F.1, F.2, F.3 and F.4, the F.1 having two 30 mm Adens with 10 seconds fire, and subsequent marks four such guns with 7.5 seconds fire.

In the definitive OR.228 referring to both the Hunter and Swift, it was stated that the aircraft was to be given *'the maximum firepower consistent with obtaining the required performance, though production of the aircraft is not to be delayed'.* The normal load was to be four Aden with 7.5 seconds fire, though in certain circumstances only two guns might be carried, and then at least 10 seconds fire per gun was required.

In the event the Hunter was given four 30 mm Adens and space for 150 rounds/gun. It was found that the feed operated more reliably if the ammunition was restricted to 135 rounds/gun, which corresponded to just less than 7 seconds fire. Due to persistent structural problems and the fact that the Hunter was 'overgunned' for ground

targets, a later modification allowed the pilot to select pairs firing (inbd/outbd). One of this writer's proposals for further Hunter development for the RAF involved the deletion of one inboard and one outboard cannon, and redesign of the gunpack to accept two enlarged shell boxes in place of the four small ones, but this concept was not proceeded with.

In the definitive OR.228 it is stated that *'provision is to be made as soon as possible for the carriage of the air-air rocket battery or ultimately Blue Sky'* (the Fairey Fireflash beam-riding air-air guided missile). It is also stated that a secondary role for the aircraft was to be ground attack, but that provisions for this role must not prejudice its performance in the primary role or delay production of the aircraft. This role required provisions for 16 three-inch (76.2 mm) rocket projectiles on zero length launchers using tier-stowage, or, when available, rockets called up in OR.1099, or two 1,000 lb (454 kg) bombs. The armament specified in OR.1099 was presumably the Matra Type 155/116M pod with 18 or 19 SNEB 68 mm rockets respectively. These pods eventually replaced the highly inaccurate 'drainpipes' of wartime vintage, although some of Hawker's experts would have preferred a faster rocket with greater penetrating power. For overseas customers the company generally recommended the 80 mm Hispano SURA rocket, although it represented far more drag than the French system.

Using the wartime three-inch (76.2 mm) RP, the normal load was 24 rocket with 12/18/25 lb (5.4/8.2/11.3 kg) heads, or 16 with 60 lb (27.2 kg) heads. The requirement said that the missiles were to be carried in addition to any fuel drop tanks. This demand could be satisfied partially with stacks of 'drainpipes' or SURA rockets, since the inboard pylon was well clear, and the outboard pylon deleted only one tier on either wing. However, Blue Sky was carried on the inboard pylons (where later the big tanks were carried as standard), and the SNEB/Matra pods were carried on any of the four wing pylons (normally the outer pair), hence they restricted external fuel.

In the context of the ground attack roles, it was required that protection should be increased to include the underside and sides of the cockpit. In the event, cockpit armour (aside from the front bulkhead and windscreen) was applied only to the FR.10 and export equivalents.

Considering other changes in the definitive OR, the section on performance added that *'it is desirable that a diving speed of at least Mach 1.2 be obtainable'*. By this stage endurance *'with permanent built-in tanks'* was not to be less than $1\frac{1}{4}$ hours, and jettisonable tanks had become a formal requirement for reinforcing and low altitude operations.

The airbrakes *'should not cause the aircraft to vibrate, snake or hunt so that the gunsight cannot be used'*. They were also to be used in rapid descents, and were *'not to affect stalling speed, or the aircraft's handling qualities at any speed'*.

Inert gas purging of all fuel tanks, including drop tanks, was required, though this was ignored by Hawker. The same was true of the requirement that a single bullet strike would not cause the loss of more than 20 per cent of remaining fuel. The company did honour the original demand for a maximum loss of 50 per cent, but the later demand would have meant a large-scale rehash of the fuel system. The MoS intention was evidently that the fuel should be fed by nitrogen pressure, with compressed air from the engine used only if the nitrogen pressure fell to an unsatisfactory level. Single-point refuelling was specified with a flow rate of 150 Imp gal (680 litres)/min, though a two-point system was acceptable if it produced any appreciable weight-saving. In the event, the single-point demand was met, using a connection in the left-hand mainwheel bay.

Sun-blinds were also required, but they were not provided. Pilots sitting in Hunter cockpits on the ground in the Middle/Far East were shielded either by sheets of canvas on ground-mounted frames, or by hand-held parasols that were simply hurled clear when the aircraft were scrambled.

The aircraft was required to have VHF radio and standby, IFF Mk 10 with coding devices or (failing that) IFF Mk 3GR. All aerials were to be suppressed. One useful innovation was that a plug and socket to OR.2044 were to be provided to allow direct landline communication with the pilot.

Chapter 6

Early Test-Flying and Records

Handsome, white-overalled Sqn Ldr Neville Duke DSO, OBE, DFC**, AFC, Czech MC, was probably the last British test pilot whose name became a household word. By the time that 'Bill' Bedford made the first flight in the P.1127 and Brian Trubshaw flew Concorde, the excitement and romance (if not all the potential danger) had left test flying, perhaps due to increasing professionalism in aircraft design and the advent of the astronauts.

In July 1951 Duke was still very new to the job of chief test pilot, but he had an impeccable background as a wartime fighter pilot, and had flown all the Hawker jet series. In the course of three operational tours in Spitfires (which in theory were restricted to 180 hours each) he had flown 712 hours in 486 sorties, including 543 hours with the Desert Air Force. Along the way he had destroyed 28 enemy aircraft, and was also credited with three probables and five damaged.

From the end of 1944 he had been attached to HAL at Langley to assist with production test flying, and in 1946 was posted to the fifth course at ETPS. This had been established in 1943 at Boscombe Down, but by this stage had moved to Cranfield, prior to settling at Farnborough in 1947. Duke left the RAF to join Hawker in June 1948, becoming deputy to Wade, who had taken over from 'Bill' Humble as CTP when the latter became sales manager. However, for a time Duke continued his association with the RAF, becoming in September 1950 the CO of No 615 County of Surrey Squadron of the Royal Auxiliary Air Force, based at the famous Battle of Britain airfield of Biggin Hill.

As recorded earlier, Duke became CTP in mid-April 1951, and was shortly afterwards joined by Flt Lt A W 'Bill' Bedford AFC as deputy CTP. Bedford had flown P-47s in India and Hurricanes in Burma, graduated from ETPS and instructed there, and had test-flown for RAE.

Three prototype P.1067s (two with Avons, one with the Sapphire) had been ordered by MoS in November 1948, and on 20 October 1950 the Ministry issued an ITP for planning for the production of 200 Avon-powered aircraft. The first production contract, for 113 Hunter F.1s, was signed on 14 March 1951, and in the following year the Hunter programme was placed on a 'Super Priority' status. Because of Hunter production commitments, HAL built only 35 Sea Hawks at Kingston, switching production to Armstrong Whitworth (AWA).

In preparing to fly the P.1067, Duke first flew the

Canberra bomber for experience of Avon engine handling, in-flight relights, etc, and then the F-86A for experience of transonics in swept-wing aircraft. Like most fighter pilots, Duke found the Sabre 'a most pleasant aircraft'. He also flew an experimental Fairey Firefly FR.4 with the powered flying control units (PFCUs) of the P.1067, and a Sea Fury with powered elevators.

The first prototype P.1067 was painted a pale green, a colour that Duke and many others refer to as 'duck egg green'. The paint was actually a slight variation of the 'sky' camouflage then used on the undersurface of Fleet Air Arm aircraft. It was developed and donated as a publicity effort by Cellon, the first two prototypes being painted this colour.

On 27 June 1951 the first P.1067 was taken by road from Kingston to the MoS airfield at Boscombe Down, which has a 9,000 ft (2,750 m) runway. Duke had never previously taken a prototype up for its maiden flight, and this may have accounted for the fact that he burned out the aircraft's brakes in the course of high-speed taxy trials.

Duke's 'maiden-maiden flight' took place in the evening of 20 July 1951. The prototype (WB188) was fitted with a spin-recovery parachute at the base of the fin, and ballast in place of the four guns and ammunition. It was a 47-minute flight in which the undercarriage was retracted and Duke simply took the aircraft up to medium level to see how it handled on the approach to the stall, then landed back at Boscombe. The only point of any technical interest on this historic first flight was that Duke had to apply 'a very considerable two-handed heave on the stick' to round out for that first landing. Britain then lagged behind in powered flying controls, and for the first flight it had been decided to keep the elevators in manual, although Duke could still trim the tailplane electrically. In the event, the tailplane trim range proved to be inadequate, hence Duke's comment on stick force.

The first prototype began life with manual rudder, and boost ratios of 14:1 and 5:1 on the ailerons and elevators respectively. The Fairey

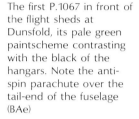

The first P.1067 in front of the flight sheds at Dunsfold, its pale green paintscheme contrasting with the black of the hangars. Note the anti-spin parachute over the tail-end of the fuselage (BAe)

PFCUs suffered considerable teething problems, but these were gradually sorted out and the Hunter eventually acquired fully-powered ailerons and elevators. In the case of the ailerons, plain spring feel was used, though the system incorporated two-speed gearing to reduce the stick loads when flying in standby manual control.

In the case of the elevators, these surfaces were also later to be fully powered. But their effectiveness decreased markedly above about Mach 0.95, hence high speed manoeuvrability was at this stage of development still significantly inferior to that of the F-86. A 'poor man's flying tail' was therefore produced by sensing elevator position with microswitches, and using the signal generated to drive the tailplane by means of the electric trim motor in a follow-up mode. Artificial feel was provided in the form of a three-gradient spring, with the later addition of a bobweight on the FGA.9. A slab tail was flown experimentally, but never became a production item.

Returning to the story of WB188, after Duke had made five flights from Boscombe, testing was

Preparing to fly: the first aircraft being refuelled via the port mainwheel bay. This unusual shot emphasizes the relatively low aspect ratio of the Hunter wing, which penalized sustained turn performance. The oversize roundels are also striking
(BAe)

transferred to Farnborough (which is much closer to the manufacturer's facilities) on August 10th and then to Dunsfold on September 7th. Having accumulated 11 hours flying time by early September, the aircraft was presented at the 1951 SBAC Show, with high-speed passes at up to 608 knots (1,127 km/hr).

Following preliminary performance tests, the aircraft was grounded for minor modifications and the installation of a production Avon RA.7 with variable swirl. By the spring of 1952 it was involved in high Mach investigations, but progress bogged down for a considerable time at an IMN of 0.97–0.98, where there was heavy aerodynamic buffet and rudder vibration. The maximum IMN in dive tests gradually edged up to 1.03 by April 1952, but by this stage the rear-end buffet and vibration were extremely severe, and further progress seemed impossible.

Various modifications were tested in efforts to increase dive speed, including vortex generators, revised boat-tail fairings, extra dorsal fin area, a reduced-span rudder, and spoilers on the fin.

Meanwhile, Duke had been looking through magazines, studying photographs of Soviet and American jet fighters, and noticed that some were equipped with a bullet fairing at the rear of the junction between the vertical and horizontal tails. He drew this to the attention of the project office, a similar fairing was fitted to WB188, and the aircraft's dive speed immediately jumped to 1.06 IMN. These dives were usually made from around 45,000 ft (13,700 m), and reached angles of 30°–45°. The elevators were completely in-effective supersonically (this was before the follow-up tail), and dive recovery was made either by throttling back or by careful use of tailplane trim.

Indicated speeds usually involve some error due to the effect of the aircraft's shape on the surrounding flow field. In transonic flight the presence of shock waves makes it even more difficult to establish true Mach No (TMN), hence up to this point HAL was not sure whether the P.1067 had actually gone supersonic. In reality it had probably not exceeded a TMN of 0.97. It was

The first prototype P.1067 illustrates the fine lines of the original design, before all the excrescences were added. It also brings out the shortness of the front fuselage, and the way the intake and the tip served to increase isobar sweep
(Cyril Peckham, HAL)

The second P.1067, WB195, was also powered by an Avon and painted pale green. It had its maiden flight on 5 May 1952, and was the first of the series to be equipped with cannon, though it was not used for the initial gunfiring trials
(BAe)

Left The first Sapphire-engined Hunter was the silver-painted WB202, seen here outside the experimental hangar at Dunsfold. It was this aircraft that gave the wholly erroneous impression that the series would have no gunfiring problems
(Cyril Peckham, HAL)

Below The first production Hunter F.1 WT555 had its maiden flight on 16 May 1953 piloted by 'Frank' Murphy. Having been chief production test pilot, Murphy later transferred to marketing, and was responsible for many Hunter exports
(BAe via Brian Isles)

widely believed within the company that North American had claimed supersonic performance for the F-86 before it was actually achieved, because the pitot-static head was inside the air intake and produced large errors.

The only way to be sure that an aircraft had exceeded Mach 1.0 was to record a sonic boom on the ground. The first flight of the P.1067 with the newly-installed tail bullet was made on 6 June 1952, and a series of dives was then made, reaching an IMN of 1.06. However, the first confirmation of true supersonic flight came only on June 24th, when the first bang was heard on the ground.

The first public demonstration of this pheno-menon took place on 10 July 1952, when the P.1067 performed at Melsbroek in Belgium. At this stage Hawker had the lead in Britain (and the rest of Europe), and the company's test pilots emphasized this fact by aiming bangs at Supermarine's South Marston airfield and de Havilland's facility at Hatfield. However, by the time the next SBAC Show came around in

September, the D.H.110 was also diving super-sonically.

By the end of 1952 HAL had three Hunters flying. The second F.1 (WB195) was also painted pale green, and was first flown (by Duke) on 5 May 1952. This was the first of the series to carry four Aden cannon and radar ranging. It proved to be something of a rogue-aircraft, as in the course of a demonstration at CFE, West Raynham (probably 4 June 1952) it developed an undamped elevator vibration in a pull-up at 590 knots (1,095 km/hr). This vibration damped out only when speed was reduced to 540 knots (1,000 km/hr). In a recurrence at Boscombe, the pitching was so bad that the pilot almost decided to eject. However, a cure was eventually found.

Such problems were investigated by a long programme of resonance testing at gradually increasing airspeeds, the pilot making a sudden input via the control column, and the resulting aircraft response being recorded for subsequent analysis. Duke seems to have made his input with *'a sharp clout of the fist'*, but Bedford got someone

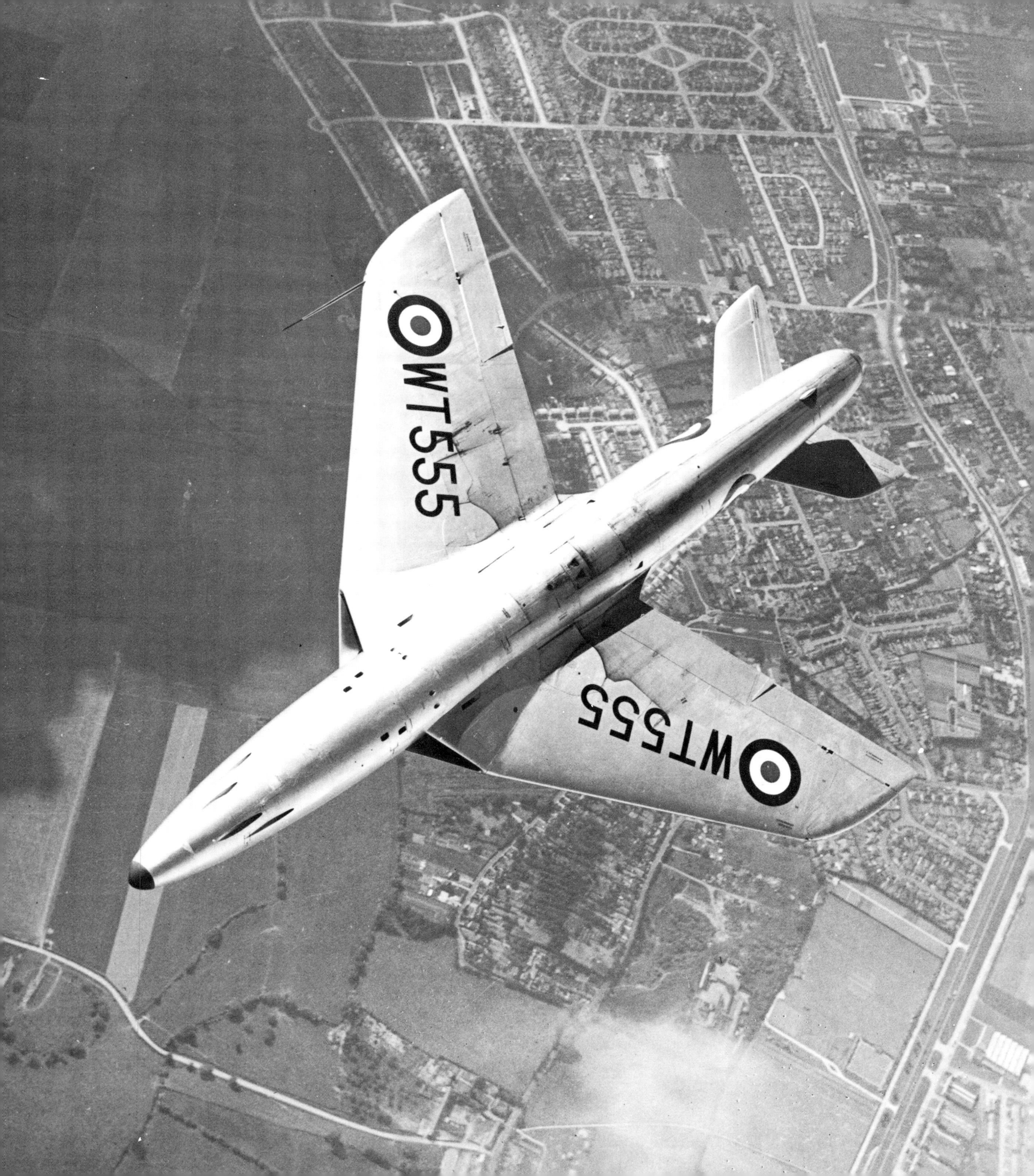
WT555
WT555

Left The first production Hunter F.1 inverted over typical English countryside. The lack of a separate airbrake is noteworthy, as is the fact that the chutes for the shell cases and links ended flush with the skin (BAe)

A later production standard of F.1 is illustrated by WT594, which first flew on 2 July 1954 (pilot 'Frank' Bullen). By this stage the ventral airbrake had been developed to a satisfactory standard, although deliveries had been delayed by a year (HAL)

to manufacture a wooden-handled brass 'bonker' for the same purpose. In later years as marketing manager, 'Bill' kept the 'bonker' on his desk, applying the slab of cold metal to his forehead as a heat-sink in more trying moments.

In December 1952, WB195 was flown to Boscombe for preliminary MoS assessment. It was later used in airbrake development and early spinning trials. The third aircraft was WB202, equipped with a Sapphire engine, and thus the first F.2. It was painted silver, and had its maiden flight (Duke at the controls) on 30 November 1952. It was (unfortunately) allocated to initial gunfiring trials, then to airbrake development and drop tank tests. It was later flown with up to four de Havilland Blue Jay (Firestreak) air-air guided missiles.

It soon became clear that development work and clearance trials would require the use of more aircraft than the three prototypes ordered. The first 21 production Hunter F.1s and the first seven F.2s were accordingly diverted for use in tests by the manufacturers, A&AEE, R-R, and RAE (Farnborough).

Ordering the aircraft 'off the drawing board' in March 1951 (four months ahead of first flight) may have been a foolish move in generating a large number of operationally useless aircraft, but it had the advantage of a rapid buildup of test vehicles in late 1953 and early 1954. A great deal of trial installation (TI) work could thus be carried out at Dunsfold, without interfering with clearance trials at Boscombe Down.

The first production F.1 (WT555) took to the air on 16 May 1953, piloted by chief production test pilot 'Frank' Murphy, a 'Kiwi' who had flown with the RAF in the Battle of Britain and later became a highly successful marketing manager for HAL, responsible for most Hunter sales. The maiden flights of the next four F.1s were spread between June and September 1953, and all were allocated to Boscombe. By the end of 1953 there were 16 production F.1s assisting in the test programme, and by 8 January 1954 the 21st (WT575) had flown, and was duly sent to A&AEE.

The F.2 had been ordered into production with an initial batch of 45 aircraft, to be built by AWA at

The original OR envisaged the use of afterburning, which was tested on WB188. Endurance was unacceptable, but the trials did allow the Hunter to win the world's absolute speed record. It is shown here taking off for the record attempt (via Brian Isles)

Top Hunter F.1 WT594 with airbrake extended. This gave far less pitching moment than the use of wing flaps, but the drag increment was limited and the airbrake could not be used in the approach (HAL)

Middle right Neville Duke in the cockpit of WB188 after the record-breaking flights in the summer of 1953. At this stage the highly-swept conical windscreen used in the record attempts had been removed, leaving a pale green patch in the blood-red paint scheme (BAe)

Middle left One of the Hunter's best features was its rapidly-replaceable gunpack, which was lowered from the aircraft on three bomb-hoists, the four barrels having been detached and left in the blast-tubes (BAe)

Bagington, Coventry. The first (WN888) had its first flight on 14 October 1953, and the seventh allocated to trials (WN894) flew on 26 August 1954.

The fact that three prototypes, 21 production F.1s and seven production F.2s were to take part in the development programme is some indication of the multiplicity of problems that had to be investigated, and the total uselessness of the initial production standard. Considering that this was a subsonic aircraft with no weapons system in the accepted sense, the Hunter initially represented a catastrophe of remarkable proportions.

Some of the problems associated with powered flying controls have already been mentioned. However, even in the early prototype flying, pilots were running into other problems that were destined to grow in significance as they were further explored, and to delay by many months the attainment of an initial operational capability.

In the course of the first series of trials with WB188, Duke's main concern had been with rear-end buffet, produced by a combination of adverse pressure gradients on the vertical and horizontal tails. The only other obvious problem was in persuading the Hunter to decelerate. The original plan had been to use the aircraft's large plain flaps, which were stressed for operation up to the maximum speed of the aircraft. They could be lowered through 80°, producing a great deal of drag, and in emergency were to be augmented by 'dive-recovery flaps' that were intended to generate a nose-up pitching moment. Unfortunately, these auxiliary flaps proved to be ineffective, and the main flaps produced a strong nose-down pitching moment that increased markedly with speed.

The Airbrake Saga

At this point of the Hunter's history, it is necessary to mention something of the role played by the RAF's Central Fighter Establishment (CFE) at West Raynham in Norfolk. This organization (which no longer exists) had an evaluation wing consisting of one squadron dealing with all-weather fighters and another for day fighters. The latter was called the Air Fighting Development Squadron (AFDS)

The first prototype, piloted by Duke and coming in to land at Tangmere after the record-breaking run. The average speed over the three-kilometre course was 727.63 mph (1,171.3 km/hr), corresponding to mach 0.943 (AP)

and at that stage was commanded by Wg Cdr (later Air Vice-Marshal) Bird-Wilson. The other side of CFE was a training wing, consisting of an instrument training squadron and the Day Fighter Leader Squadron (DFLS), which came into the Hunter story later.

The scheme of things was that, once A&AEE had checked that a new fighter met the specification, AFDS would (in Bird-Wilson's words) 'test and combat-evaluate' it as an operational aircraft, tell the squadrons how to operate it tactically, and request any modifications felt to be necessary for operational reasons. Sometimes AFDS would make its assessment in parallel with the testing done at Boscombe. As an example of their work, just prior to the advent of the Swift and Hunter, AFDS had been testing two stripped Venoms, one of which climbed to 59,000 ft (18,000 m). These trials were aimed at investigating the problems of high level interceptions of subsonic bombers, and they found that visual sightings were extremely difficult due to glare at extreme altitude.

To digress, the standard Venom could outclimb the Sabre, but, having got to altitude at 350 knots (650 km/hr) and 0.7 IMN, it then took a quarter of an hour to accelerate to a useful speed. The Venom also had excellent manoeuvrability, out-turning the Meteor, but the latter was idiot-proof, whereas both the Vampire and Venom had a nasty flick.

On 28 September 1953 Air Cdre Wallace Kyle, Director of Operational Requirements at the Air Ministry, gave orders for Wg Cdr Bird-Wilson and Flt Lt Alan Jenkins to go to Dunsfold and fly the first production Hunter (WT555). Four flights were made to evaluate the wing trailing edge flaps as airbrakes. When the flaps were selected down at high speed and low-level, the nose of the Hunter went hard down, and 'the pilot headed for the canopy'. The trim-change was such that for operational use it was totally unacceptable, an unpalatable fact that was passed on by Air Cdre Kyle to Sir Sydney. In fact, as a result of the preliminary AFDS assessment, the RAF categorically refused to accept a single Hunter until the airbrake had been redesigned. For historical interest, Kyle also brought bad tidings to Kingston in 1954, when he announced cancellation of the P.1083.

As recalled by 'Fred' Sutton, then flight test manager at Dunsfold, HAL had been aware since May 1952 that the company had 'got it wrong' in regard to airbrakes, hence the lateral brakes that

were tested on WB188. However, the first approach had been to try to retain the use of wing flaps as airbrakes, but to find some way to trim out the pitching moment they generated. The company tested a top flap (on WB195, in May 1952), the dive-recovery flaps, and even opening the nosewheel doors, but without satisfactory results. Other tests between mid-1952 and late 1953 included perforations in the flap surface and reduced-span flaps.

In late 1953 the most promising solution appeared to be a one-third span flap (on WB202), although this gave a strong nose-down trim change around 550 knots (1,020 km/hr) IAS in combination with 0.95 IMN. However, as far as can be judged from Duke's later accounts, even though the trim change was in most circumstances acceptable, there was still a change in the aircraft's trimmed attitude, which was clearly a problem in gunfiring.

Since wing-mounted airbrakes were not going to generate the necessary deceleration without unacceptable pitch effects, the company turned to fuselage-mounted brakes. As mentioned above, they were tested first on the sides of the rear fuselage of WB188. These lateral brakes were first flown in July 1953, then removed for the record attempts, and refitted in November that year. They were later tested on XF379 (an F.6), but they were rejected due to excessive pitch change (presumably caused by a change in downwash on the tailplane), buffet, and directional problems. Considering that lateral airbrakes worked on the F-86, this was naturally disappointing.

In order to minimize the interaction of airbrake and tailplane, it was then decided to locate the brake under the rear fuselage. In general there are two possible locations for a ventral airbrake that will produce no pitching moment: one just ahead of the wing, and one just aft of the wing. In the case of the MiG-21, both locations are used, which makes possible quite small brakes. For the Hunter, only the aft location was used, for simplicity and to avoid interference with access to the gunpack and engine.

In establishing the correct location for a ventral airbrake, a TI was carried out on WT566 (the 12th production F.1). To allow for adjustment of the hinge-line, the airbrake was mounted on two rails, which were drilled with mounting holes. For the first flight with the ventral airbrake on 6 February 1954 (pilot 'Frank' Murphy) wind tunnel tests had indicated an approximate position for the hinge-line, but the exact position was (on Sutton's recollection) chosen by 'Frank' Cross to be in line with a strong fuselage frame. Having gone to all the trouble to allow adjustment of the hinge-line, it was found that this first position was acceptable! Murphy operated the brake up to 1.05 IMN and 610 knots (1,130 km/hr) IAS, and pronounced the trim change and buffet levels acceptable, though more drag was necessary.

Bird-Wilson's notes indicate that longitudinal hinge-line variations were tried that February. However, Sutton says that it was not until April (when the production airbrake was already flying) that the hinge-line was moved 12 inches (30.5 cm) forward and aft with no difference in characteristics.

Whatever the truth of this matter, in the light of Murphy's comments the airbrake deflection angle was increased first to 67° and then to 75°, and the brake was fitted with longitudinal strakes (a device later used on the Harrier and Hawk) to increase drag. However, serious problems then arose with trim change and/or buffet at high Mach No. The extension angle was therefore reduced to 60° and the strakes deleted.

Bird-Wilson returned to Dunsfold to make a series of eight airbrake assessment flights in February 1954, in the course of which he tested various modifications. Sutton's records show that Bird-Wilson flew the 60°, no-strake configuration on the 20th, the report noting that '*He was impressed with the small trim changes and low buffet level, but considered more drag desirable at high Mach and altitude, as previously reported by our own pilots*'.

Lengthening the airbrake chord proved unsatisfactory, and it was not until the production version was flown on WT573 (the 19th production F.1) that it was discovered that the fairing fixed just ahead of the airbrake had a significant effect on trim change. By modifying this fairing shape (between April and June 1954) HAL managed to increase airbrake angle to 67° and maintain acceptable trim changes and buffet levels.

Although the Rolls-Royce Avon proved the better choice in the long run, the Armstrong-Siddeley Sapphire initially gave the Hunter somewhat better performance and vastly superior resistance to surge
(Rolls-Royce)

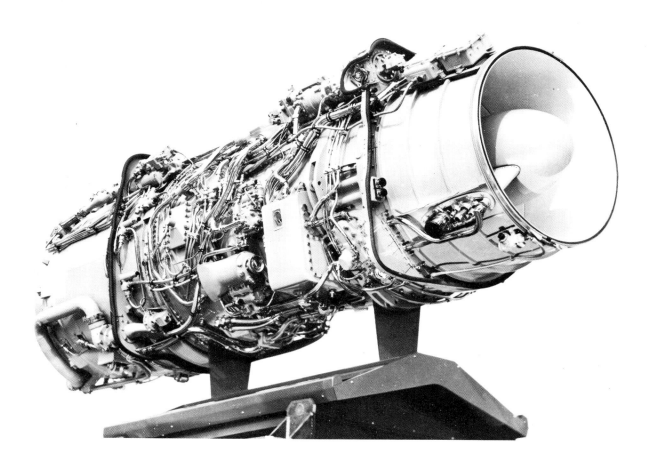

The Hunter thus eventually received an acceptable airbrake (which remained important when the aircraft was switched to the ground attack role), but it came along so late that it had to be applied externally, and it never gave as much drag as the pilots really wanted. One important disadvantage of the rear ventral brake arrangement was that it could not be extended in landing, due to ground clearance considerations. In June 1954 tests were run on an airbrake on rails under the front fuselage of WT566 (which would have overcome the landing problem), but there was a strong nose-up pitch trim change for various hinge-line positions, and the scheme was abandoned.

The only consolation to be gained from this protracted phase of flight development was that the wing trailing edge flaps, having been stressed from the outset for operation at 620 knots (1,150 km/hr), could be used as combat flaps, giving not only a higher lift coefficient, but also a better lift/drag ratio, due to the reduction in aircraft attitude in a turn.

Early Gunfiring

What Duke had no opportunity to detect in the course of the initial flight tests was that the Avon-Hunter had gunfiring problems. By an unfortunate coincidence, gunfiring trials were allocated to the third prototype, while the two Avon-engined aircraft looked at performance and handling. As it happened, the third prototype (WB202) had the Sapphire, which at that stage provided not only better performance but vastly superior handling.

The prototype gunfiring trials went extremely well, but then Boscombe tried firing the guns on a production F.1. At altitude the engine surged, and it was later found that it could be made to surge at any height. It resulted in the Avon Mk 113 of the Hunter F.1 (and later the Mk 115 in the F.4) being given a height restriction of 25,000 ft (7,600 m), which was clearly absurd for a high altitude interceptor. The F.1 problem arose just as the aircraft was entering service with No 43 Sqn, hence it could hardly have come at a worst time. It was eventually cured by reducing fuel flow while the trigger was depressed ('fuel-dipping'), but it exacerbated the delays caused by the airbrake problem, and worsened the aircraft's declining reputation. Moreover, the engine surge was soon found to be only the first of a whole series of problems associated with Aden gunfiring. The Hunter had got off to a very bad start.

Thin Wings

To add to the Hunter's many practical problems, there was also the fact that it happened to be already on the way to obsolescence. North American had quickly followed up the F-86 with the F-100 Super Sabre, equipped with an afterburning P&W J57 engine and a 45° swept wing of 7 per cent thickness/chord ratio. This combination provided supersonic capability in level flight. It peaked at only Mach 1.3, and level supersonics were restricted to a fairly narrow height band, but it was nonetheless a very significant advance. The YF-100 had its maiden flight on 25 May 1953, less than two years after the P.1067. The Soviet MiG-19, though a much smaller aircraft than the F-100, has a similar speed capability, and is believed to have flown in prototype form on 18 September 1953.

Hawker had been studying the idea of giving the Hunter an afterburning engine and a thinner, more swept wing since 1950. The outcome of these studies was the P.1083, which was ordered in prototype form and allocated the serial WN470. Whereas the standard Hunter has a 40° quarter-chord sweep and a t/c of 8.5 per cent, this 'Thin-Wing Hunter' had 48.6° of sweep and a t/c of 6.0 per cent. Because of the high fuel flow rates associated with afterburning, it was planned to add fuel tanks in the wings. A maximum level speed of Mach 1.2 was estimated, a reasonable figure in view of the fact that only the wings and powerplant had been changed. Construction of the P.1083 wings began in october 1952, but in July 1953 the project was cancelled.

It is sometimes held that the reason for this cancellation was that Supermarine had a vastly superior project, the Type 545 (Spec F.105D2), with a wing of compound sweep, varying in t/c from 8 per cent at the root to 5.67 per cent at the tips. Its Avon RA.14R was to be fed by two intakes in the sides of the nose, thus avoiding the drag of the boundary layer diverters. The Type 545 was estimated to reach Mach 1.3, and construction of prototype XA181 was nearing completion when cancellation came in 1955. Supermarine also proposed an improved version with an area-ruled fuselage and an RB.106 engine, giving a maximum speed of Mach 1.68. In this case a chin intake similar to that of the F-86D was projected.

To return to the P.1083, many at Kingston regretted its passing, but the retention of the original wing and the adoption of the non-afterburning 200-series Avon were undoubtedly the right decisions in the light of the RAF's change in emphasis from air defence to ground attack in the late 1950s. The highly swept wing would not have been as tolerant of external stores as the moderately-swept original. The P.1083 would nonetheless have been an interesting technology demonstrator. Kingston has long been painfully aware that, although it has led the world in V/STOL, it has no experience of developing a supersonic fighter with an afterburning engine.

Record Breaker

During the short life of the P.1083 programme, it was decided to investigate the use of an afterburning Avon in the first prototype, WB188. This experiment was aimed at providing an initial indication of the performance gains offered by reheat (as originally envisaged in OR.228). It also provided the basis for Hawker to win the world's absolute speed record, beating the figure of 715.75 mph (1,151.64 km/hr) established by the USAF with an afterburning F-86D on 16 July 1953.

In place of the standard production 7,500 lb (3,400 kg) Avon RA.7, the P.1067 was fitted in the first half of 1953 with an RA.7R that produced 6,750 lb (3,061 kg) 'dry' and 9,500 lb (4,310 kg) with afterburning. The aircraft was also fitted in late July/early August with a pointed nosecap, and a conical, highly swept outer windscreen. Fuel was increased from the normal 334 Imp gal (1,518 litres) to 440 Imp gal (2,000 litres) by the addition of eight small bag tanks in the inboard leading edge, similar to those later used as standard on the F.4 and F.5.

Designated F.3 and painted blood-red, the aircraft flew in its modified form on 12 August 1953, and was based at Tangmere on the south coast for an attempt on the speed record. The official course was three kilometres long (just less than two miles), and established off the coast at Rustington, near Littlehampton in West Sussex.

On August 30th, a delay occurred because the right main gear came out of the wing during a high-speed run, an incident that kept the aircraft on the ground for six days. However, on September 7th it was in the air again, and Duke

The lateral airbrakes were removed for the record attempts, and reinstated in November 1953, at which stage the rear end of the aircraft was repainted and the serial repositioned above the airbrake actuator fairing (BAe)

established a new record of 727.63 mph (1,171.3 km/hr). This corresponded to Mach 0.943, which was a good sea level speed for 1953, though only marginally better than the later F.6 could achieve with the non-afterburning 200-series Avon, despite blast deflectors, link collectors, the ventral airbrake and all the other excrescences that came with time.

On the 19th Duke established a record for the 100 km (62.15 statute miles) closed circuit, averaging 709.2 mph (1,141.1 km/hr) around the course. After these record flights the second windscreen was removed due to condensation problems, and the lateral airbrakes (which had been tested briefly in July) were reinstated for further trials.

Performance Comparison

Since the RAF's original intention was to explore the potential of both the Avon and Sapphire, and to have afterburning on later marks, it is interesting to compare the performance figures for the F.1, F.2, and F.3, using official data from MoS Form 2110 for each type.

Looking first at weights and thrust, the Hunter F.1 with 7,500 lb (3,400 kg) Avon RA.7 had a clean take-off weight of 16,350 lb (7,415 kg) with 2,540 lb (1,152 kg) of fuel. The Hunter F.2 with 8,000 lb (3,628 kg) Sapphire Sa.6 weighed 16,300 lb (7,392 kg) with 2,390 lb (1,084 kg) of fuel. According to Form 2110, the F.3 weighed 17,850 lb (8,095 kg) with 3,080 lb (1,397 kg) of fuel, although information available to this writer suggests that WB188 with wing tanks actually carried 3,475 lb (1,575 kg).

Following the line taken by OR.228, most of the performance data relate to what might be termed a 'reference altitude' of 45,000 ft (13,700 m). For readers not familiar with this class of aircraft, it should perhaps be emphasized that maximum Mach No in level flight is normally obtained at the tropopause (the height above which atmospheric temperature is constant), which in standard conditions means 36,080 ft (11,000 m). Maximum true airspeed (TAS) occurs at sea level, where the speed of sound is highest.

Looking first at the time taken to reach this reference height, this varied from 11.65 minutes for the F.1 and 9.3 minutes for the F.2 down to 5.7 minutes for the afterburning F.3. For comparison, the aim of OR.228 was to achieve a time-to-height of 6.0 minutes from pressing the starter button.

These Form 2110 times appear to be from the start of climb (rather than button-push), so the comparison with the requirement is even worse than these figures suggest.

The official figures indicate that, in comparison with the F.1, the Sapphire-engined F.2 reduced climb time (measured from pull-up) by 20 per cent, and the afterburning F.3 by a total of 50 per cent. However, not even the F.3 came anywhere near meeting the requirement.

Comparing residual rates of climb at the reference height, the F.1 was still going up at 1,150 ft/min (5.84 m/sec), the F.2 at 1,600 ft/min (8.13 m/sec), and the F.3 at 2,800 ft/min (14.23 m/sec). These figures are quoted for take-off weight, which was somewhat unfair, as none could carry external stores, hence they would all be rather lighter on reaching this height.

At the reference height the OR called for a level speed of 547 knots (1,104 km/hr). The official figures were 524 knots (971 km/hr) for the F.1, 527 knots (976.5 km/hr) for the F.2, and 542 knots (1,004.2 km/hr) for the F.3.

The requirement also called for a minimum climb rate of 1,000 ft/min (5.08 m/sec) at a height of 50,000 ft (15,250 m). The actual altitudes at which these initial marks attained that climb rate were 45,900 ft (14,000 m) for the F.1, 47,800 ft (14,575 m) for the F.2, and 50,700 ft (15,460 m) for the F.3. Only the afterburning aircraft met the service ceiling demand.

One might conclude from these figures that the F.3 came close to OR.228 in level speed and service ceiling. However, one may also suspect that the Form 2110 data relate to WB188 as prepared for the record attempt, rather than an operational version with the standard radar ranging nose and unfaired gun-ports. In addition, it must be remembered that the OR called for a combat endurance of at least 1.25 hours, including 10 minutes of combat at reference height. The official figures for the F.1 were a maximum endurance of 1.3 hours and a combat endurance of 0.55 hours. Although the afterburning F.3 had more fuel, its combat endurance would almost certainly have been less than this. It was thus far removed from the aircraft the RAF had envisaged.

It may well be that the Air Staff had simply called for a redesigned Sabre in which the emphasis was to be placed on climb rate and performance at altitude, imagining that a bigger engine would transform these characteristics without a dramatic reduction in endurance. The reality of the situation was that the state of the art was not changing that quickly; more engine inevitably meant less fuel, and thus less endurance. It is relevant to note that the F-86A with two drop tanks had a mission time of 1.62 hours, including 20 minutes combat.

The performance of the F.3 may be of purely academic interest, since the concept of an afterburning Hunter was abandoned in 1954 on endurance grounds. The comparison of F.1 and F.2 is perhaps more important, being germane to the intriguing question of why the Sapphire-powered Hunter was not preferred to that with the Avon. The F.2 may have had little speed advantage over the F.1, but it had a far better climb rate and operational ceiling, and vastly superior engine handling. Despite this clear superiority, the F.2 and the later F.5 (with wing fuel and two pylons) were produced in only small numbers, and were quickly phased out of service.

To summarize the performance differences, the F.2 took 20 per cent less time to reference height, had 40 per cent more residual climb rate at that height, and an operational ceiling 1,900 ft (580 m) higher than that of the F.1. After more than 30 years it is impossible to be sure why the decision went against all the evidence. The 'Derby Mafia' undoubtedly had more political influence than Armstrong Siddeley, and this may well have been the critical factor. In addition, it is possible that, despite the incredible bitterness generated at Kingston by the Avon's surge problem, Sir Sydney may have maintained his faith in Rolls-Royce's ability to overcome technical difficulties. The outstandingly successful Merlin piston engine had in the pre-war days been just as trouble-prone as the Avon now was proving.

There are two aspects to this matter of the choice of the Avon for the Hunter. The first is that it appears to have gone against all the technical evidence. The second is that those observers who regarded it as a dubious decision at the time now appear to be quite convinced that the choice ultimately proved to be the right one. The Avon 200-series was one of the finest military engines of the period.

The original Rolls-Royce RA.21 Avon Mk 115, as used in the Hunter F.4, and rated at a minimum thrust of 7,815 lb (3,545 kg) at 7,950 rpm. These '100-series' Avons had separate combustion chambers and a three-shot cartridge starter in the nose (Rolls-Royce)

Chapter 7

In RAF Hands

The year 1954 was to have been a turning-point for Fighter Command, with both the Swift and Hunter entering service, placing the RAF among the leading swept-wing air forces. Unfortunately, both of these debuts were catastrophes.

The prototype of the Supermarine Type 541 Swift (WJ960) had first flown on 1 August 1951, only 12 days after the P.1067. The production aircraft initially appeared in two forms, the two-gun F.1, and the four-gun F.2 with cranked leading edge. Some 20 and 16 were produced, respectively. The Swift entered service with No 56 Sqn in Feburary 1954, powered by the same Avon RA.7 as in the Hunter F.1.

Bird-Wilson's connection with the Swift began on 1 October 1953, when he flew the aircraft at Supermarine's development centre at Chilbolton. He carried out what he regarded as ordinary operational turns at low airspeed and high AOA, at 40,000 ft (12,200 m). The Avon promptly 'blew out', and the same thing happened on his second flight, on the following day. Incredibly as it seems, it was subsequently established that such a manoeuvre had never been undertaken either by the company's pilots, or by test pilots at A&AEE.

There is little doubt that the Swift had been rushed into service for political reasons, since the RAF wanted the cachet of a swept-wing fighter. Two aircraft (WK201 and 202), powered by the Avon RA.7 Mk 105, had been delivered to Boscombe in early 1954. The result was a CA Release remarkable for the limitations it placed on the aircraft. Below 5,000 ft (1,525 m) the Swift was restricted to a maximum of 520 knots (1,020 km/hr) IAS. Above this height the limitation was 0.90 IMN or 600 knots (1,112 km/hr) IAS. Maximum load factor was set at 6G. The most bizarre aspect was that Britain's new high altitude interceptor was restricted to a maximum altitude of 25,000 ft (7,600 m)!

Boscombe criticized the aircraft for severe pitch-up at modest G-values above this height, buffet onset at modest turn-rates, loss of elevator control above the speed limitation, heavy pitch control forces at high IMN, a marked nose-down trim change on airbrake extension above 0.94 IMN (0.96 TMN), wing drop between 0.92–0.94 IMN (0.93–0.96 TMN), and a tendency to engine surge with or without gunfiring. On approaching the stall, the Swift generated dangerously high rates of descent, and exhibited very strong pro-spin tendencies.

One of Bird-Wilson's officers at AFDS was Flt Lt

Duncan Simpson, who was later to become CTP at Dunsfold (following Bedford and Merewether). Swifts had begun to arrive at CFE in early February 1954 (the first four on the 13th of the month), but Simpson's first experience was in delivering one from South Marston to No 56 Sqn at Waterbeach toward the end of the month.

Simpson's impression was that the aircraft was quite pleasant to fly at 5,000–10,000 ft (1,525–3,050 m), which was subsequently to make it acceptable for the photo-reconnaissance role, although the later Hunter FR.10 proved much better. The flap, which Simpson recalls as 'perhaps the best part of the aircraft' could be used very effectively as an airbrake without significant trim change, although the aircraft's attitude did change.

However, the wing design was 'agricultural', and the fuselage retained the plump dimensions of the Types 510 and 535 (which had been designed to take the centrifugal Nene), although this was to give the Swift better fuel volume and endurance than the Hunter. Incredibly, the tailplane of early production aircraft was fixed. Simpson sums it up neatly as 'Meteor aerodynamics with a swept wing'.

The aircraft would go supersonic in a 30°–40° dive, but, as Mach No increased, the stick came back, and there was nothing left for manoeuvre. In Simpson's view, the Hunter was a much more refined aircraft. When Bird-Wilson asked him which of the two aircraft he would like to specialize in, there was no doubt in his mind that the Hunter was *the* aeroplane, although the airbrake affair had admittedly left the programme running somewhat late.

In March and April of 1954 Boscombe tested WK124, an example of the Swift F.2, which had the extra two Adens and the extension to the inboard leading edge. However, the forward movement of aerodynamic centre appears to have exceeded the CG movement due to the two additional guns. Pitch-up characteristics were even worse than for the F.1, and longitudinal handling in general was assessed as falling below the standards required by the service.

A modified Swift F.2 (WK216) was assessed

The Swift F.1 was issued to No 56 Sqn in February 1954, becoming the first British swept-wing fighter to enter service, although restrictions on its use were severe (Vickers)

between early June and mid-August 1954, but it was still considered to be quite unsuitable and unsafe for operational fighter duties. The F.2 was nonetheless issued to No 56 Sqn that August, with the same severe restrictions as for the F.1, the aim being limited to acquiring flying and service experience, in the hope that there would ultimately be a Swift that could be cleared for operational use.

To complete the Swift story, the F.3 had an Avon RA.7R Mk 108 with afterburning giving 9,500 lb (4,310 kg), and a leading edge extension toward the tips, while the F.4 added a taller fin and (finally) a variable-incidence tailplane. The F.3 (WK248) went to Boscombe in November 1954, but was judged to have inadequate longitudinal control. With modifications, it was found by mid-January 1955 that the elevator control forces had been reduced, pitch-up at high Mach Numbers was controllable, and the aircraft could reach 40,000 ft (12,200 m) in six minutes. However, the engine was still prone to surging, and fuel consumption in afterburner led to a very short sortie.

The F.4 prototype (WK198), flown by 'Mike' Lithgow, had set a world speed record of 737.7 mph (1,187 km/hr) on 25 September 1953,

benefitting from the high temperatures available at Castel Idris in Libya. Duke gives the TMN as 0.930, compared to 0.943 for the Hunter F.3. However, the F.4 was judged by A&AEE to be unsuitable for high altitude interception duties, and likely to be out-turned by other fighters, even at medium altitudes.

The only Swift variant to be cleared for service use was the FR.5 with a three-camera nose, two guns, a modified saw-tooth wing, and a ventral drop tank. It was powered by an Avon Mk 114, giving 7,175 lb (3,255 kg) dry and 9,450 lb (4,285 kg) with afterburning. Some 62 FR.5s were built, and they served with Nos 2 and 79 Sqn in Germany from 1956 to 1961, when they were superseded by the Hunter FR.10. The Swift F.7 was used briefly for operational trials with the Firelfash missile, as discussed later.

It is difficult to view the Swift as anything but one of the great disasters of British fighter design. Nevertheless, in the period between the first flights of the Hunter and Swift and their delivery to the service, Supermarine was felt to be the favoured contender. That company was also perceived to be the favourite of Rolls-Royce, since Supermarine was dedicated to afterburner development,

A beautiful load of trouble: the Hunter F.1. A limited CA Release was finally granted on 1 July 1954, almost three years after the first flight of the P.1067, a virtually unprecedented delay for a straightforward day fighter
(BAe)

Top In order to improve the high-Mach characteristics of the Swift, the leading edge root was extended forwards and a wing fence was added. The example shown here, WK198, was the prototype of the F.4. Flown by Lt Cdr Lithgow, it established a world speed record of 737.7 mph (1,187 km/hr) on 25 September 1953 (Vickers)

The Swift was soon phased out as an interceptor, but the FR.5 served in the low level photo-reconnaissance role with Nos 2 and 79 Sqn in Germany. It differed from earlier marks in having a longer nose, fully-glazed canopy and outboard leading edge extensions (Vickers)

whereas HAL was constantly advocating the big dry engine.

Sir Sydney never forgot that for several years it had looked as though the Swift would be ordered in quantity and the Hunter abandoned. He attributed this swing largely to the USAF evaluation (of which more later), although it is probably true that the American pilots said only the same as those from A&AEE and CFE, but even more forcibly. As representatives of the leading Western air force, their opinions were probably listened to more carefully than their domestic equivalents.

Enter the Hunter

In November 1953 three Hunter F.1s (WT555, 573 and 576, the 1st, 19th and 22nd production aircraft) were flown from Dunsfold to Boscombe for CA Release trials. The initial reaction was that lateral stick forces at high IAS and high IMN were too high, and in the following month the aileron system was therefore changed from power-assistance to full power. Boscombe also confirmed the initial AFDS assessment, that the Hunter could

not be accepted without a new form of airbrake. These early aircraft were fitted with a variety of Avon models, the principal forms being the 7,500 lb (3,400 kg) RA.7 Mk 107, and the 7,600 lb (3,447 kg) RA.21 Mk 113.

Aside from lateral stick loads and the airbrake, Boscombe criticized pitch-up at high Mach Numbers, and a tendency to engine surge when turning or accelerating, the tendency being aggravated by gunfire. Elevator control loads were felt to be excessive at high IAS, and the early introduction of Dunlop Maxaret (anti-skid) wheel-brakes was recommended, although the principal effect was to reduce tyre wear.

On the other side of the coin, the F.1 was praised for its climb performance, reaching 40,000 ft (12,200 m) in approximately seven minutes from wheels rolling. Boscombe also approved of the F.1's level speed of Mach 0.93 TMN at altitude, and the cockpit's comfort and general design. The field of view was praised, aside from some reservations about view directly aft, which was certainly inferior to that of the F-86. It was estimated that the Hunter's maximum practical combat altitude was 45,000 ft (13,700 m).

Following a limited CA Release on 1 July 1954, three Hunters out of a batch of 12 allocated to CFE were flown from Dunsfold to West Raynham on the 5th. The pilots were Sqn Ldr D H Seaton, Flt Lt J M Calvey and Flt Lt D M S Simpson.

Simpson recalls having lunch at the mess at Dunsfold, and a lightning brief on the Hunter F.1, and then being taken out to the aircraft on the ORP. They took off and flew straight across London (and Air Ministry) back to CFE. On taxying in, they were met by the Commandant, Air Cdre 'Paddy' Chrisham, who told them he had just received a phone-call from the Air Ministry. Expecting to get a rocket for flying over the city, the three pilots were surprised and relieved to hear that the call had been simply to congratulate CFE on getting three Hunters airborne together for the first time!

Shortly afterwards, pilots from AFDS flew Hunters in the annual Fighter Command air defence exercise (Exercise Dividend), which began on July 18th. Simpson remembers that the weather was appalling, and that the Hunter's shortcomings showed up immediately. Shortage of fuel was very much in their minds when flying intercepts over the North Sea, and returning to West Raynham for GCAs. Canopy misting and icing were appalling, especially in descents: 'How we didn't lose one, I don't know!'.

The second unit to receive the Hunter F.1 was No 54 Sqn at Odiham, deliveries taking place in January 1955. This was the first squadron to form a Hunter aerobatic team, a four-aircraft section operating throughout the summer of that year (Russell Adams, Gloster Aircraft)

The third production Hunter F.4, WT703, was used for external stores trials at Dunsfold and Boscombe Down. It is seen here with 100 Imp gal (454 litre) drop tanks on the inboard pylons, and a full load of 24 three-inch (76.2 mm) rockets (HAL)

Four RAF Hunter F.4s in close formation with airbrakes extended. The F.4 was the first series to have a useful operational capability, since it had wing fuel and provisions for up to four pylons, or two pylons and rocket projectiles (HAL)

The Hunters were flying in pairs, and transparency misting ('*the most persistent I have ever experienced*') made operations extremely dangerous. After the exercise the pilots insisted on some of the company's technical experts sitting in an F-86 to experience both the mass flow and the distribution of that aircraft's air conditioning system.

Simpson flew against B-45s, B-47s, Canberras, F-86s and Meteors, his last intercept of the exercise being against a B-45 on July 25th, when he was flying as wingman to Bird-Wilson. In the course of 'Dividend' he had two complete R/T failures, and in another sortie his leader lost R/T. He also had an engine surge above cloud. Such teething problems did not endear the Hunter to the pilots, but it remained clear to Simpson at least that the Hunter (in spite of everything) had very good potential.

Even as CFE was making its operational assessment of the Hunter F.1, similar aircraft were being delivered to the first squadron, No 43 Sqn at Leuchars. Next came No 54 Sqn at Odiham in January 1955, then No 222 Sqn at Leuchars in March, and No 247 at Odiham in June. Other F.1s went to No 229 OCU at Chivenor, No 233 OCU at Pembrey in South Wales, and No 5 MU at Kemble.

Several F.1s were used as TI aircraft, including WT571, an RAE experiment with 'Area Rule' bulges on the rear fuselage sides, and WT656 with 'blown' flaps. Others were used to develop the leading edge extensions, link collector tanks, and wing pylons. It may be noted that the first unit to form a Hunter aerobatic team was No 54 Sqn, with a four-aircraft team operating from March to October of 1955.

One of the main concerns regarding the Hunter in its early service days was endurance in a combat sortie, since neither the F.1 nor F.2 had wing tanks or provisions for drop tanks. This problem was to result in the loss of at least two F.1s in the course of the first 12 months of service due to fuel starvation, the pilot being killed in both cases. These aircraft were WT590 of No 43 Sqn, near Leuchars on 22 October 1954, and WT628 from ETPS on 18 July 1955, near Farnborough. Two aircraft from No 54's aerobatic team were lost in November 1955 for similar reasons. However, the Hunter's endurance deficit was to be most strikingly dramatized by a multiple accident on 8 February 1956, when six aircraft out of an exercise involving eight F.1s went down in the course of eight minutes.

The eight Hunters from DFLS had taken off from West Raynham at 10:50 hr, the pilots consisting of two instructors and six students, who had been briefed to carry out a four-vs-four dogfight at 45,000 ft (13,700 m). There was some low cloud and widespread mist, though the weather situation was expected to improve. A less formal assessment was that the weather was foul, so bad that AFDS would not fly at all. As the eight aircraft taxied out, old hands from AFDS expressed the view that this time DFLS had pushed their luck too far!

The aircraft climbed to altitude, formed up into battle formation, made two or three turns, and then had to return to base as their fuel was running low. By the time they got back they found that, instead of the weather improving, the cloud base was down to 400 ft (120 m) and surface visibility was only 800–1,000 yd (730–915 m). The aircraft were overhead West Raynham at 20,000 ft (6,100 m) at 1115 hr, with fuel for 20–25 minutes, and they were clearly going to have to land somewhere else.

The two possible diversions were Marham, 10 nm (18.5 km) south-west, and Waterbeach, 30 nm (55.5 km) in the same direction. With hindsight, if they had gone to Waterbeach, all might have been well. In fact, a Meteor and Vampire were successfully diverted from West Raynham to Waterbeach while the Hunters were going down at Marham. Unfortunately, Marham, at that time a Canberra station, had just lost its good GCA to Fighter Command, and received in its place an early and inferior model. The view has also been expressed that the controllers at Marham were (quite naturally) not accustomed to dealing with fighters that were almost down to the fumes.

In any event, the decision was made to divert to Marham, in the expectation that the Hunters would be able to carry out a visual circuit and landing. Having descended to 2,000 ft (600 m) over West Raynham, the Hunters set off for Marham with 30-second intervals between pairs. During the few minutes that it took for them to cover the distance, fog formed, and the scene was set for a disaster that would go down in RAF history.

Red One and Two overflew Marham at 1,000 ft (300 m), made a quick circuit and broke cloud at 500 ft (150 m). Red Two (an instructor) lost his leader, but pressed on and landed at 1132 hr after 42 minutes in the air. Red One flew three timed circuits before he saw the runway, and landed successfully, though his engine stopped from fuel

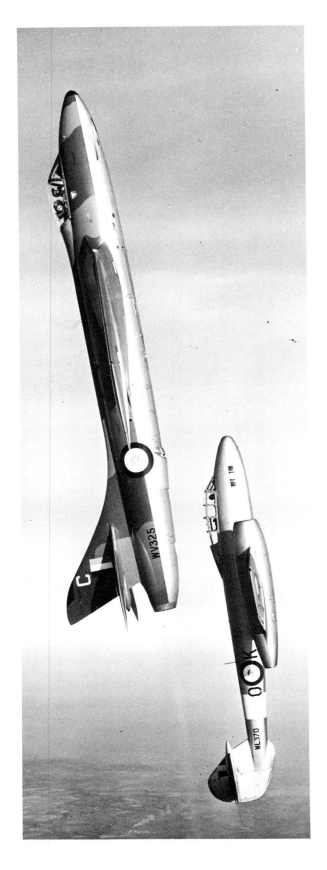

Far left A Hunter F.4 looping with a Meteor T.7. This F.4 first flew on 13 June 1955 (pilot Hugh Merewether) and was delivered to CFS in the following month. It later became a Jordanian FGA.73A, serial 846 (Russell Adams, Gloster Aircraft)

Top left The fifth production Hunter F.5 from a batch of 105 built by Armstrong Whitworth, WN958 was supplied to Boscombe Down for trials with various external stores. It is seen here with the original small tanks and tiers of 'drainpipes' (HAL)

Middle left A Hunter F.5 with tanks and eight tiers of RPs. Since the standard F.5 was never given provisions for any type of rocket, this was probably WN958, which was used as an armament TI aircraft (HAL)

Bottom left The proposed use of a slab-tail eliminated the possibility of manual reversion, so HAL ran tests on a ram-air turbine (RAT) that would maintain hydraulic pressure following engine failure. A TI is shown on WT772, a production F.4 (HAL)

Hunter F.4, XF310, was delivered in July 1956 to Fairey Aviation for trials with that company's Blue Sky (Fireflash) beam-riding air-air missile. The aircraft's nose was extended slightly to house a modified radar ranging set (BAe via Brian Isles)

starvation as he taxied in. As he stepped from the cockpit, he is reported to have made the far-sighted remark: *'There'll be a row about this!'* Two aircraft had been saved; the other six were doomed.

Yellow Three could see only glimpses of the ground from 500 ft (150 m), so climbed and ejected. Yellow Four was killed when his aircraft crashed into a field.

Yellow Two (the other instructor) lost his leader, and, with 12 Imp gal (55 litres) remaining, climbed and ejected. Yellow One was forced to climb when he saw trees in his path, but let down again to 150 ft (45 m) and saw the runway. His engine flamed out as he turned on finals, and he force-landed straight ahead.

Red Four likewise lost his leader, having descended to 600 ft (180 m) without seeing the ground. He climbed, and ejected as the engine flamed out at 2,500 ft (760 m). Red Three climbed to 4,000 ft (1,200 m) and ejected. The last Hunter hit the ground at 1140 hr, exactly 50 minutes after take-off.

This short duration clearly said something about the internal fuel capacity of the F.1, but the fact that the six aircraft were lost is arguably more of a comment on the way that DFLS was run. The idea behind DFLS training was that officers who were to lead fighter squadrons had to know how to fly their aircraft to the limits, hence this squadron seems to have ignored normal safety procedures. Over the years, the belief had probably grown that the unit had some special dispensation in this respect, though this was not the case. To give one example, DFLS flew to a 50 ft (15 m) minimum altitude, whereas any other RAF aircraft was supposed to be nose-up below 250 ft (75 m). A number of well-qualified observers felt that it was only a question of time before DFLS experienced a serious accident because of the way they flew, and that the fact that they happened to be flying Hunters on this occasion was largely coincidental.

To The Squadrons

Despite its shortcomings, production of the F.1

had gone ahead at Kingston and Blackpool, and that of the Sapphire-engined F.2 at Coventry. Although less serious than engine surging, gunfiring problems, and difficulties with the powered flying control units (PFCUs), there were teething problems with the landing gear, notably with sequencing of the 'D-doors' hinged at the sides of the fuselage to cover the lower halves of the mainwheels when retracted.

Production of the F.1 was covered by a contract signed on 14 March 1951 for 113 aircraft to be built at Kingston. A supplementary contract covering 26 F.1s to be constructed at Blackpool was signed on 15 August 1953. The first Hunter produced at Blackpool, WW599, had its maiden flight on 7 July 1954.

The F.1 had an Avon Mk 107 or 113 with a BTH cartridge starter, TR1985 and 1986 VHF radios, Green Salad CHF homing, IFF Mk 3, DME, and radar ranging Mk 1. It had no provisions for external stores. The Mk 1 had three pairs of fuel tanks in the fuselage, with 101 Imp gal (459 litres) in each of the front pair, 36 Imp gal (164 litres) in each mid-fuselage tank, and 30 Imp gal (136 litres) in each aft tank. This gave the very modest total of 334 Imp gal (1,518 litres). For interest, the pilot was supposed to rejoin the circuit with 80 Imp gal (363 litres) remaining.

Production of the F.2 was limited to 45 aircraft built by AWA as Coventry, the first production aircraft (the silver-painted WN888) flying on 14 October 1953. Equipment standard was similar to that of the F.1, but the Sapphire Mk 101 had a Rotax cartridge starter. Use of the aircraft was limited to two squadrons at Wattisham, No 257 Sqn receiving the F.2 in September 1954 and No 263 in February 1955.

All the six squadrons that received the initial marks of Hunter converted from the Meteor F.8, although subsequently RAF units were generally to convert from the Canadair-built Sabre (and in a few cases the Venom FB.4) to the Hunter. For those moving up from the Meteor, the change was welcomed in view of the performance improvement, but conversion from the well-established Sabre was viewed with mixed feelings.

Four and Five

The Hunter F.4 was basically an F.1, but with the Avon Mk 115 or 121, and with fuel added in eight small bag tanks in the inboard leading edge, although the rear fuselage tanks of the F.1 were

deleted. Provision was made from the outset for two (inboard) wing pylons that could take 100 Imp gal (455 litre) tanks, 1,000 lb (454 kg) bombs, or napalm. Part-way through production, Mod 228 was introduced, adding the two outboard wing pylons, and provisions for eight tiers of RPs, to meet the ground attack requirement specified in later issues of OR.228. The F.4 was also the first Hunter to have the 'follow-up tailplane', in which movement of the elevators activated the tailplane trim motor. Some F.4s were retrofitted with the leading edge extension that was developed for the F.6, to cure the relatively gentle pitch-up from which the Hunter family suffered. The F.4 is also listed as having an autostabilizer, ie, a yaw damper working on the rudder trim, though this appears to have been of only marginal value in improving target tracking in turbulence.

The introduction of wing fuel provided 70 Imp gal (318 litres) per side, and increased the total internal capacity to 414 Imp gal (1,882 litres), a 24 per cent improvement. Having been designed initially simply to carry lift loads and to house the main undercarriage, the wing was full of structure that made it extremely difficult to add internal tanks or underwing pylons. As an improvement on the wing bag tanks, HAL designed and ground-tested an integral leading edge tank, but evidently failed to win MoS support for the scheme.

An RAF F.4 with link-collectors or 'Sabrinas'. This aircraft, XE665, was one of a batch of 100 F.4s built at Blackpool. It was delivered to No 5 MU in May 1955, then issued to No 118(F) Sqn at Jever in which unit markings it is shown (MoD via Brian Isles)

A total of 367 F.4s were built in the UK, roughly evenly divided between Kingston and Blackpool. These were the days when Hunter production peaked, with 90 aircraft completed in the second quarter of 1955 at these two plants.

The first F.4 was WT701, which had its maiden flight on 20 October 1954, with Frank Murphy at the controls. The first F.4 from Blackpool (WW646) followed on 20 January 1955. Five days later Murphy was involved in a tragic accident when making a belly landing at Ford NAS, near Chichester, following a failure to achieve relight after a booster pump check. With a dead engine and the batteries flattened by his relight attempts, he was unable to lower the flaps, and made a wheels-up landing at 200 knots (370 km/hr). Unfortunately, the aircraft swung off and went through a caravan park, killing two people. It then crossed a road, breaking into three pieces (it appears to have broken at the transport joints), and the front fuselage rolled for a considerable distance before coming to rest. Murphy's helmet was split from front to back, and he spent many months in hospital recovering from his injuries.

It was a bad year for Hawker test pilots. In August Duke was flying an F.1 (WT562), carrying out gunfiring trials off Littlehampton, when he experienced a power failure. He managed to get the Hunter down at Ford (a feat for which he received the Queen's Commendation), and it was fitted with a new engine. However, on collecting the aircraft on the 6th, he had an almost total power failure over the town of Chichester at a height of only 1,000 ft (300 m). Duke's options were limited and he made a forced landing at Thorney Island. Touching down fast on the grass surface, the aircraft went into a series of horrific bounces, so he retracted the undercarriage. Only one main gear came up, and the aircraft bounced on, through the perimeter fence, and down into a dip in the ground, where it came to an abrupt halt. Duke's spine was badly damaged, and (even after hospital treatment) he found that he was still in pain when flying the Hunter in turns. He therefore resigned from the CTP position in October 1956, handing over to 'Bill' Bedford.

Deliveries of the F.4 began in early 1955. One of the first units to receive it was No 111 Sqn at North Weald, which (when at Northolt in 1938) had been the first squadron to receive Hawker's Hurricane. 'Treble One' had marked the arrival of the Hurricane by the CO (Sqn Ldr J W Gillan) establishing a speed record from Edinburgh back to his base, averaging 408 mph (656.5 km/hr). In keeping with this tradition, the new CO (Sqn Ldr Roger Topp) flew an F.4 (WT739) from Edinburgh to London at an average speed of 714.5 mph (1,149.6 km/hr).

The Hunter F.4 equipped no less than 22 RAF squadrons, of which 13 were with 2ATAF in Germany and the remainder were based in the UK. In Germany, Geilenkirchen housed Nos 3 and 234 Sqn, Jever Nos 4, 93, 98, and 118 Sqn, Oldenburg Nos 14, 20, and 26 Sqn, and Brüggen Nos 67, 71, 112, and 130 Sqn.

In the UK, Nos 54 and 247 Sqn were based at Odiham, No 111 at North Weald, Nos 43 and 222 Sqn at Leuchars, Nos 66 and 92 Sqn at Linton-on-Ouse, No 74 Sqn at Horsham St Faith, and No 245 at Stradishall.

The F.4 was altogether a much more practical fighter than the F.1 and F.2 had been, yet it remained in front-line service for only a short period. The phase-out began in late 1956, and the last RAF unit with this type was re-equipped in early 1958.

Quoting data from Form 2110, the Hunter F.4 had an RA.7 Avon of 7,500 lb (3,400 kg) and weighed 17,000 lb (7,710 kg) with 3,150 lb (1,429 kg) of internal fuel. It could reach 0.904 TMN at sea level, and 0.91 TMN at 45,000 ft (13,700 m), at which height it had a residual climb rate of 1,000 ft/min (5.08 m/sec). It took 12.5 minutes to reach this height.

The F.5 was the Sapphire-engined equivalent of the pre-Mod 228 F.4, with provisions for only two pylons. Only 105 were built, but the first example (WN954) narrowly beat the F.4 into the air, making its first flight on 19 October 1954.

Deliveries to No 263 Sqn at Wattisham began in March 1955, this unit being later joined by the F.5s of No 257 Sqn. Nos 1 and 34 Sqn flew the F.5 from Tangmere, where No 208 also had the F.5 very briefly in early 1958. Biggin Hill's last operational squadron was No 41 Sqn, with Hunter F.5s. Waterbeach had the F.5s of No 56 Sqn. As discussed later, F.5s of Nos 1 and 34 Sqn were deployed to Akrotiri in Cyprus at the time of the Suez crisis of October 1956, but this exercise served mainly to underline the need for larger drop tanks. Phasing-out of the F.5 took place between early 1957 and mid-1958.

Some of these improved Hunters were used as TI aircraft. One F.4 (WT780, which first flew on 6 April 1955) was retained by HAL, and was used to test the Plessey ram air turbine (RAT). This equipment was located in the starboard rear fuselage, and extended into the airflow when the hydraulic pressure fell below a preset level. The aim of the RAT was to provide emergency hydraulic power for a slab tailplane that was developed to replace the rather crude follow-up tailplane arrangement described earlier. The slab-tail was more effective transonically, though at low speeds it was probably a retrograde step, in view of its lack of camber. It also eliminated the possibility of manual reversion. In 1956 the slab-tail programme was cancelled, and the need for the RAT disappeared.

The same aircraft was used as a basis for a private-venture fighter-reconnaissance variant, in which the radar ranging was deleted and the space in the nose used to accommodate a 'fan' of five Vinten F.95 cameras. Such a TI was easy to carry out, since the nose back to frame 3A was detachable. The installation consisted of two high obliques, two low obliques, and one forward-looking camera protected by two retractable 'eyelids'. Despite teething problems with window misting, it was a successful project, eventually leading to the three-camera Hunter FR.10.

A later F.4 (XF310) was employed as a TI aircraft for the Fairey Fireflash air-air missile, code-named Blue Sky. The plan called for two Fireflash to be carried on the inboard pylons. The need for a modified radar ranging set, to generate a modulated beam along which the missile could ride, led to a more pointed nose shape, but in other respects the aircraft was unchanged externally. However, acceptance trials with Fireflash demonstrated an unacceptably low kill rate, largely due to the failure of the external boost motors to separate in around one-third of cases, and frequent premature firings of the weapon's radar proximity fuze.

Within the scope of OR.228, the Swift F.7 was developed under specification F.105D&P3 to carry two Fireflash missiles and radar ranging Mk 2, provisions for guns and RPs being deleted. The original plan called for 75 Swift F.7s to be produced, but the Fireflash trials fiasco led to only 10 being completed (XF113-124). These aircraft were used briefly by the Guided Weapons Development Squadron at RAF Valley in North Wales, to gain experience of operating a GW-equipped unit prior to the introduction of the Javelin and Lightning with the vastly superior Blue Jay (Firestreak). In the context of the Hunter, the Fireflash tests with XF310 led nowhere.

Another F.4 (WT798) was used for drop tanks development work, including the first flights with the private-ventured 230 Imp gal (1,045 litre) steel tank. This was one of the most important steps in the development of the aircraft, since it finally gave the Hunter a useful amount of fuel in a low-drag installation.

Comparing these big tanks with the standard 100 Imp gal (455 litre) Bristol plastic tanks, it was reckoned at the time that on the inboard pylons the small tanks added 1 per cent to profile drag, while the big tanks added 3 per cent. The outboard station created a great deal of drag for various reasons that were probably never fully understood. Four small tanks were estimated to add 15 per cent to the profile drag of the basic aircraft, and the combination of big tanks inboard and small tanks outboard added 25 per cent. The use of outboard drop tanks was only marginally profitable, but they were nonetheless employed in the ferry configuration.

Aside from the need for sway-bracing to restrict pylon loads in rolling manoeuvres, the only real problem with the big tank was that initially it was short of internal bulkheads to limit fore-and-aft fuel movement. This deficiency was reckoned to have been responsible for the fatal crash of a Hunter in the Middle East, the aircraft failing to recover from a dive in a ground attack operation.

The final ferry configuration was two 230 Imp gal (1,045 litre) tanks inboard and two 100 Imp gal (454 litre) tanks outboard. It is shown here on an aircraft that was used for demonstrations in Switzerland (BAe)

Later figures (quite possibly not consistent with the above drag estimates) indicated that comparing the definitive ferry configuration of two big tanks and two small ones with the original concept of four small ones, the aircraft had 7.6 per cent more fuel, but achieved 20 per cent more range. A great deal of work was later done to further improve ferry range, though the RAF's need for intercontinental deployments was fast disappearing. In February 1962 HAL and Flight Refuelling made proposals for IFR using probes in the noses of the big tanks. Although only the two drop tanks were replenished, it was possible to quote a ferry capability of over 3,000 nm (5,560 km) with two refuellings.

The idea of stretching the big tank to 350 Imp gal (1,590 litres) was studied in 1960, and such tanks were flown on G-APUX. To the best of this writer's recollection, the aim was to persuade Portugal that the Hunter could be ferried to colonies in Africa, but nothing came of the exercise. one of the most promising developments of the period was a long 144 Imp gal (655 litre) tank

that cured the flow separations that were largely responsible for the very high drag on the outboard 100 Imp gal (455 litre) tank. Unfortunately, by the early 1960s the RAF was not willing to fund such developments, and Kingston was pouring its money into V/STOL.

Other F.4 'specials' included WT770, which was sold to Sweden for evaluation and became a Mk 50, serial 34001, and WW591, which became the first Danish Mk 51. The F.5s were less frequently employed as TI and demonstration aircraft, but WN958 appears to have been given Mod 228 wings for weapon trials, and WN955 flew briefly with a 10,000 lb (4,535 kg) Sapphire Sa.7.

Comparisons

As indicated earlier, the Hunter was basically a replacement for RAF Meteors, Sabres and Venoms. Before continuing with the history of the Hunter, it may therefore be worthwhile to consider what sort of improvement this aircraft provided, relative to its predecessors.

The Gloster Meteor F.8 first flew on 12 October

The Hunter was basically a replacement for the Gloster Meteor F.8, which is seen here in ground attack configuration. Relative to early Meteors, the tail design had been cleaned up, as has the cockpit enclosure, although rear view was restricted
(Russell Adams, HSA)

1948, and entered service with the RAF in 1950, No 245 Sqn receiving its first F.8s on June 29th. In RAF service the F.8 replaced the earlier F.4 version and the Vampire FB.5. The main criticisms to be made of the Meteor are that deliveries of the F.8 began over a year after those of the F-86A to the USAF (in February 1949) and that it had asymmetric flight problems. It appears that if the Meteor under-carriage was lowered with one engine out, there was a risk of the aircraft entering a dive, which below 600 ft (180 m) was irrecoverable. A similar problem arose if one engine failed just after take-off, especially at high weights and below 170 knots (315 km/hr). In the approach the problem was eventually solved by ensuring that the aircraft was very precisely trimmed in straight and level flight before the gear was dropped.

The Meteor F.8 was powered by two 3,500 lb (1,590 kg) R-R Derwent 8s. It had an empty weight of 10,625 lb (4,820 kg) and a clean gross weight of 15,700 lb (7,115 kg). It had an initial climb rate of 7,000 ft/min (35.5 m/sec) and a service ceiling of 44,000 ft (13,400 m). It could reach 30,000 ft (9,150 m) in 6.5 minutes, and 40,000 ft (12,200 m) in 11.6 minutes. Maximum level speed was 0.78 TMN at sea level and 0.81 TMN at 30,000 ft (9,150 m).

The RAF's Sabre was the Canadair-built version, equivalent to the F-86E. A total of 430 were produced for the UK, partly funded by MDAP.

Deliveries began in late 1952, and the series entered service with No 67 Sqn in May 1953. In all there were 10 RAF Sabre units in Germany (Nos 3, 4, 20, 26, 67, 71, 93, 112, 130, and 234 Sqn), and two in the UK (Nos 66 and 92). After the Hunter had replaced the straight-wing fighters, it replaced the Sabre in 1955–56. Most of the RAF Sabres were then passed to Italy (180 aircraft) and Yugoslavia (121 aircraft).

The Sabre was a somewhat smaller, lighter aircraft than the Hunter, though level speed capability was similar. It was a real 'pilot's aeroplane' with superb longitudinal handling at high Mach (the tailplane and elevators being linked mechanically from the outset). It also had an excellent rear view, a great deal of internal fuel, and a 'Rolls-Royce' cabin conditioning system. However, its usefulness in the RAF air defence role was limited by its very slow engine start (using external power) and its poor rate of climb.

From an engineering aspect, the Hunter was far less reliant on ground equipment, but the maintenance men, accustomed to the Sabre's self-bleeding hydraulics, took a dim view of having to pump any air bubbles out of the Hunter's system by hand, whenever the aircraft's rear fuselage was detached. It was also a sore point that the Hunter's rear fuselage was attached with over twice as many bolts as that of the Sabre.

The first production series of the Canadair Sabre was the Mk 2, illustrated here by CAF aircraft 19183, and equivalent to the F-86E with the J47-GE-13 engine. The first Mk 2s for the RAF arrived in Britain in October 1952 (Canadair via Robert F Dorr)

Preceding page Freshly painted in attractive Training Command colours, a vic of Hunters from No 4 FTS at RAF Valley head towards the South Stack lighthouse off Holyhead, North Wales, on 25 June 1973. Lead is T.7 XL567, flanked by a pair of F.6s (XG185 to port, XF383 starboard). These aircraft entered service with No 4 FTS in 1958
(Norman Pealing)

This page A T.79 trainer (foreground) with two of the three FGA.78s being prepared in the paint shop at Dunsfold before delivery to Qatar in the Arabian Gulf
(HSA via Mike Stroud)

A Hunter with a varied past: Lebanese FGA.70A L282 began life as F.6 serial WW594, which tested the radar nose shape of the P.1109. It was converted to an FR.10, and was bought back in 1974, becoming G-9-423 before delivery to the Lebanon in late 1975. Marine Corps TAV-8A Harrier, bureau number 159379, in background (BAe via Brian Isles)

Top The blood-red WB188 (redesignated F.3) set a new world speed record of 727.63 mph (1,171.3 km/hr) on 7 September 1953. Interestingly, Hawker CTP Neville Duke actually achieved 751 mph (1,201.6 km/hr) during one of the 12 runs he made along the coure. Details of the records set by WB188 can be found on page 81. Pictured outside the RAF St Athan museum in August 1983, this renowned machine made its last flight on 12 January 1954 (Robbie Shaw)

Above An immaculate FGA.9, XG228/'56' of No 79 (shadow) Sqn, No 1 TWU, about to make a perfect landing at its home base of Brawdy in South Wales in June 1984. By the end of the month, No 1 TWU had completely re-equipped with the Hawk T.1A (Robbie Shaw)

Right Led by ex-'Red Arrows' team leader Wg Cdr Brian Hoskins, these ex-No 1 TWU Hunters are being ferried to RAF St Athan for storage on 24 July 1984 (Geoffrey Lee, BAe)

These pages Resplendent in desert camouflage and displaying the flags of satisfied customers under the cockpit, G-BABM appeared at the 1976 Farnborough Air Show. Previously FGA.9 XF432 with the RAF, this aircraft was bought back by the company as G-9-363 and became an FR.74B for Singapore, number 526. The 'towel-rack' antenna under the rear fuselage (right) is associated with the Marconi AD.722 radio compass, an option for export customers. Note the shadow on the starboard wing (above) from the Handley Page Hastings camera ship (Air Portraits)

Top left An FGA.59 for Iraq taxying at Dunsfold after a pre-delivery test flight
(BAe via Brian Isles)

Left Led by Sqn Ldr 'Pete' Mercer, the F.6-mounted 'Blue Diamonds' were the RAF's premier aerobatic display team in 1961–62. After being bought back by the company in 1966 as G-9-216, a rather weathered XG232/'G' taxies out for a test flight from Dunsfold prior to refurbishment. It subsequently emerged as an FGA.71 for Chile, delivered on 19 June 1968 coded J-714
(BAe via Brian Isles)

This page The Hunters operated by the Sultan of Oman's Air Force (SOAF) are painted in particularly garish camouflage. Configured for an air defence mission, this FGA.9 is fitted with two 230 Imp gal (1,045 litre) combat tanks and a pair of AIM-9P Sidewinder AAMs
(Rolls-Royce)

Fitted with the Integrated
Flight Instrumentation
System (IFIS), Hunter T.7A
XF967 serves with No 237
OCU at RAF Lossiemouth,
Scotland, to assist pilots
converting to the
Buccaneer S.2 maritime

strike aircraft, a type
which lacks a dual-
control training version
(Tim Laming)

Another specialized Hunter trainer: two T.8Ms are operated by No 899 Sqn of the Fleet Air Arm to acquaint students with the Ferranti Blue Fox radar system fitted to the V/STOL Sea Harrier FRS.1 multi-role fighter. Based at RNAS Yeovilton in Somerset, XL580 (pictured) and XL602 were converted from T.8s in 1979–80 (Air Portraits)

Top left Kuwait received four FGA.57s and five T.67s, but the single-seaters were transferred to the Sultan of Oman's Air Force in 1975 after the arrival of A-4KU Skyhawks. This factory-fresh FGA.57 is parked at Dunsfold before delivery (BAe via Brian Isles)

Left One of the 12 ex-RAF Hunters delivered to the Royal Rhodesian Air Force in 1963, '58' (ex-XF416) is still in service with No 1 Sqn, Air Force of Zimbabwe. Photographed at Malta in March 1984 in ferry configuration with two 230 Imp gal (1,045 litre) and two 100 Imp gal (454 litre) wing tanks, this aircraft is probably en route to Zimbabwe after

a major overhaul by Airwork Services (Robbie Shaw)

This page A smash hit at UK air shows and a founder member of Michael Carlton's Hunter One Collection, G-HUNT was originally one of a batch of 30 new-build F.51s supplied by HAL to the Royal Danish Air Force, serial E-418. After

flying some 3,573 hours with Esk 724, it was bought back by the company after the unit disbanded in 1974 and allocated the 'B' Condition registration G-9-440. The aircraft was sold privately to Spencer Flack and it flew for the first time as G-HUNT in March 1980 following an impeccable restoration at Elstree by ex-Hawker

employee Eric Hayward. After its acquisition by Michael Carlton in 1981, G-HUNT was later retrofitted with saw-tooth wing leading edges and a tail parachute installation. Sadly, Michael Carlton was killed in a flying accident in Zimbabwe on 31 August 1986 (Tim Laming)

Top left Toting an AGM-65B Maverick infrared-guided air-surface missile on the outboard pylon, Swiss Hunter F.58 J-4082 is on finals for its home base at Dubendorf where it was originally delivered on 18 December 1959.

The enlarged 'Sabrinas' are believed to contain flare/chaff dispensers (Robbie Shaw)

Left Parked in front of a Mirage IIIS, F.58 J-4087 displays an impressive array of rockets and

bombs, plus a Maverick missile on a pallet. This aircraft was delivered on 14 January 1960 (Heinz Meier)

This page T.68 J-4207 taxies past a hardened shelter at Dubendorf in April 1984 (Heinz Meier)

Overleaf A Hunter GA.11 (WW654/'VL833') of the Yeovilton-based Fleet

Requirements and Air Direction Unit (FRADU) approaching the Needles off the Isle of Wight over a flat calm sea in September 1985. Note the tailhook (Robbie Shaw)

Comparison with the Hunter in dogfight terms is difficult, since the Hawker aircraft needed external tanks, whereas the Sabre had a credible endurance on internal fuel. It is said that the early Sabre could generate a very high initial turn rate by using its leading edge slats, but that it then had to dive to get these automatic slats to retract. The Hunter would therefore simply pull up and wait for the Sabre to dive.

It is also reported that the Sabre's controls were badly harmonized at medium speeds, being very light laterally and heavy longitudinally. At high IAS the Sabre's stick movement per G was very small, and there was a risk of pilot-induced oscillations (PIOs). In one incident recounted to this writer, the Sabre began porpoising at 500 knots (925 km/hr), bent one wing and lost an elevator.

It seems likely that the Sabre was more easily overstressed than the Hunter. Being built like a battleship, with a structure weight to match, the Hunter never broke up in flight. There was a well-known incident in Germany, in which a ham-fisted pilot somehow managed to achieve an estimated 14G in a turn. His nose bled, the pitot-static head was bent, and the needle of the G-meter was pressed against the right-hand stop, but the aircraft remained in one piece.

It should perhaps be explained that the Hunter had a design load factor of 7.5G, ie, it was to sustain this value without permanent distortion, and 50 per cent more (11.25G) without structural failure. On this occasion it had exceeded requirements by a significant margin.

The indestructible nature of the Hunter was also illustrated by a Danish aircraft (serial 415), which suffered a flame-out on the approach to Skrydstrup. The pilot ejected three miles (five kilometres) from the airfield, where the aircraft landed itself wheels-up, and was flying again within a month.

In RAF service at Oldenburg in Germany, a Hunter stalled on the approach and swung off, reducing to scrap two Mercedes fire tenders, the runway caravan and the crash jeep, with very little damage to itself aside from the loss of one undercarriage leg. As discussed later in the context of development for ground attack, the Hunter's structural qualities were very much appreciated after the Venom, which was regarded as distinctly fragile and fatigue-prone.

To revert to the Sabre, this aircraft had been designed as a long-range escort fighter (in the tradition of the same company's P-51 Mustang), hence its wing planform emphasized aspect ratio, which also helped sustained turn rate. Having chosen a quarter-chord sweep of 35°, its designers originally hoped to employ an aspect ratio of 6.0, relying on leading edge slats to prevent tip-stall. However, stability considerations forced them to reduce this to 4.79, compared to the Hunter's 3.33. The basic wing area was 287.0 sq ft (26.75 m²), and thickness/chord ratio was 11 per cent at the root, tapering to 10 per cent at the tip, compared to the Hunter's constant 8.5 per cent.

The RAF's Sabre Mk 2 and 4 had the J47-GE-13 engine of 5,200 lb (2,360 kg) thrust, and weighed 11,100 lb (5,035 kg) empty and 14,640 lb (6,640 kg) at clean gross. Sea level rate of climb was stated to be 7,250 ft/min (36.8 m/sec), but it took 9 minutes to reach 30,000 ft (9,150 m) and 18 minutes to 40,000 ft (12,200 m). In level flight it could reach 0.89 TMN at sea level and 0.905 TMN at 35,000 ft (10,670 m).

Another quite well designed contemporary of the Hunter was the Dassault Mystère IVA, which had a slab tail, and was a very clean aircraft. It could initiate manoeuvres very quickly, could run away from a Hunter in a dive, and could recover without any problem. On the other hand it had far less power, was roughly 0.01 mach slower in level flight, and had a poor rate of climb, especially at altitude. In simulated combat, the Hunters would use climbing turns to gain the initiative over the Mystère. Its rear view was no better than that from the Hunter.

When the Mystère was formally evaluated at Boscombe, the air conditioning system was criticized: the transparencies misted and the pilot got cooked. In turbulence, the airbrakes set up a violent oscillation, reaching + 12G and − 4G, in the course of which the radios were torn loose from their mountings.

The Mystère IVA had a Hispano-Suiza Verdon centrifugal turbojet derived from the Tay and producing 7,710 lb (3,500 kg) thrust. It had an empty weight of 12,950 lb, a clean gross weight of 16,530 lb (7,500 kg) and a wing area of 344.5 sq ft (32 m²). It was armed with two 30 mm DEFA cannon. Published data includes a maximum level speed of Mach 0.91 at sea level and 0.93 at altitude.

Chapter 8

Bad News and Good News

Having outlined how the Hunter entered service with the RAF, and how new variants with increased fuel were quickly introduced on the production lines, one cannot avoid recalling that the Hunter was still riddled with problems as the numbers of aircraft built up. Once the new airbrake was introduced, the aircraft was given a limited release, but other serious problems remained to be solved.

First in order of priority was Avon engine surging at high AOA or due to gunfire. As is customary in such cases, the airframe manufacturer blamed the engine company for producing a powerplant with no surge margin, and the engine manufacturer claimed that the aircraft's intakes produced so much flow distortion that it was impossible to operate a respectable powerplant behind them. However, the fact that the Sapphire had no such surge problem was a strong indication that R-R was in the wrong on this occasion.

It says a great deal for the reputation and influence of R-R that, despite the evidence of the Sapphire, the company won MoS support for the idea of taking three Hunter F.4s to Tripoli in Libya, to test a variety of intake 'fixes' designed by that company to straighten out the flow to the engine. This was purely concerned with Avon surging under G at altitude, and the trials were presumably mounted in a hot climate because high temperature on the ground usually means low temperature above the tropopause. Surging generally occurs at high rpm and low temperature, and the two modified aircraft were compared with the standard F.4 as they manoeuvred at high level. However, this very expensive trial served only to prove that it was the 100-series Avon that was at fault, not the Hunter intakes.

In the end, the Avon's tendency to surge at high AOA was cured by derating the engine, while surge due to gunfire was cured by fuel-dipping activated by the trigger being depressed. The overall result was something of a lash-up, but the F.4 was regarded as an interim type, pending the advent of the F.6, hence the RAF judged the result acceptable. The Boscombe report on engine handling and the effects on the engine of gunfiring for the F.1 and F.4 said that (with Avon 113 and 115 respectively) these aircraft had been restricted to a maximum height of 25,000 ft (7,600 m) when firing high velocity ammunition. However, 'with the Mk 121 with "Stage A" modifications (ie, fuel-dipping and air-bleed), which was tested in F.1 WT612 and F.4s WT704 and WV276, it was reported that the

Hunter could be given an unrestricted clearance for gunfiring over the practical flight envelope of the aircraft'.

There was a whole series of other problems associated with the four Aden guns. Having had no prior experience of firing four such powerful cannon, it was found that extensive fatigue-cracking occurred in the surrounding structure, a problem that was tamed by local reinforcements of stainless steel, and later by allowing the pilot to fire one pair of guns at once.

Hot gases from the breech accumulated in the front fuselage and on one occasion exploded, blowing the nose-cap out of place. This problem was cured by arranging that an air-scoop on the lower surface of the gunpack was opened electrically whenever the trigger was depressed, ventilating the entire area.

In the initial design (again through lack of experience) the empty shell cases and belt links were simply released through chutes that ended flush with the aircraft skin. This produced the minimum of drag, but there was virtually no control over where this debris went. Being light, the links were blown directly aft, battering the airbrake fairing (and the airbrake itself, if extended), and scratching the rear fuselage. The cure was to collect the links in two blister fairings, which the RAF knew as 'Sabrinas' after an unusually well-endowed young starlet of the 1950s.

It was judged impractical to retain the empty cases, but the chutes were extended and modified to direct them well clear of the aircraft. There was an unconfirmed report at the time that one case had passed straight through a plastic drop tank on the inboard pylon. The combination of link-collection and case jettison has worked well, but the Swiss were later reported to be concerned that their practice firings took place over farming land, and that this risked damage to farm machinery, even if no workers or animals were present at the time. Swiss Hunters are thus said to have enlarged 'Sabrinas' for weapons training, collecting both links and cases.

In 1956, when it finally seemed that the end of

One of the Hunter F.4s built by Fokker-Aviolanda in 1955–56. N-156 is reported to have served with No 323 Sqn at Leeuwarden, a unit now equipped with F-16s. The silver tail-cone appears to have been a feature of Belgian and Dutch-built Hunters
(Koninklijke Luchtmacht)

the gun-firing problems might be in sight, a Hunter pilot fired a long burst at altitude, and discovered that the nose of the aircraft dipped by approximately one degree. It was easy to confirm on the back of an envelope that this order of pitch-down due to gunfire was to be expected. With a reaction of around 3,000 lb (1,360 kg) acting 1.4 ft (42.7 cm) below the CG, the aircraft acquired a new trimmed attitude 0.6° nose-down. With reduced damping at altitude, it would clearly overshoot to something like the pilot-estimated pitch angle. The project office suggested various means to eliminate pitch-down due to gunfire, including a somewhat hare-brained scheme for upward-firing rockets in the rear fuselage. However, in the end simple blast deflectors were introduced, identical in principle to those of the traditional gangster's Thompson submachine gun, but turning the blast downward, rather than upward.

These blast deflectors became standard fit on Hunters (and subsequent Kingston aircraft), though in low level use they were deleted to reduce drag. It is argued by some observers that, even in the air-air role, it takes a long burst (not used operationally) at altitude with no control column restraint to produce measurable pitch-down.

Far left This photograph of a Hunter F.4, WV325 (first flown 13 June 1955 by Hugh Merewether), serves as a reminder of the clean lines of early production aircraft. At this stage the only excrescences were the airbrake and tail bumper (Russell Adams, Gloster Aircraft)

Above Illustrative of some of the gun-firing modifications, this FGA.9 from the Tactical Weapons Unit at Brawdy in South Wales has blast deflectors, link collectors, and chutes to direct the empty cases clear of the airframe (Peter Hudson, RAE Bedford)

A Fighter for NATO

In the early 1950s the US was concerned that Euro-NATO air forces should have modern jet fighters in service at the earliest possible time, and a policy decision was made to use a fighter construction programme to assist in the post-war recovery of West European industry. In July 1952 the Mutual Security Agency therefore earmarked a sum of $245 million to purchase European-designed combat aircraft for NATO, with delivery to take place by June 1955.

At that stage the RAF favoured the Swift F.4 with afterburning and variable-incidence tail, basically because it carried more fuel than the Hunter. There were 375 Swift F.1s and F.4s on order, and it was anticipated that the MSA order would add to this total. However, MSA relied for technical advice on the USAF, and in 1952 the service sent a team of test pilots to the UK to evaluate both the Swift and the Hunter, flying them against the F-86. The Swift may have been favoured up to this point, but the situation was about to change.

The evaluation team was headed by Brig Gen 'Al' Boyd, and included 'Chuck' Yeager, 'Fred' Asani, and about 10 engineers. Their visit to Dunsfold was supervised by 'Bob' Marsh, who was later to become assistant chief engineer at Kingston. Marsh was responsible for all the details of the visit, down to the general's lunchtime pint (568 cc) of milk. It was also left to Marsh to explain to Boyd that the reason he was forced to land with the ailerons in 'manual' on his first Hunter flight was entirely due to his mishandling of the system!

It should be explained that to select 'power' for the flying controls after flying in 'manual', a pawl in the release unit adjacent to the PFCU had to engage in a groove in the hydraulic ram. Successful engagement was indicated to the pilot by a black 'doll's eye'. If the pawl did not enter the groove (ie, in the event of a 'false lock'), the pilot had to move the control column vigorously until engagement was effected, otherwise the aircraft remains in 'manual'.

In spite of its limitations, the Hunter appears to have impressed the USAF team with its potential. Thanks largely to its more advanced wing design, it

The Mk 50, built for the Swedish Air Force in the UK, was a standard F.4, aside from having an Avon Mk 1205 with a Plessey IPN starter, and Swedish avionics. A total of 120 were purchased to supersede the Vampire and J-29 (HAL)

could always dive away from the F-86 which had to be vertical to reach Mach 1.0. Boyd reported that 'the Hunter handles as well as any aircraft in the world today'. The team decided that the improvements necessary for the Swift could not be completed in time for the MSA deadline, whereas the Hunter could be produced in time. Nine changes were proposed at meetings sponsored by MoS, but most of the modifications were already in the pipeline. The most significant change was the deletion of the two small fuel tanks in the rear fuselage for safety reasons, although the USAF seems to have changed its mind about this danger by the time the F-16 made its appearance. Nitrogen tank-purging was requested, but was never accepted for the Hunter.

The aircraft selected in 1953 for procurement under MSA funding was the Hunter F.4, with wing fuel replacing the rear fuselage tanks, and provisions for drop tanks. Although the full details of this offshore procurement programme do not appear to have been made public, the US is believed to have funded (or contributed to the funding of) up to 958 Hunters, including some for the RAF and 30 for Denmark.

However, the most important effect was to establish in Belgium and the Netherlands production lines on which a total of 445 Hunters were built (this figure representing a slight reduction on the originally planned 460). The principal companies involved were Fokker, Aviolanda, SABCA, and Avions Fairey. The plan was that for the Belgian Air Force the US would pay for 64 and the Belgian government a further 192, while for the Royal Netherlands Air Force the US was to fund 48 aircraft and the Dutch government an additional 156. In 1957 production switched from the F.4 to the F.6, with the result that roughly half the total built corresponded to the later model. The best information available to this writer is that Holland completed 96 Mk 4s and 93 Mk 6s, while Belgium built 112 Mk 4s and 144 Mk 6s. However, one Belgian and one Dutch F.4 appear to have flown first in the UK.

The RNAF F.4s had serials running from N-101, and the F.6s from N-201. The Netherlands also purchased 10 two-seat T.7s (N-301 to -310) from HAL and 10 from MoS (N-311 to -320). These Dutch Hunters served with Nos 324 and 325 Sqn at Leeuwarden and No 327 Sqn at Soesterberg. In 1960 12 Hunters were taken on the aircraft carrier *Karel Doorman* to Dutch New Guinea, and there were reports that a further 10 were shipped out in

the following year. However, in 1962 the colony was transferred to Indonesia. In 1966 the last Dutch Hunter unit (No 325 Sqn) received NF-5s. Some 47 Dutch Hunters and 10 two-seaters were bought back by HSA in the course of the 1960s.

The Belgian Air Force (BAF) Hunters served with the 1st Wing at Beauvechain, the 7th at Chièvres, and the 9th at Bierset. Serials for the Mk 4 ran from ID-1, and for the Mk 6 from IF-1. The 1st and 9th Wings kept their Hunters only briefly, but the 7th flew the aircraft until 1963. Belgium was not a case where the Hunter covered itself in glory, since deliveries had begun at a very early stage in the aircraft's history, when it was still deep in teething problems, and HAL was fully occupied in satisfying the complaints of the RAF. In Belgium the Hunter acquired a reputation for bad reliability and non-existent product support, and the BAF simply dumped it at the earliest possible opportunity. Many aircraft were placed in storage with less than 50 flying hours on the clock.

Kingston's reputation in Belgium was not enhanced when the company bought back a total of 94 BAF Hunters, paying only scrap-metal prices. What was less well publicized was the fact that HSA paid the Belgian government an additional fee in the event that a buyer could be found for the aircraft, when refurbished. However, judging by figures quoted in Parliament in Brussels early in 1963, this second payment was less than generous. It was said that 32 F.6s that had originally cost BFr 14 million ($280,000) each were sold back for an initial sum of BFr 1.6 million ($32,000) each, with a follow-on sum of BFr 650,000 ($13,000) if HSA resold them. It must have been obvious that Belgium would have done far better if SABCA had been allowed to refurbish and resell these Hunters, but this was clearly outside the terms of the contract.

Export Fours

Just before the first Hunter F.1 was issued to an RAF squadron, on 29 June 1954 Sweden signed a contract for the purchase of 120 aircraft (serials 34001-34120). This series was known to HAL as the Mk 50 and to the Swedish Air Force (SAF) as the J-34. It replaced the Vampire and J-29. The first Mk 50 (34001), which had begun construction as WT770 for the RAF, was flown by 'Frank' Murphy on 24 June 1955, and was delivered to Sweden on August 26th. The first 24 were built at Kingston and the remainder at Blackpool.

The Mk 50 was based on a post-Mod 228 Mk 4, but it had an Avon 1205 with Plessey IPN liquid fuel

Top left This Belgian Air Force F.4, ID-8, was the eighth built by Avions Fairey and SABCA. The 7J-J code denotes the 7th *Ecole de Chasse* at Chièvres. A white horse insignia is painted on the red nose flash

Left The Swedish Mk 50, exemplified here by the first production aircraft, 34001, was one of the most photogenic Hunters ever built. It equipped four day fighter wings, and was modified in Sweden to carry Sidewinder (HAL)

starter for reduced scramble time, and Swedish VHF radios. It was later modified in Sweden to carry Sidewinder. As the J-34 it was issued to four day fighter wings: F8 at Barkaby, F9 at Säve, F10 at Ängelholm, and F18 at Tullinge. In 1962 this last unit formed an aerobatic team, the 'Acro-Hunters'. The aircraft appears to have been well-liked, and was particularly complimented for its low-speed handling and spin-resistance, though pilots would have preferred nosewheel steering to differential braking. Press reports suggest that the SAF's only problem with the J-34 was to keep the avionics working.

One Mk 50 (serial 34085) was used as a TI aircraft for an afterburner developed by Svenska (now Volvo) Flygmotor. It was modified to what the SAF termed J-34B standard, and first flew in this form on 6 May 1958, with Plt Off Lars Erik Larsson at the controls. External changes were limited to a sawn-off tailcone and small dorsal intakes. The Swedish afterburner was designated EBK-56U (EBK being an abbreviation for *Efterbrännkammare* or afterburner).

Reports indicate that time-to-height was roughly halved, the J-34B taking only four minutes to 39,360 ft (12,000 m). Pilots who flew this aircraft are said to have enthused about its climb performance and turn rate, but there were difficulties in keeping the afterburner working at altitude: it flamed out at 42,000 ft (12,800 m). The final flight was made on 6 June 1958. The programme was abandoned, since it was felt the fuel consumption was too high, and the aircraft's radius of action too small. In addition, the J-35 Draken would shortly be available.

The J-34 remained in first-line service until 1966, when most of these aircraft were literally cut up for scrap, to the great chagrin of HSA. A few were retained for weapon training until the late '60s. In 1962 we discovered that there had been a mistake in the Swedish contract, as a result of which there was nothing to stop Sweden reselling these aircraft anywhere in the world. There was a rumour that Sidewinder-equipped Mk 50s were going to the Lebanon, but Sweden appears to have decided to avoid the stigma of arms dealing. It may be explained that Hunter export contracts normally included a clause giving HSA the first option, in the event that the customer decided to resell. This was supposed to prevent the aircraft falling into Communist hands (a difficult point to make in selling to Chile's then left-wing government), but in practice it assured the company of a steady

supply of low-cost pre-used Hunters.

On 3 July 1954, only four days after the Swedish signing, Denmark signed a contract for 30 Hunters.. These aircraft were built at Kingston, designated Mk 51, and given serials E-401–430. The first Mk 51 had its maiden flight on 15 December

This Mk 50 (serial 34085) was modified to take a Svenska Flygmotor EBK56U afterburner and was redesignated as a J-34B. Flight tests in 1958 showed major improvements in climb rate, but the effect on radius of action proved unacceptable (SAF via Ewald Wedin)

Top left This photograph taken at the military aircraft test centre at Linköping shows the Swedish afterburner inside a wooden framework simulating the modified rear fuselage (SAF via Ewald Wedin of Volvo Flygmotor AB)

Left The Danish Mk 51s formed Esk 724, which disbanded in 1974, when 20 were bought back by HSA. Some are seen here at Dunsfold, awaiting refurbishing. The Midland Air Museum received E-425 and Peter Warren of Biggin Hill bought E-424 (Mike Stroud)

1955, and the first two aircraft were delivered to Denmark at the end of January 1956. These aircraft served with Esk 724, initially at Aalborg, then at Karup, and finally at Skrydstrup and Vaerlose. The Mk 51 was essentially a post-Mod 228 F.4 with an Avon 120, ARC-34 UHF and STR.9X VHF radios, Mk 10 IFF and ARA.25 radio compass (ie, ADF). Denmark also had two T.53s (serials ET-271 and -272), and later two slightly modified T.7s (ET-273 and -274). The squadron was disbanded in March 1974, at which stage 20 serviceable Hunters were bought back by HSA.

In 1955 plans for the phasing-out of RAF F.4s in favour of the F.6 made some of these earlier Hunters available for resale abroad. Peru signed for 16 ex-RAF F.4s, which were slightly modified and redesignated Mk 52s (serials 630-645). These were pre-Mod 228 aircraft with only two pylons, and no RP provisions. They retained the standard VHF radios, but Green Salad was deleted and they were fitted instead with Bendix ARN-6 radio compass, which necessitated a small bulge in the canopy fairing. The first conversion (WT717, becoming No

630) was flown by 'Frank' Bullen on 1 December 1955. Deliveries were made by sea during 1956. Peru also had an ex-RAF F.4 converted to a two-seat Mk 62 (No 681), basically a T.7 with the same navaid change as on the single-seaters. This aircraft was flown by 'Don' Lucey on 15 September 1959, and delivered in 1960. The Peruvian Hunters served with one squadron of a mixed fighter wing (Grupo 12) at Limatambo and Talara, the other squadrons having the F-86F and T-80C.

At Farnborough in 1966 there were preliminary discussions on the possible supply of refurbished F.6s to Peru, and quotes were requested on 8 and 16 aircraft. However, at that time Chile had a one-month option on all the 21 aircraft available (including the two-seat demonstrator G-APUX), and quickly converted that option into a firm sale. Following the supply of Mirage 5Ps in 1968–69, the Peruvian Hunters were switched to the ground attack role (for which these two-pylon aircraft were very badly suited), and in 1976 they were replaced by the Sukhoi Su-22.

Chapter 9

At Last An Engine

This account has earlier recorded that in mid-1953 HAL was ordered to cease work on the afterburning, thin-wing P.1083, and to channel Hunter development toward use of a more powerful 'dry' Avon.

Geoffrey Wilde's record of early Avon development states that by 1950 there was an urgent need for a more powerful version to supersede the RA.7 of 7,500 lb (3,400 kg). By late February 1951 design work had started on the RA.14, a 'second generation' Avon aimed at a thrust of around 9,500 lb (4,310 kg). Since this involved a large-scale rehash, it also provided the opportunity to introduce a new compressor design that (if successful) would eliminate the part-speed stall and surge characteristics of the basic RA.3, the engine without variable inlet-whirl and interstage bleed.

The Avon's only competitor for RAF orders was the Sapphire, which R-R believed to have 'greatly superior' flow/pressure ratio characteristics to those of the Avon. Fortuitously, Armstrong Siddeley had recently approached Lord Hives for assistance in connection with mechanical problems on the Sapphire. The way was thus clear for an exchange of information on the Avon and Sapphire, which took place in December 1950. As part of this exchange, R-R was given details of the aerodynamic design and performance characteristics of the Sapphire, which were undoubtedly far better than those of the RA.3. The addition of interstage bleed and variable inlet-whirl on the RA.7 had reduced the superiority of the Sapphire, but Armstrong Siddeley's compressor was unquestionably a better design.

At the risk of over-simplification, one major difference between the two designs appears to have been that the loading on the first four Sapphire compressor stages was less than half of the corresponding figure for the Avon. The Sapphire blades were thus running nowhere near the stall, and could tolerate a large increase in AOA due to a reduction in axial velocity. However, the Sapphire blading was subject to mechanical vibration due to aerodynamic flutter. The functioning of the Sapphire was also helped by the fact that the compressor had a constant outside diameter, whereas the Avon was waisted to accommodate the auxiliary gearbox and accessories within the minimum possible frontal area.

Aerodynamic design of the RA.14 compressor began in February 1951. Wilde states that 'it was

The P.1099 prototype in
flight, illustrating once
again the attractive lines
of the original F.6. The
reason for the dark bands
at the rear transport joint
and in the middle of the
rear fuselage is not
recorded
(Rolls-Royce)

*decided to follow the aerodynamic design of the
Sapphire exactly in the first four stages, but to follow
these with 11 stages of new aerodynamic design,
allowing for the progressive reduction in compressor diameter for a low-drag installation, and to give a
straight flow into the combustion chamber'.*
Combined with this basic compressor was to be a
refined version of the variable inlet-whirl and the
interstage bleed used on the RA.3, which came in
progressively as a function of engine speed. The
RA.14 would thus enjoy the fruits of previous
compressor experience on both the Avon and
Sapphire.

Design of the RA.7 for the Hunter F.1 and F.4,
and the Canberra, had commenced in March
1949, and tests of the first complete 100-series
Avon had begun in August 1950. Start of the detail
design for the RA.14 occurred at the end of April
1951, and by July (the month that WB188 flew) the
first compressor rig tests were being carried out.
The results were highly successful, and it was
found that, by optimising the setting of the inlet-
whirl vanes, the mass flow and pressure ratio
exceeded the design values by a worthwhile

margin, allowing the engine to be uprated to at
least 10,000 lb (4,535 kg).

Bench-testing of the first complete RA.14 engine
began on 17 November 1951, and quickly
confirmed earlier predictions. The 150-hour Type
Test was carried out in April 1952, and trials in a
flying testbed commenced exactly a year later. The
first production RA.14 was delivered in July 1953.

However, as far as HAL was concerned, the first
'Big Avons' (ie, the 200-series) still handled badly
and had a low surge margin. It was only when a
much more sophisticated fuel control system was
added in the RA.28 that what Marsh recalls as *'a
shattering improvement'* was actually achieved. In
his words, *'the new Avon got the reputation of
being virtually surge-proof against all types of
vicious mishandling and gunfiring combined'.*

At last HAL was to have an engine that not only
produced far more thrust, but also gave the pilots
an aircraft in which they could fire the guns at any
altitude, reach high AOAs, and slam the throttle
backwards and forwards, all without fear of the
engine surging. It began to look as though we
might just have an aeroplane, after all.

Top left The 200-Series Rolls-Royce Avon had an RA28 rating of 9,950 lb (4,515 kg) at 8,000 rpm, and is distinguished from the 100-Series by its tubo-annular combustion system. With a sophisticated fuel control system it provided a shattering improvement (Rolls-Royce)

Top The exhaust louvres in the sides of the rear fuselage. In principle, the high tail of the Hunter made it more suitable for the installation of a thrust reverser, but a braking parachute was less expensive (Rolls-Royce)

Left The P.1099 prototype for the Hunter F.6 series first flew on 23 January 1954, and in mid-1956 was used for tests with a Rolls-Royce thrust reverser, aimed at reducing landing ground roll (Rolls-Royce)

Hunter Six

Following termination of work on the P.1083 prototype, (WN470), it was agreed that HAL could use the centre fuselage, front fuselage and tail from that aircraft to speed the construction of the P.1099 based on the RA.14 engine. The P.1099 (XF833) was to be the prototype for the F.6 series, and it made its first flight on 23 January 1954, piloted by Neville Duke. Due to the airbrake saga, this was six months ahead of the F.1 entering service. It was also nine months ahead of the maiden flight of the F.4, which was simply ordered into production without a prototype. In essence, the F.4 was merely a new build standard, whereas the F.6 might well be termed a 'second generation Hunter'. Before leaving the subject of XF833, it may be added that in mid-1956 this aircraft was used as a TI for a Rolls-Royce thrust reverser.

Due to the re-arrangement of engine accessories on the 200-series Avon, the Hunter's small centre fuel tanks had to be deleted. In their place, two 25 Imp gal (114 litre) kidney-shaped tanks were introduced in the rear fuselage on either side of the jetpipe. The front tanks and wing tanks of the F.4 were retained, giving an internal fuel volume of 390 Imp gal (1,775 litres).

The production F.6 was fitted with the 10,150 lb (4,603 kg) Avon Mk 203 or 207, which had IPN liquid-fuel starting. This was faster, cheaper and more reliable than the earlier cartridge starters, though it initially led to some rear fuselage fires and other teething problems. This mark also had ARC-52 UHF radio as an alternative to VHF. It also had TACAN, and provisions for SNEB/Matra rocket batteries. A few F.6s had provisions for target-towing using a drag launch, and six were fitted with braking parachutes. Some early F.6s had the old variable-incidence tail, but most had the follow-up tailplane arrangement described earlier.

With the F.6, HAL finally got down to curing the mild pitch-up that had characterized earlier marks. Trials were conducted on an F.1 (WT568) with various fixes, including wing fences, but the ultimate solution was an outboard leading edge extension, which incidentally increased wing area from 340 to 349 sq ft (31.60 to 32.43 m²). At high

The initial production standard of F.6 is illustrated by WW593, the second aircraft off the Kingston line. It was first flown on 19 August 1955 by Frank Bullen, and in 1961 became an FR.10. Note the absence of leading edge extensions (HAL)

Top left Static tests with the thrust reverser, showing the outer wing immersed in engine efflux. In practice, the use of reversed thrust would probably have been limited to fairly high speeds to restrict airframe buffeting
(Rolls-Royce)

Top Believed to have been first suggested by David Lockspeiser, the HAL pilot primarily responsible for armament development, this twin-Sidewinder installation on the gunpack would have left the wing pylons free for other stores
(BAe)

Left The leading edge extensions that were developed to cure the mild pitch-up of earlier marks are well illustrated by XE588, seen here over Selsey Bill. It first flew on 19 March 1956, and served with No 263 Sqn
(HAL)

speed this extension worked by reducing the local lift coefficients and weakening the shock waves (due to the lower t/c), and at low speeds the discontinuity stopped the inboard spread of the leading edge vortex. It was such a beautiful idea that it seemed a pity it had not been on the wing from the outset.

By now the Hunter was becoming a serious aeroplane, and a major series of intensive gunfiring trials was carried out to provide a complete clearance for the gunpack. The aircraft involved were F.6s XE543, 558 and 598. Duke writes of flying 16 sorties per day for two consecutive days in March 1956, firing off the full load of ammunition on each flight at maximum IAS. This was part of a five-day programme that involved the firing of over 40,000 rounds.

The total number of F.6s supplied was 383 aircraft from the Kingston and Coventry factories, this figure evidently including seven 'Interim Mk 6s' diverted from the F.1 production line. One early problem during flight development was fatigue failures of compressor blades, which was over-

come by derating the engine from the original 10,500 lb (4,762 kg) to the definitive figure quoted earlier. The precise thrust in common usage rounded out to 10,000 lb (4,535 kg), and the 200-series Avon was always referred to in this manner. In addition to derating, fatigue was tackled by the introduction of steel rotor and stator blades toward the rear of the compressor. As mentioned earlier, handling was improved by a new fuel control system, and the Boscombe assessment of RA.28 Avon 203 handling in early 1956 stated that *'the engine can be regarded as free of any surge tendency'*. In the course of five years, the Avon had come a long way.

Quoting data from Form 2110, the F.6 had a clean take-off weight of 17,400 lb (7,890 kg) with 3,000 lb (1,360 kg) of internal fuel. Maximum speed at sea level was 0.94 TMN, and even at 45,000 ft (13,200 m) it was still capable of 0.92 TMN. (Though not mentioned on this form, it peaked at 0.945 TMN). It reached this reference height in 7.1 minutes, and then had a residual rate of climb of 1,700 ft/min (8.63 m/sec) at clean take-off weight.

This artist's impression shows de Havilland Propellers' Firestreaks gunpack-mounted. The artwork was based on the photograph of XE588 on the previous page, printed in reverse, and with a fictitious serial added inverted! XE288 was actually a Bristol 173 helicopter (BAe)

Not a pretty sight! The Hunter (exemplified here by an F.6) had many bad features, including the fact that the control column handle tended to obscure the compass, and that some avionics switches were inaccessible (BAe)

At this same weight, 1,000 ft/min (5.08 m/sec) service ceiling was 47,500 ft (14,500 m).

The first of seven 'Interim Mk 6s' (WW592) from the F.1 production line, fitted with pre-Mod 228 F.4 wings, was first flown on 23 May 1955 by 'Bill' Bedford, and the first real production F.6 (XE526) was flown by Hugh Merewether on October 11th that year. There was later a Mk 6A variant, which was effectively a half-way house to the FGA.9, having provisions for two 230 Imp gal (1,045 litre) tanks and increased oxygen, but not the other modifications.

The F.6 was granted a CA Release at the end of May 1956, and deliveries then began to No 19 Sqn at Church Fenton, which phased out the Meteor F.8 in October that year. The F.6 served with 19 RAF front-line squadrons within Fighter Command and 2ATAF, primarily in the air defence role. Most F.6s were phased out around the end of 1960, but Nos 14 And 19 Sqn retained this Hunter until late 1962, and No 92 Sqn kept it until April 1963.

Of all the RAF Hunter units, the best remembered is probably No 111 Sqn, with its aerobatic team of nine black-painted aircraft. The 'Black Arrows' made their first major demonstration at the 1957 SBAC Show. In the following year, augmented by aircraft from No 43 Sqn, 'Treble-One' looped 22 Hunters in immaculate formation, a feat very rarely equalled and never surpassed.

The F.6 was used as the basis for a number of developments. One of the most interesting was the P.1109, equipped with AI.20 nose radar and two de Havilland Blue Jay (Firestreak) air-air missiles on underwing pylons, cannon armament being reduced to two guns in view of the extra weight in the nose.

The company was encouraged by MoS to spend private venture money on the P.1109, presumably to safeguard against the possibility of Gloster failing to transform the Javelin into an acceptable aircraft. Two F.6s were converted, the P.1109A (WW594, the third F.6) having the radar but not the missiles, and the P.1109B (XF378) having the complete system, and being used in firing trials. In the event the Javelin went ahead, and the money

An early RAF F.6 configuration is shown here on XF389, with 100 Imp gal (454 litre) tanks and 24 three-inch (76.2 mm) RPs. This aircraft served with 92 Sqn, DFLS, 56 Sqn and 229 OCU, and ended as Jordanian FGA.73A serial 829 (HAL)

Top left The 'Black Arrows' of No 111 Sqn will long be remembered as one of the RAF's finest aerobatic teams. They made their debut at Farnborough in 1957, and performed at all major airshows in the UK for the next three years

Left Taking off from the main runway at Farnborough, the nine Hunter F.6s of 'Treble One' prepare to form up for their display. As illustrated here, slow gear retraction was a Hawker characteristic
(HSA via Brian Isles)

Right The nine aircraft of the 'Black Arrows' in their immaculate formation. As fighter costs escalated, the role of the RAF's premier aerobatic team was taken over by trainers, first the Gnat and later the Hawk
(MoD)

Above The third production F.6, WW594, was used as a trials vehicle for the AI.20 radar that was to equip the Firestreak-armed variant. In the writer's view one of the most attractive Hunters, it was designated P.1109A (BAe)

Left The later F.6, XF378, was equipped with the complete AI.20/Firestreak weapon system and designated P.1109B. It was employed for trials at Hatfield and RAF Valley in 1957, but cannibalized two years later after a rear fuselage fire (BAe)

spent on the P.1109 (mainly in 1957) was wasted. The company also proposed some two-seat Hunters to be armed with Firestreak, the P.1114 being based on the Avon and the P.1115 on the Sapphire.

In this writer's view, the P.1109 was the most attractive of Hunters in plan-view, the standard single-seater being spoiled by the short nose necessitated by the one-ton gunpack. 'Bob' Broad, who flew the 'Hunter night fighter' at CFE, recalls that the radar was poor, but that the aircraft was an outstanding performer at altitude, flying with less rpm and turning tighter than the standard short-nose F.6. In fact, in May 1956 Merewether zoomed the P.1109A from a height of 52,000 ft (15,850 m), where he was flying at 0.86 IMN and 200 knots (370 km/hr) IAS to a quite remarkable 55,000 ft (16,770 m), at which point his speed had wound down to 0.68 IMN and 140 knots (260 km/hr) IAS. This was almost certainly the greatest altitude ever reached by a Hunter of any type.

To digress on the subject of long-nose derivatives of the F.6, the company was en-couraged by CFE (although this was strictly outside their terms of reference) to make proposals for an improved F.6 with two guns and radar ranging removed, additional ammunition for the two remaining cannon, increased internal fuel, and a braking parachute. Tasked with formulating the proposal, this writer explained to Sir Sydney that moving the whole front fuselage forwards to allow enlarged main tanks just behind the front transport joint would significantly improve the appearance of the aircraft, which was obviously disproportionately short ahead of the wing. This gratuitous advice on Hunter aethetics went down like the proverbial lead balloon. Sir Sydney did not speak to this writer for several days, and the CFE Hunter was quietly forgotten.

The desire to increase the fuel load of the Hunter without using the underwing pylons was a constant factor in the aircraft's development. One F.6 (WG131) was flown with tip tanks in 1956. Designed on the best available advice from RAE Farnborough, these tanks produced an extremely high buffet level at very modest lift coefficients,

The P.1109B with nose enlarged to house the AI.20 radar, and two Firestreaks. Unfortunately, sortie endurance in this configuration was extremely limited (HAL)

Above Wingtip tanks had the attraction that they would leave all four pylons available for armament. They were tested on F.6 XG131, which first flew on 16 August 1956, but proved to be aerodynamic disasters
(HAL)

Left With its finer fuselage the P.1109B outperformed the standard F.6 at altitude. As shown here, two cannon were removed to offset the CG movement caused by the weight of the radar in the nose
(HAL)

and were quickly abandoned.

This TI was so dramatically unsuccessful that even today Kingston is loath to add any foreign object to the tip of a swept wing (eg, for the Sea Harrier or Hawk). In the case of the original P.1127 there was no avoiding having the outrigger fairings project ahead of the tip leading edge, and the result was another aerodynamic catastrophe, although the fault in this case was largely due to the appalling design of the basic wing.

With the prospect of the Lightning entering service in 1960, the role of the Hunter was clearly swinging to ground attack, although it was to remain useful as a day fighter in the Middle and Far East for many years. The demand for external armament locations, increased radius of action (as demonstrated in the basing of F.5s on Cyprus in 1956), and long-range reinforcement capability, all encouraged the development of larger drop tanks.

The HAL-designed 230 Imp gal (1,045 litre) mild steel tanks were flown briefly on F.4 WT798, and then on an F.6 (XF374) for full trials. In the first of a series of overseas proving sorties, on 4 May 1957

this latter aircraft was flown nonstop from Dunsfold to Turin. On June 6th it flew nonstop from Dunsfold to Elba, with the two big tanks and two small ones outboard, a configuration that was to become standard for ferry missions.

On October 2nd Hugh Merewether flew XF374 with these four tanks from Dunsfold to El Adem. The straight-line distance is 1,588 nm (2,943 km), but Merewether was forced to fly a dog-leg course of 1,609 nm (2,980 km). The flight took 3 hr 24 min, and he landed with 450 lb (204 kg) remaining. It had been a fairly marginal exercise (the return flight against the wind proved impossible nonstop), but the Hunter had shown that in emergency it could cover the vital leg from the UK to Cyprus without refuelling.

Some consideration had been given to the idea of flying with four of the big tanks, but such plans were then abandoned. The aircraft was really quite heavy enough in the ferry configuration. By the time the aircraft reached FGA.9 standard, empty weight had grown to 14,530 lb (6,590 kg), giving a clean gross weight of 18,310 lb (8,305 kg), and a

Improved ferry range was a major consideration until the RAF withdrew from the Middle East. This Hunter is shown with four 230 Imp gal (1,045 litre) tanks, a configuration that was tested but never cleared (HAL)

Above Fatigue problems with the RAF's de Havilland D.H.112 Venom (illustrated here by the first production aircraft) led to urgent demands to replace it in the ground attack role in the Middle and Far East
(HSA)

Left This F.6, XK161, was actually completed as Indian Hunter Mk 56 serial BA205, following the cancellation of the last 100 F.6s for the RAF in 1957. This combination of 1,000 lb (454 kg) bombs and RPs was never employed by the RAF
(HAL)

ferry weight of 24,422 lb (11,075 kg) with two big tanks and two small ones. This was quite an increase for an aircraft that began life with a maximum take-off weight of 16,350 lb (7,415 kg).

One of the major events in the UK during 1957 was the publication of a Defence White Paper that marked a watershed in the RAF's attitude to the manned fighter. In essence, Defence Minister Duncan Sandys said that the only sure defence against nuclear strikes was to rely on a nuclear deterrent. The forthcoming Lightning was thus to be the RAF's last manned fighter. The case against the manned fighter was argued very logically, but the document failed to recognize the fact that there will always be smaller conventional wars, hence there will always be a need for a ground attack aircraft.

It may be added that the USAF had earlier fallen into the same trap of planning for only an all-out nuclear war, and in consequence found itself fighting what began as a COIN war in SE Asia with aircraft designed either to drop a nuclear weapon or to intercept a high altitude nuclear bomber. As a result, the USAF had to commission modified US Navy equipment, such as the A-7D attack aircraft and the F-4E air combat fighter.

One immediate effect of the 1957 DWP was a reduction in RAF needs for Hunter F.6s by 100 aircraft. This brought about the closure of the Blackpool factory, and forced HAL to make a major effort to win export sales. For the longer term, the prospects for further work on Hunters for the RAF revived with the decision to replace the fast-fatiguing Venom in the ground attack role in the Middle and Far East. Reports at the time indicated that the Venom had a safe life of around 200 hours in such duties, which amounted to perhaps one year of operations.

Believing that the Venom could be replaced cheaply and effectively either by the lightweight Gnat or by an armed derivative of the Jet Provost basic trainer, the RAF mounted competitive trials in Aden in 1958. The aircraft were flown by AFDS pilots, and the idea was to assess these aircraft under typical service conditions and with various ground attack loads. When HAL proposed that the

It was anticipated by Air Ministry that the most cost-effective replacement for the Venom would be a small aircraft such as the Folland Gnat, seen here as the third of five development aircraft, XK740

An Indian Air Force Hunter Mk 56, probably at Dunsfold, with a maximum RP load of 36 three-inch (76.2 mm) rounds. This was a very high-drag, short-range configuration, and it seems unlikely that it was used
(HAL)

Below The Hunter's win in Switzerland was particularly important in view of the broad spectrum of aircraft competing for the order, and the fact that the selection was made on merit alone. An HSA demonstrator is shown here on a mountain airfield
(HAL)

Hunter should also be considered, the company was told that it would be a waste of time, since an aircraft as expensive as the Hunter could not possibly compete with these cheap, lightweight aircraft in cost-effectiveness. At the company's insistence, two F.6s were nonetheless flown to Aden for evaluation. The aircraft were XK150 and 151, and they were standard RAF Hunters, aside from having braking parachutes, which had proved very useful in the Swiss trials of the previous year.

The results of the Aden trials were easily predictable. The Gnat might have done well as a clear weather point defence fighter if it had been developed some years earlier, but it had no other possible role. Nor did it have the necessary ferry range: the Gnat was broken down and taken to Aden in a Beverley. External loads that the Hunter barely noticed had the Gnat and Jet Provost using the full length of the runway to get in the air, and cruising at piston-engine speeds. It was a no-contest affair, with the Hunter the clear winner. The outcome was the Hunter FGA.9, which had a

fatigue life 10 times that of the Venom, and (unfortunately for HAL) was produced by modifying the F.6.

Export Sixes

The first overseas customer for the F.6 was the Indian Air Force, which in April 1956 sent an evaluation team to Dunsfold to assess both the F.4 and F.6. In July 1957 India signed for 160 Hunters similar to the F.6 (15 were ex-RAF Mk 6s), but fitted with a braking parachute and designated Mk 56 (serials BA201 onwards). The first aircraft, BA201 had its first flight on 11 October 1957. Deliveries began on October 25th, when the first two aircraft were flown out. This quick response was a direct result of the RAF cancellation, and of the fact that the Mk 56 differed from the F.6 only in camouflage and national markings. The Indian Hunter initially served with Nos 5 and 17 Sqn at Poona and Nos 7, 20, and 27 Sqn at Ambala. Later reports refer to Hunters with Nos 14 and 37 Sqn, and performing target-towing duties with Nos 3 and 31 Sqn. In 1982 there were references to six blue and white

In the early 1970s Switzerland again bought Hunters, but in this case they were refurbished Aircraft that were fitted out by the Federal Aircraft Factory to the latest Swiss Air Force modification standard (F + W, Emmen)

Above Every Hunter-driver's favourite: a Mk 58A, throttled back and airbrake out, desperately trying to hold station with a flat-out Harrier GR.1. The Swiss aircraft was actually escorting the GR.1 demonstrator and its HS.125 support aircraft

Left The 80 mm Hispano SURA rocket is used on Swiss Hunters, and was recommended by HAL to export customers in preference to the RAF's 68 mm SNEB, although it clearly represented a higher drag penalty (BAe)

Hunters forming a *Thunderbolts'* aerobatic team.

Some 53 FGA.56As were subsequently delivered in 1966–70 as attrition replacements, and corresponded to FGA.9 standard. India was the first country to order the Two-Seater with 200-series Avon, some 12 T.66s being ordered in 1957 and 10 more in 1960 (serials BS361-376 and BS485-490). Like the single-seater, the trainer had the braking parachute. Further orders consisted on 12 T.66Ds, which were delivered in 1966–67 with a later standard of VHF radio and provisions for the large tanks, and five T.66Es, which differed in having IFF Mk 10 and Bendix DFA-73 radio compass. This final variant was delivered in 1973. The Indian trainers are believed to have been mainly used by the OCU at Kalaikunda.

The second overseas buyer for the F.6 was Switzerland. Although the order was smaller than that for India, the Swiss contract was of crucial importance in establishing the Hunter's outstanding capability as a multi-role combat aircraft. Switzerland has always been an influential customer, since it is a major incorruptible buyer

that takes equipment selection very seriously. It was also significant in the sense that its neutral position threw the contest open to both East and West. The Hunter was thus evaluated not only against the Canadair Sabre F.4 and Mystère IVA, but also the Czech-built MiG-15, the Swedish J-29 and Switzerland's own P-16.

The Swiss evaluation of 1957, involving Hunter F.6s XE587 and 588, was incredibly thorough, including measurements of radius of turn (using kinetheodolites) and weapon delivery accuracy. On this occasion the HAL sales team was led by George Anderson, the PR manager. The selection of the Hunter was one of the most important milestones in the programme, undoubtedly influencing several other customers.

The immediate outcome was the signing of a contract in January 1958 for 100 Hunter Mk 58s (serials J-4001 to -4100). The first 12 were ex-RAF Mk 6s, but the remainder were new-build aircraft. First delivery took place in April 1958. The Hunter served with Nos 1, 4, 5, 7, 8, 11, 18, 19, and 21 Sqn. In 1970 five Hunters from No 11 Sqn formed the

One of the original batch of new-build Mk 58s. These were some of the best equipped Hunters produced at Kingston, with braking parachutes, Saab BT-9 bombing computers, and Sidewinder provisions (Swiss Air Force)

Above The Swiss have carried out tests to assess the feasibility of operating Hunters from various types of roadway. This aircraft appears to be using an unusually large flap setting for a clean take-off
(Swiss Air Force)

Left Fighters of three nationalities, serving with the Swiss Air Force. In the foreground a Hunter Mk 58A (J-4141), which appears to be carrying drop tanks inboard and bombs on the outer pylon. Beyond, a Mirage IIIS and an F-5E Tiger II
(Swiss Air Force)

Right Swiss defence planning includes the use of heavily defended mountain airstrips with aircraft housed in caverns blasted out of the rock. To economize on floor space, some aircraft are hung from gantries
(Swiss Air Force)

Left The power cables on the right and the surrounding mountains illustrate the hazards associated with off-airfield operation. Note the distinctive mountings for the 80 mm Hispano SURA rockets under the outer wings
(Swiss Air Force)

The *Patrouille de Suisse* aerobatic team was formed on the Hunters of No 11 Sqn in 1970, and became one of Europe's best known display items. Here two Mk 58s are shown flying a 'mirror-image' formation with undercarriage down
(Norman Pealing)

Patrouille de Suisse aerobatic team.

The Mk 58 corresponded closely to the F.6, but had Swiss UHF radios and STR.9X VHF. It also had Wilcox 914X-1 radio compass and a braking parachute, the latter to facilitate operations from small mountain airfields. At a later stage they were fitted in Switzerland with the Saab BT-9 bombing computer and provisions for Sidewinder on the outboard pylons.

There was a certain irony in this last modification, as in 1960 this writer was in the US trying with only limited success to obtain installation information for the AIM-9, while the Dutch, Swedes and Swiss had already modified their aircraft to take it. The other irony about the Sidewinder situation was that RAF Hunter squadrons were screaming for it, while MoD took the view (from 1960 onwards) that there was no point in modifying the Hunter, since the aircraft had only two years left with the RAF! It was to be more than 10 years before this became reality. In December 1971 the FGA.9 was finally withdrawn from the last operational unit, No 8 Sqn, although

it remained in use with the shadow squadrons of the TWUs.

Returning to the subject of Swiss Hunters, in the early 1970s some 52 refurbished aircraft were ordered under the designation Mk 58A (serials J-4101 to -4152), the main difference being the use of the Avon 207 in place of the 203. These aircraft were fitted out at the Federal Aircraft Factory at Emmen. Switzerland also had eight T.68s with Avon 207s and the same operational equipment as the single-seaters. Of this batch (serials J-4201 to -4208), four had flown originally as F.4s and the others as Swedish Mk 50s.

In 1982 Switzerland embarked on a 'Hunter-80' programme to update the type's operational equipment and armament. Modifications included the addition of a radar-warning receiver, flare/chaff dispensers, and provisions for the Hughes Maverick air-surface guided missile.

Chapter 10
Yet More Variants

The outcome of the 1958 trials in Aden to choose a Venom replacement for the RAF was the ordering late that year of the first 30 of a series of 102 conversions of the F.6 to a new fighter/ground attack standard, the Hunter FGA.9, with the first to be delivered before the end of 1959. This variant was to have provisions for the inboard carriage of the large tanks, a braking parachute of 13.5 ft (4.1 m) diameter, extra mass flow for the air conditioning system to deal with higher temperatures, local fatigue modifications in the fuselage, the addition of a bobweight in the longitudinal control system, some 200 lb (91 kg) of ballast in the front fuselage, and a third 750-litre oxygen bottle to give an endurance of $3\frac{1}{2}$ hours. Blast deflectors were deleted on the basis that they were not required at low level. In regard to the avionics suite, DME as retained and Marconi AD.722 radio compass was added (hence the 'towel-rail' aerial under the fuselage), while TACAN and Green Salad were deleted. The FGA.9 was seen by the RAF as a rocket-launching aircraft, although all four pylons could in principle carry practice bombs or napalm.

The first Hunter FGA.9 conversion (XG135) made its first flight on 3 July 1959, and in January 1960 deliveries began to No 8 Sqn at Khormaksar (Aden). In all, the FGA.9 served with seven operational squadrons, Nos 208 and 43 joining No 8 Sqn in Aden, No 20 Sqn based at Tengah (Singapore), and No 28 at Kai Tak (Hong Kong). At home, Nos 1 and 54 Sqn served as the fighter-bomber element of 38 Gp of Support Command, tasked with reinforcing NATO's flanks and existing RAF units in other areas. The FGA.9 was the longest-serving RAF Hunter, the last unit (No 8 Sqn) finally relinquishing its aircraft at the end of 1971. However, from 1972 to 1976 the FGA.9 served with Nos 45 and 58 Sqn for tactical training duties.

The FGA.9 was only marginally heavier than the F.6, the later variant having a basic weight of 14,530 lb (6,590 kg), a clean gross of 18,310 lb (8,305 kg) and a maximum take-off weight of 24,422 lb (11,075 kg) in the ferry configuration. The performance was virtually unchanged from that of the F.6, aside from the effects of the big tanks. In clean configuration the FGA.9 reached Mach 0.92 at sea level, and could still grind along at Mach 0.88 with all four tanks. However, for much of their lives RAF FGA.9s carried six RP rails (which allowed the outboard pylons to be fitted) and used the large inboard tanks as virtually a permanent fit,

Overleaf Hunter FGA.9s of No 1 Sqn, photographed over Norway, the role of this unit being to reinforce NATO's northern and southern flanks. Both XE584/W and XE624/B were built as F.6s in 1956 and converted to FGA.9s in 1960
(HSA)

This FGA.9 of No 54 Sqn, XF523/N, was almost the last F.6 built in the UK, and was written off in a crash on 24 June 1963. Note the steep fall of its 'drainpipes', which appear to have 60 lb (27 kg) warheads
(MoD)

hence their cruise speed was a much more modest figure. Typical figures used by 38 Gp were 0.89 Mach at altitude and 420 knots (778 km/hr) at sea level. The manufacturer's brochure refers to a less common configuration, with two big tanks and eight 3-inch (76 mm) rockets with 60 lb (27 kg) warheads. In this condition the FGA.9 had a maximum speed at sea level of 575 knots (1,065 km/hr) or Mach 0.87. The RAF was initially interested in the Hispano rocket as a replacement for the WW2 'drainpipe', but dropped this idea in 1962 due to a reported 122°F (50°C) limit on the propellant, and adopted the 68 mm SNEB instead.

In the air defence role, the clean aircraft had an initial climb rate of 16,500 ft/min (83.8 m/sec), reducing to 13,200 ft/min (67 m/sec) with two small tanks. In the high altitude patrol-intercept sortie, these small tanks increased endurance (with 10-minute combat allowance) from 60 to 93 minutes, and the two big tanks gave 150 minutes.

The brochure for the FGA.9 supports the view that it made a good long-range strafing aircraft, and could deliver rockets (though not bombs) at a

useful radius. The point was that the Hunter needed the big (inboard) tanks to go anywhere, but the RAF aircraft was never cleared to release bombs from the outboard pylons. Some foreign operators (including the Swiss) dropped bombs from the outers, though (since the pylon was aft of the CG) it is believed that the clearance was limited to a narrow speed band.

Equipped with all four tanks, the FGA.9 had a brochure HI-LO-HI strafing radius of 545 nm (1,000 km). With two 1,000 lb (454 kg) bombs inboard and the small tanks outboard, which was not a configuration used by the RAF, brochure radius dropped to a modest 215 nm (400 km). With two large tanks and eight 3-inch (76 mm) rockets with 60 lb (27 kg) heads, the radius went up to a more useful 385 nm (715 km). The actual radius quoted by 38 Gp for the aircraft with two large tanks and 16 'drainpipes' was 164 nm (305 km) LO-LO, and 286 nm (530 km) in a HI-LO-HI.

Ferry range with the four tanks was 1,445 nm (2,680 km) according to the brochure, though 38 Gp normally operated to a maximum of 1,250 nm

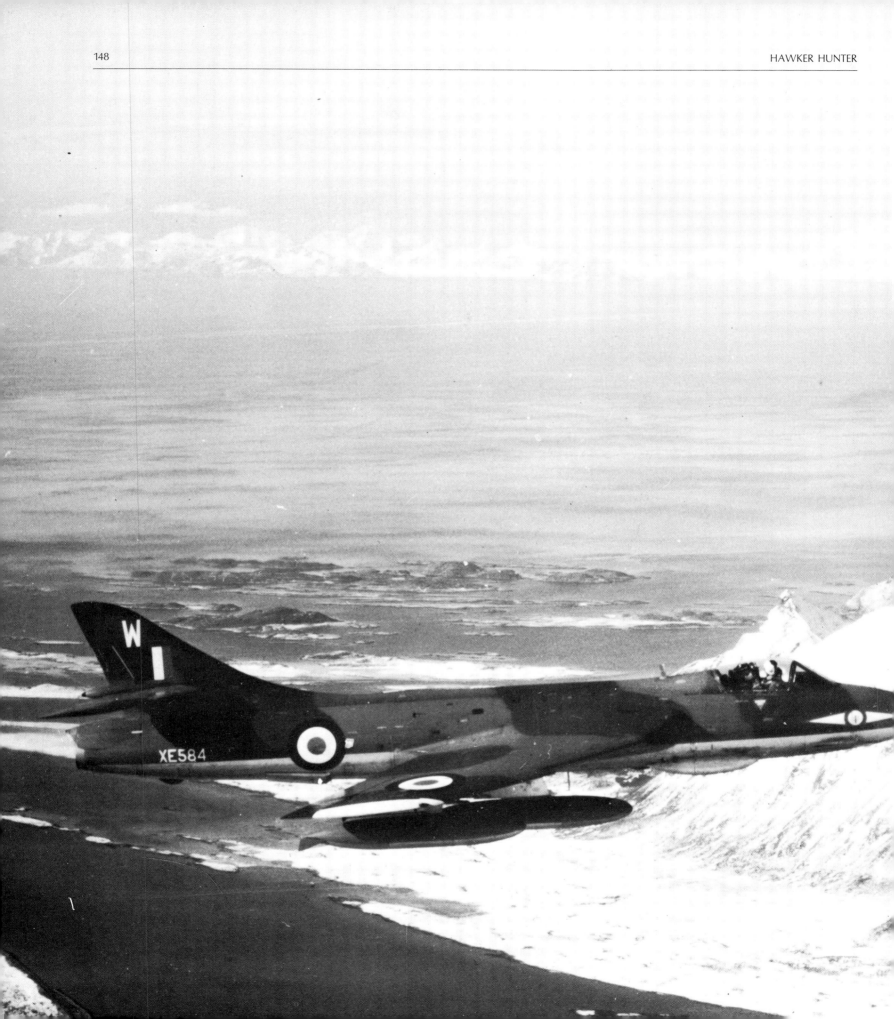

(2,315 km), or 1,400 nm (2,595 km) in the event of a tailwind and suitable alternates.

Aside from the fuel-sloshing problem with the big tanks, the FGA.9 was a comparatively trouble-free development. However, in 1960 there were several incidents that initially appeared to be due to tailplane runaways. As far as this writer can establish, the real cause was slipping of the clutch in the tailplane actuator in high Mach dives, this clutch having been introduced to prevent overloading of the electric motor.

Fighter-Reconnaissance

The Hunter FR.10 was a tactical reconnaissance aircraft based on the FGA.9. It used the latter's ferry configuration to achieve a LO-LO radius of 240 nm (445 km) and a HI-LO-HI of 570 nm (1,055 km). Radar ranging was deleted to make space for three cameras in the nose. The FR.10 retained the braking parachute and most of the equipment of the FGA.9, though DME was deleted, as were provisions for rocket armament. A Wirek voice recorder was added for visual reconnaissance. Armour plate was added under the cockpit floor as ballast to offset the removal of radar ranging.

Developed to specification FR.164D, the Hunter FR.10 was a converted F.6. The first conversion (XF429) had its maiden flight on 7 November 1958, and a total of 43 F.6s were modified to this standard. The FR.10 served with Nos 2 and 4 Sqn in Germany, replacing the Swift FR.5, though detachments were sent briefly to No 8 Sqn at Khormaksar and to No 79 Sqn of No 2 TWU. The two units in Germany kept the FR.10 in service from early 1961 to 1971/72, No 2 Sqn becoming a Jaguar unit with special responsibilities for tactica reconnaissance, and No 4 Sqn a Harrier unit. In mid-1962 the RAF formally requested from HSA information on the use of Sidewinder on the FGA.9 and FR.10, but nothing came of it.

Naval Single-Seaters

In the early 1960s the Royal Navy established a need for some low-cost tactical training aircraft

Pairs of FGA.9s conducting 30 mm strafing attacks on vehicles positioned on a firing range. Although typical of 1960s tactics, these Hunters appear to be dangerously high by modern standards

that would smooth the transition from the Gnat advanced trainer to operational aircraft such as the Buccaneer and Phantom, and would carry appropriate equipment such as TACAN. It was therefore decided to convert a total of 40 ex-RAF Hunter F.4s. Of these, 24 were pre-Mod 228 standard, and thus had provisions for only two pylons, while the remaining 16 could carry 4 pylons and had provisions for RP rails.

All 40 aircraft were given facilities to fire pods of 2-inch (50 mm) naval rockets. Cannon armament, radar ranging, DME and Green Salad were deleted, as were provisions to drop any kind of bomb aside from practice bombs. The VHF radio was changed to TR.1936B. All 40 aircraft were fitted with TACAN and a hook for arrested (airfield) landings. Most of these aircraft were designated GA.11 and used for surface attack training and radar calibration, with a Harley Light in the nose to facilitate visual acquisition. The remainder of these F.4 conversions were equipped by Shorts with camera noses and were designated PR.11s.

The first GA.11 conversion (XE712) flew in April 1962. This variant appears to have been used by various training units, including Nos 738, 739, and 764 Sqn, before being allocated to FRADU (Fleet Requirements and Air Direction Unit) at RNAS Yeovilton, where they have been operated by Airwork Services and later by Flight Refuelling. Press reports indicate that some of these Hunters will be equipped with additional pylons to take MEWSG (Maritime Electronics Warfare Support Group) electronics countermeasures pods so that they can participate in EW exercises. It also appears that four Hunters are flown by the Royal Naval Reserve Air Branch at Yeovilton.

Two-Seaters

In the early post-war years it was the custom in the UK to develop a fighter as quickly as possible, and to produce a two-seat training version almost as an afterthought. In the case of the Hunter, the general idea seems to have been that RAF student pilots could convert perfectly easily from the Meteor T.7 or Vampire T.11 to the Hunter fighter,

A Hunter FR.10 of No 54 Sqn, probably photographed at Gütersloh, XF428/C was later bought back by the manufacturer and refurbished to be sold as a Mk 74B (serial 525). It was delivered to Singapore in 1977 (A. le Nobel)

despite the fact that the Hunter possessed a completely different order of acceleration and high-subsonic performance.

Project studies of a two-seat derivative began only two years after the Hunter's first flight, at which stage there was no clear guidance from the RAF as to whether tandem or side-by-side seating was preferred. Tandem seating is now generally agreed to be better for advanced flying training for the fast jets, since the student's cockpit layout and field of view on both sides (which is important in formation flying) are virtually the same as in a single-seater. On the other hand, side-by-side seating may be preferable for tactical training, since the instructor can use as much depression angle in weapon aiming as the student, which is especially useful in teaching the delivery of retarded weapons. It seems that both Sir Sydney and Neville Duke would have preferred tandem seating, although this would have required an increase in the Hunter's vertical tail, which is arguably somewhat small, even for the single-seater.

The first three-view drawing of a two-seat Hunter (the P.1101) was done in the project office by 'Ron' Williams, working under the guidance of Vivian Stanbury. It appears to have been Stanbury who decided on side-by-side seating (which facilitated balance) and Stanbury's car that was measured as a guide to cockpit width! However, after the P.1101 was begun, other drawings were made in the DO on the basis of tandem seating.

In designing the P.1101, the company accepted what turned out to be an excessively difficult criterion, viz, that the new aircraft would be identical with the single-seater aft of the front transport joint. Interpreting this literally, it was necessary to taper a wide, deep cockpit enclosure down to a small spine fairing (which housed only the control rods to the tail) in an extremely short distance. The result was predictable: virtually as soon as Duke had made the first flight in XJ615 on 8 July 1955, it was found that there were shock-induced flow separations over the rear of the hood above Mach 0.84, causing a totally unacceptable buffet level.

Left Pictured during exercise 'Royal Flush 1970', a Hunter FR.10 (XF438/E) of No 4 Sqn RAF is shown with (top to bottom) an RF-104G of No 306 Sqn RNethAF, a Belgian RF-84F of No 42 Sqn, an RF-4C of 38TRS USAF, a German F-104G of AKG.52, and a CF-104G of No 439 Sqn CAF

With guns and associated excrescences deleted, this RN GA.11 (WV380) presents a much cleaner appearance than contemporary RAF Hunters. Built as an F.4 in July 1955, it was converted to a GA.11 in 1962 and sold to Switzerland as a Mk 58A (J-4119) in 1972 (HSA)

Various modifications were tried in vain attempts to cure the problem without changing the aircraft aft of the transport joint. In the end it was clear that the task was impossible, and that it had been a foolish objective from the outset, since all that was at stake was a change in the shape of an unstressed fairing. The buffeting was eliminated in early 1956 by means of a large, Area-Ruled canopy fairing designed by 'Cliff' Bore, who went on to become head of research at Kingston.

The Area-Ruled hood fairing was one of those cases where the use of technology provided precisely the desired result. In consequence, although the Two-Seater has more profile drag at low speed than the single-seater, the former aircraft's drag rise is delayed, hence at high subsonic Mach Number the drag of the Two-Seater is less than the original. In the case of Hunters with 100-series Avons, maximum level speed is not high enough for this delayed drag increase to be of any practical value, hence the F.4 and T.7 speeds are virtually identical. However, the 200-series Avon takes the Hunter beyond the crossover-point on the drag curve, hence the T.66 is marginally faster than an F.6 in level flight.

The first prototype had two guns and a 100-series Avon, one gun subsequently being eliminated and the recoil of the remaining cannon rendered harmless in pitch and yaw terms by means of an angled blast deflector. The second prototype (XJ627) first flew on 17 November 1956 and had the 200-series Avon of the F.6 and FGA.9. It was obvious that the big-engined Two-Seater was the aircraft best suited to train pilots for the single-seater, but the RAF nonetheless adopted the 100-series Avon for its lower cost. The resulting T.7 was ordered into production, the first (XL563) of 45 new-build aircraft being flown on 11 October 1957 by 'Frank' Bullen. Deliveries began in the following year. This initial order was supplemented by some F.4 conversions, giving a total of 73 aircraft for the RAF. The majority of T.7s were allocated to No 229 OCU and later the TWUs. Some were operated by the Fleet Air Arm, one RN T.7 being fitted with an arrester hook, and most RAF Hunter units had one or more T.7s.

Seen here with something approaching the final hood fairing shape, XJ615 is still unpainted, having only a coat of pale green primer. The wings and vertical tail may well have been salvaged from an RAF Mk 4 (HAL)

Right The prototype P.1101 (XJ615) under construction, illustrating the very rapid change in cross-section of hood fairing needed to attain the original aim of retaining a standard aircraft aft of the front transport joint
(BAe)

Below The first Two-Seater taking off at an early stage of the development programme, evidently fitted with one of the many hood variations flown in efforts to cure the noise and buffeting produced by shock-induced flow separations
(BAe)

Top In order that hood and fairing variations could be tested quickly, the first aircraft was flown with a metal canopy, despite the restrictions that this imposed on lateral and upward vision (BAe)

Above left Although a production T.7, XL574 (which flew on 18 April 1958) was used by Boscombe Down for CA release trials, then returned to HAL for windscreen rain dispersal, de-icing and tropical trials. It was finally used for fatigue tests

Left As mentioned above, Hunter T.7 XL574 was employed for various trials, and was finally tested to destruction in the fatigue rig at Kingston. It is seen here alongside a single-seater (BAe)

The T.7 was, in effect, a two-seat version of the post-Mod 228 Mk 4, with an Avon Mk 122. It added ARC-52 or PTR.175 UHF radio, Marconi AD.722 radio compass, TACAN, provisions for rocket pods, and a braking parachute. Basic weight was increased to 13,500 lb (6,122 kg). The T.7A was a trials vehicle for OR.946 servo-operated instruments, which came in around the time of the Buccaneer. The gun, radio compass, and all provisions for bombs and rockets were removed from this variant. Four were converted from the standard T.7.

The company was greatly disappointed that the T.7 was not accepted by the RAF as a replacement for the Vampire T.11, the Folland Gnat Trainer being taken in its place. Although the Gnat was far less expensive, and looked good in the hands of the Red Arrows on account of its small size, it was regarded at Kingston as a heap of rubbish that was not representative of any operational aircraft flown by the RAF, 'a good trainer only for the Gnat fighter'. The fact that the RAF had Hunter T.7s at Valley (to train pilots who could not fit inside the Gnat) was some indication of what a Mickey Mouse aeroplane the Folland product was. The Gnat was also totally unsuited to weapons instruction, so the TWUs had to be equipped with Hunter T.7s. The choice of the Gnat T.1 as a Vampire replacement was undoubtedly one of the worst decisions ever made by the RAF.

The Hunter Two-Seater was one of the great training aircraft of its generation, especially in the T.66 form pioneered by India. Equipped with the big engine and two guns, this aircraft also had a useful operational capability. Whereas XJ615 topped out at around 49,000 ft (14,940 m), Bedford took XJ627 to 52,000 ft (16,000 m) in the course of demonstrations in Switzerland in early 1957. Although vastly inferior to the T.66, the RAF's T.7 became quite a popular aeroplane. When the plan was announced to phase out the T.7 in favour of the Hawk, which flies its weapon training sorties 50 knots (93 km/hr) slower, car-stickers appeared saying 'FORGET THE HAWK – FLY HUNTER!'.

To revert to the story of T.7 development, as part of a major effort to have the aircraft accepted

Equipped with the Area-Ruled hood fairing designed by 'Cliff' Bore, the Two-Seater became far better aerodynamically and aesthetically. This production aircraft, XL571, was first flown on 29 March 1958 by Hugh Merewether (HAL)

A visitor from No 4 FTS at Valley, Hunter T.7 XL600 basks in a spell of sunshine during an air show at RNAS Yeovilton in 1976
(Roy Braybrook)

for the advanced flying training role, HAL had tried to get a clearance for spinning training, which could be done on the Vampire (though it had a very nasty spin). The T.7 was eventually cleared for intentional spinning, but the clearance was revoked after only 10 days, when a pilot was killed at Chivenor. The aircraft had entered an inverted spin from an erect spin, and the control actions for recovery had been mistimed. One pilot bailed out and was killed, but the aircraft recovered once it had lost the canopy, and the other pilot survived.

Following a trials programme involving approximately 1,200 spins, improved corrective actions were developed and it was found that Hunter spins presented no problem if the appropriate action was taken within the first two turns. The Hunter is spin-resistant, and it is probably true to say that no-one has ever been killed in an accidental spin in this aircraft, because it is very easy to stop the motion before the spin is fully established.

'Bill' Bedford played a major role in the spinning programme, and at Farnborough in 1959 and '60

demonstrated spins of up to 12 turns. However, the Hunter has never been cleared for intentional inverted spinning, and it was never spun solo by students at ETPS.

The original RAF order was to have been for 65 T.7s, but this number was reduced to provide trainers for Holland and allow 10 two-seaters, designated T.8, to be delivered quickly to the Fleet Air Arm. However, before any of these new-build aircraft flew, a naval prototype (WW664) was produced by converting an F.4, which in this form had its maiden flight on 3 March 1958. The first new-build T.8 (XL580) had its first flight on May 30th that year.

A total of 41 T.8s, T.8Bs and T.8Cs were built. The T.8 differed from the T.7 in having no radio compass or DME, though it was equipped with a hook for arrested (airfield) landings. The T.8C was also an RN aircraft, but appears to have had no VHF radio or radar ranging, though TACAN was introduced. The T.8B is listed as an RAF aircraft, similar to the T.8C, but with the OR.946 instruments of the T.7A. At a much later stage two

Left Instead of adopting the Hunter Two-Seater to replace the Vampire T.11, the RAF economized by purchasing the Folland Gnat T.2, an aircraft that was not representative of any RAF operational type, could not accommodate the full range of pilots, and could not be used for weapons training
(Central Press)

Right The cockpit of the T.7. The great advantage of the Hunter Two-Seater over most trainers was that the instructor had exactly the same field of view as the student for weapons instruction
(BAe)

T.8s (XL580 and 602) were converted to T.8Ms to assist in the development of the Ferranti Blue Fox radar for the Sea Harrier, and subsequently with pilot training in the use of the Sea Harrier's operational equipment. A third T.8M (XL603) was subsequently produced for use in pilot training.

Export two-seat Hunters based on the 100-series Avon (Mk 122) were the Mk 53 for Denmark (two of), the Mk 62 for Peru (one of), the Mk 75 for Singapore (four of), the Mk 77 for Abu Dhabi (two of), and the Mk 79 for Qatar (one of).

Within the company there was a great deal of enthusiasm for the Hunter Two-Seater with the 200-series Avon, but the only UK order for such an aircraft was the Mk 12, a converted single-seater with some of the operational equipment planned for the TSR.2. One Mk 12 (XE531, which had previously been an F.6 and an FGA.9) was delivered to RAE Farnborough in 1963 to assist in TSR.2 systems development, but cancellation of that programme two years later eliminated the need for further Mk 12s to act as crew trainers. The Mk 12 was used by RAE for a wide variety of tests,

including (in 1973) a three-axis quadruplex electrically signalled flight controls system. It was equipped with the Avon Mk 207 and was unarmed, but it had head-up displays (HUDs), and a vertical camera that produce a slight bulge in the upper lines of the nose. In a distinctive green and white paint scheme, it became one of the best-known of UK Hunters.

Even better known than XE531 was G-APUX, the company's Two-Seater demonstrator, which for much of its life was painted red and white, and was one of the few aircraft on the UK civil register (perhaps the only one) to be fitted with two 30 mm Aden cannon. The front fuselage had been new-built for display at Paris in 1959, but the remainder of the airframe was a mixture of components from two crashed Belgian F.6s (IF-19 and -67). Designated Hunter Mk 66A, G-APUX made its first flight on 12 August 1959, with 'Bill' Bedford at the controls. It was equipped with an Avon Mk 207, TR.1036 and/or STR.92/100 VHF radio, Bendix ARN.6 radio compass, and DME. It had an enlarged braking parachute, and full armament provisions

Left Built originally as an F.6 (serial N-204) by Fokker-Aviolanda in the late 1950s, this aircraft was bought back by HAL, becoming G-9-82 before being delivered to India as a T.66D (serial S-572) (HAL via Mike Stroud)

Below Built as an F.4, WW664 was converted into a Two-Seater and became a prototype for the Royal Navy T.8. It is seen here with four 100 Imp gal (454 litre) tanks, arrester hook and a single cannon (HAL)

Top Probably the best-looking Hunter ever built, XL580 was the first production T.8 for the Royal Navy. It first flew on 30 May 1958 with David Lockspeiser at the controls, and was mainly used as an 'Admiral's Barge' by the Flag Officer (Flying Training) at RNAS Yeovilton
(HAL)

Above left Three Hunter T.7s of the Royal Netherlands Air Force, pictured alongside a Fokker S-14 Mach-Trainer, a Derwent-powered basic jet trainer. The T.7s were all built by HAL at Kingston

Left Second of a batch of 20 Hunter T.7s constructed for Holland, this aircraft was first flown by Duncan Simpson on 30 May 1958 and was delivered to Twente on July 18th that year

was deleted.

The Mk 66A was intended primarily for demonstration purposes, but it was also employed for a number of flight trials, including those for a nosewheel braking system and the big tanks stretched to give a capacity of 350 Imp gal (1,590 litres). The aircraft was loaned to various Middle East air forces in the mid-1960s, and eventually sold to Chile in 1967 as a Mk 72.

Export Two-Seaters

As explained earlier, few export Two-Seaters had the 100-series Avon of the T.7. The basis for most overseas Hunter trainer sales was the Indian T.66, which was derived from XJ627. Some 22 T.66s were built, equipped with the Avon 203 and two guns. This model had the TR.1936 VHF radio and Green Salad, plus DME. Like the T.7, it was equipped with a braking parachute and full armament provisions, except for rocket pods. Further Indian orders covered 12 T.66Ds with TR.1987A VHF radio and big tanks, though no IFF, and five T.66Es, which were like the Ds but had Mk 10 IFF, and Bendix

DFA.73 radio compass in place of DME.

Four T.66Bs were sold to Jordan, a mixture of new-build and converted aircraft. They were similar to the Indian aircraft, but had provisions for the big tanks, PTR.175 UHF and VHF radio, and Marconi AD.722 radio compass in place of DME. Three conversions for the Lebanon were designated T.66Cs. Again, they were like the Indian aircraft, but had the same VHF as the T.7, provisions for the big tanks and Hispano rockets, though IFF was deleted.

The remaining export Two-Seaters had the Avon 207 and two guns, and (with the exception of the Swiss aircraft) provisions for big tanks. The T.67 for Kuwait (five of) had ARC-52 UHF and Marconi AD.722 radio compass. The T.68 for Switzerland (eight of) had ER.76A and RG7-70 UHF and STR.9XM VHF, Wilcox 914X-1 IFF, the Saab BT.9 bombing computer and Sidewinder provisions. The T.69 for Iraq (five of) had Marconi AD.722 and Hispano rocket provisions. The T.72 for Chile (five of) had provisions for Hispano rockets and Bendix avionics, including RTA.41B

Hunter T.8 XL580 later became the first T.8M, used initially for Blue Fox radar development and then to assist in training Sea Harrier pilots. Both the T.8M and the Sea Harrier are shown here with SN231 air combat telemetry pods on their outboard pylons (BAe via Brian Isles)

Top Peru had only one Two-Seater, an F.4 (WT706, the sixth production aircraft, which first flew on 13 December 1954) and was converted by HAL to a Mk 62, serial 681. In this form it was flown by 'Don' Lucey on 15 September 1959 and was delivered to Peru in February 1960. The ventral blister is associated with the Bendix ADF
(HSA)

Above left The Two-Seater demonstrator, G-APUX, in which many Hawker guests (and this writer) had their first experience of supersonic flight
(HAL)

Left Built with components from several different Hunters, G-APUX was the only twin-cannon aircraft on the British civil register
(BAe)

VHF radio, DFA.73 radio compass, and VOR/ILS. The T.75A for Singapore (five of) had PTR.175 VHF/UHF, Mk 10 IFF, and provisions for Hispano rockets and target-towing. Finally, the T.81 for Kenya (two of) had Bendix RTA.42A VHF radio, Marconi AD.370B radio compass, Bendix VOR/ILS, and RCA DME.

Further Exports

This discussion has already dealt with variants of the F.4 and F.6 that were sold abroad, and with licence-manufacture in Belgium and the Netherlands. Beyond this phase, there was a much later wave of exports based on the FGA.9, and produced mainly by converting F.6s. The following provides an outline of this second wave, on a country-by-country basis.

Abu Dhabi

In 1969 orders were placed for seven FGA.76s, three FR. 76As and two T.77s, the single-seaters being converted from ex-RAF F.4s and F.6s, and the Two-Seaters from ex-Netherlands T.7s. The single-seaters had Avon 207s and provisions for big tanks and Hispano rockets, while the trainers had the Avon 122. All these Hunters had target-towing provisions and braking parachutes, PTR.170 and 175 UHF and VHF, Marconi AD.370B radio compass, and Collins VOR/ILS. The Hunter squadron was based at Sharjah, but in 1975 the aircraft were loaned to Jordan to replace Hunters destroyed by the Israelis in the Yom Kippur War of 1973, their place in Abu Dhabi being taken by Mirages.

Chile

Based on contracts signed in 1966 and '69, Chile acquired a force of 28 FGA.71s, six FR.71As and five T.72s. All were conversions, using the Avon 207. All had provisions for big tanks and Hispano rockets. The FGA.71s were fitted for smoke-making, since an aerobatic team was planned, and the FR.71As had provisions for target-towing. All had Bendix RTA-41B VHF radio, and the same company's DFA.73 radio compass and VOR/ILS.

A Dutch T.7 landing illustrates the generous dimensions of the split flaps and the housing for the braking parachute (HAL)

They formed two squadrons based at Antofagasta, but availability rate is believed to have suffered as a result of the UK arms embargo declared in 1974.

A number of details have emerged concerning the supply of Hunters to Chile by the British Government during and after the Falklands conflict. It has been alleged (rightly or wrongly) that these 12 Hunters, together with three Canberras, were part-payment for the use of Chilean bases by RAF reconnaissance Canberras and helicopter-borne SAS teams against Argentine facilities. Some of the allegations made against HMG in this context were ill-founded. For example, it is not true that the arms embargo was still in force in early 1982. Nor is it true that these were the first ex-RAF Hunters to be exported without passing through the manufacturer's hands. On the other hand, it was quite clear at the time that Britain would use any measure short of nuclear weapons to ensure victory, and that it was essential to have access to bases in South America, in case one of the RN carriers was lost.

It may be recalled that the Falklands conflict began with the landing of the first Argentine unit near Port Stanley in the early hours of 2 April 1982, and that the Argentine surrender came on June 14th. Britain's carrier battle group sailed for the South Atlantic on April 5th. On April 6th eight Hunters were transferred from No 1 Tactical Weapons Unit at Brawdy to Abingdon, where they were checked over and crated. On the 18th the first four were taken by road to Brize Norton. On the 24th these aircraft (XE546, XE582, XF442, and XJ686) were loaded on Flying Tiger 747 N806FT and departed for Chile via San Juan, duly acquiring the FAC serials 739, 740, 742 and 743 respectively.

The second batch of four consisted of XF376, XJ688, XK137 and XK138, which were moved by road to Brize Norton on May 9th, and departed in Flying Tiger 747 N810FT on the 22nd being redesignated by FAC 741, 744, 745 and 746 respectively. It is understood that in November of 1982 four further Hunters were delivered to Chile, XF445 becoming 747, XG291 becoming 748, XJ687 becoming 749, and XK141 becoming 750.

India
As discussed earlier, India ordered 160 Mk 56s based on the F.6, 53 FGA.56As based on the FGA.9, and some 22 T.66s, 12 T.66Ds, and five T.66Es.

Iraq
Following the Arab-Israeli War of 1956 several 'front-line' air forces in the Middle East made efforts to modernize their equipment. As part of this programme, Iraq purchased 15 ex-RAF Hunter F.6s on a government-to-government basis, reportedly using funds provided by the US. Iraq was evidently so pleased with these F.6s that a series of orders were placed with HAL for conversions based on the FGA.9. These contracts eventually totalled 24 FGA.59s, 18 FGA.59As, four FR.59Bs and five T.69s. All four models had the Avon 207 and Marconi AD.722, and provisions for Hispano rockets and the big tanks. The FGA.59 appears to have been delivered without IFF, whereas the 59A had IFF Mk 10, but DME was deleted, as were provisions for target towing.

Jordan
A further instance of a country receiving ex-RAF Hunters from the UK Government, then buying improved variants from HAL, was Jordan, which initially had 12 F.6s and eight FGA.9s, in addition to four T.66Bs purchased from HAL. Jordan lost all but two of these aircraft in the Six-Day War of 1967, but was given three single-seaters by Saudi, and ordered two FGA.73s, seven FGA.73As, and 12 FGA.73Bs. All were equipped with PTR.175 UHF and VHF, and Marconi AD.722, and had provisions for Hispano rockets and the big tanks. They appear to have differed only in minor respects, the 73A having DME, and the 73B lacking provisions for rocket pods. In 1975 some additional aircraft were received from Abu Dhabi, but later that year most of the remaining Jordanian Hunters were passed to Oman. It seems likely that the Abu Dhabi Hunters were simply returned there and placed in storage.

Kenya
In 1974 Kenya purchased four FGA.80s and two T.81s from Millbank Technical Services (ie, the Crown Agents). They were equipped with Bendix RTA.42A VHF radio, Marconi AD.370B radio compass, Bendix VOR/ILS, and RCA DME. The single-seaters were equipped for target towing. These aircraft were replaced by F-5Es and disposed of to Zimbabwe.

Kuwait
A small number of Hunters were operated by Kuwait between the mid-1960s and mid-1970s as a deterrent to Iraqi aggression, pending the availability of A-4KU Skyhawks, which had better bombload-radius performance. Kuwait purchased four FGA.57s and five T.67s. These were standard aircraft, aside from having ARC-52 UHF radio in addition to VHF, Marconi AD.722 radio compass,

Top One of four T.66Bs purchased by Jordan, this aircraft (serial 800) was probably converted from a Dutch or Belgian-built F.6
(BAe)

Above left Illustrating the outboard carriage of 19-round Matra Type 116M rocket pods with 68 mm SNEB projectiles, this Indian Air Force F.56 (serial BA239) was built as an RAF F.6 (serial XE600). Delivered to India in March 1958, it was apparently rejected and returned to HAL. Converted into an FGA.9, it crashed in June 1962
(BAe via Brian Isles)

Left Iraq was one of the best customers for refurbished Hunters. In 1964–65 three T.69s were delivered, all being conversions from Belgian-built F.6s. This example began life as IF-84 and was renumbered 567 for Iraq
(BAe)

Top This Iraq Air Force FGA.59, serial 570, was the first of 24 Two-Seaters converted from F.6s built in Belgium and Holland. It began life as IF-6 and was delivered to Iraq in March 1964
(HAL)

Above left Two further aircraft built as Belgian F.6s and converted into FGA.59s for Iraq. Seen here in temporary UK registrations, G-9-95 first flew as IF-142 and became serial 582, while G-9-93 began as IF-126 and became serial 585. Both were delivered to Iraq in December 1964
(HSA via Mike Stroud)

Lebanese FGA.70A serial L282 began life as F.6 serial WW594, which tested the radar nose shape of the P.1109
(BAe)

and provisions for Hispano rockets and the big tanks.

Lebanon

Like Iraq and Jordan, the Lebanon received some ex-RAF F.6s (six, in this case) in the late 1950s under US funding, and subsequently order some improved conversions from HAL. Orders totalled four FGA.70s, six FGA.70As and three T.66Cs. These were fairly standard export aircraft with provisions for big tanks and Hispano rockets, but the 70A was distinguished by its Collins 618M VHF radio (hence the large blade aerial just aft of the cockpit) and Marconi AD.370B radio compass.

Oman

No Hunters were refurbished specifically for the Sultan of Oman's Air Force (SOAF), but in the course of the 1970s this service acquired 31 from a variety of sources. These included ex-RAF FGA.9s, ex-Jordanian FGA.73s, and ex-Kuwaiti FGA.57s. Around half were held in storage, while the remainder formed No 6 Sqn at Thumrayt.

Qatar

In 1969 Qatar ordered three FGA.78s and one T.79, the trainer being based on the T.7, with an Avon 122 and a single gun. The FGA.78 was based on the Abu Dhabi Mk 76, being fitted with PTR.175 UHF and VHF, Marconi AD.370B, and Collins VOR/ILS. All four aircraft had provisions for Hispano rockets and target towing, and the single-seaters could take the big tanks. The aircraft are based at Dohar at time of writing.

Rhodesia/Zimbabwe

In February 1962 Rhodesia placed an order for 12 ex-RAF F.6s to be refurbished to FGA.9 standard, for delivery in 1963. These aircraft played an important role in the COIN operation that ended with the Lancaster House Agreement. Following independence in 1980, Zimbabwe obtained four FGA.80s and one T.81 from Kenya. A number of Hunters were destroyed in a guerilla attack on Thornhill Airbase on 25 July 1982. The remaining Hunters are maintained by Field Aviation Services.

One of 12 ex-RAF F.6s that were converted to FGA.9s for the Royal Rhodesian Air Force and played a major role in that country's struggle against insurgent forces. This aircraft, which was built as XE560, is now designated 1286 in the Air Force of Zimbabwe (BAe)

Left An Omani FGA.9 on patrol armed with AIM-9P Sidewinders. **Below** A fitter working on an Avon engine with a Hunter in background (Rolls-Royce)

Saudi Arabia

In 1966 under a government-to-government deal with the UK (the 'Magic Carpet' programme), Saudi ordered four refurbished ex-RAF Hunter F.6s and two T.7s, pending delivery of a much larger force of Lightnings. As a stop-gap measure these Hunters were deployed to deter incursions by Egyptian aircraft, but in 1969 the three remaining single-seaters were donated to Jordan. The Two-Seaters were retained to facilitate transition to the Lightning, but in 1974 were returned to the UK.

Singapore

In the late 1960s Singapore placed orders totalling 12 FGA.74s, four FR.74As, 22 FGA.74Bs, four T.75s and five T.75As, all of these aircraft being conversions. The basic Mk 74 had PTR.175 radio, Marconi AD.722, DME, and provisions for big tanks, target-towing and Hispano rockets, although they seem to have been flown mainly with SNEB/Matra rocket pods. The Mk 74A had a camera nose and Reifler D.6.B voice recorder, and the Mk 74B differed from the 74 only in having a

Marconi AD.370B radio compass. The Hunters equip No 140 (Osprey) Sqn and No 141 (Merlin) Sqn at Tengah. These aircraft have been the subject of an extensive armament upgrade programme by Lockheed Aircraft Services, involving additional weapon stations and the use of Sidewinder.

Somalia

Reports indicate that in 1983 Somalia received from Abu Dhabi that country's remaining Hunters, viz, seven FGA.76s, one FR.76A, and one T.77. These aircraft are reportedly flown by ex-Rhodesian Air Force pilots and maintained by Airwork Services.

The Royal Saudi Air Force operated two F.6s and two T.7s briefly in 1966–67 as a stop-gap effort pending the delivery of Lightnings. The F.6, serial 60-602, began life as XE591 (HSA)

Chapter 11

Later Developments

By the standards of its time, the Hunter was a relatively low-cost, high performance aircraft with good operational flexibility and very few restrictions on the way it was flown. It therefore made sense to further exploit the potential of the Hunter rather than develop a new aircraft from scratch, unless some performance breakthrough demonstrated the need for a radical change in airframe or engine.

Supersonic performance at altitude was one possible avenue of development, and would logically have led Hawker to an aircraft in the class of the Dassault-Breguet Mirage F.1, an excellent multi-role fighter. However, it could be argued that Vietnam saw very little combat at supersonic speeds, and that there are still many areas of the world where supersonics are not needed. From a 1960s viewpoint, there was thus a strong case for further development of the Hunter, rather than investing large sums in a heavier supersonic aircraft. The other performance breakthrough was in V/STOL, which required a completely different powerplant and airframe. In the event, Kingston chose to invest its financial and technical resources in this line of development (with the P.1127/Harrier series). However, it has to be said that the V/STOL market for first-generation aircraft proved extremely disappointing, basically because advanced composite materials were needed to bring the penalty of V/STOL down to a level that operators would tolerate.

In spite of the company's main effort being directed to the V/STOL programme, in the late 1950s and early 1960s some studies were made of possible Hunter derivatives. With hindsight, many of these projects ignored the fact that the Hunter had a very high structural weight, or that it would take more than a new wing to give the Hunter a good supersonic performance.

What the market really wanted was an improved Hunter with more hardpoints, providing a warload-radius performance that would compete with a late-model A-4, while retaining the superior dogfight capability of the Hunter. The late 'Charlie' Cray, the armament section leader in the production drawing office, for many years tried to get support for a series of proposals that would have enhanced considerably the effectiveness of the aircraft. Although the company had spent millions on the P.1121 and P.1127, it would not fund improvements for the Hunter, partly because a 'Super Hunter' would have made the P.1127 look even more useless. In the end some of Cray's ideas were developed in Singapore by Lockheed Aircraft Services. This was done with assistance from ex-Hawker personnel, notably the late 'Bill' Weetman from the stress office and David Lockspeiser, the test pilot who had specialized in armament.

Going back to the 1950s, most of the preliminary design work on possible Hunter derivatives was done by Ralph Hooper and John Fozard, though in the later years of the decade they were to become project engineers for the P.1127 and P.1154 respectively. Aside from the P.1083 (which was cancelled in 1953), there were several other Hunter variants aimed at supersonic performance. The P.1090 was based on the Gyron engine. The P.1091 was a Hunter of tailless delta configuration. The P.1097 was a P.1083 with the RB.106 in place of the Avon. The P.1100 of 1955 had a thin wing, an afterburning Avon, and two liquid rocket motors in the trailing edge roots, an installation similar to that proposed for the much larger P.1103 interceptor project.

When it became obvious that no-one was going to fund a supersonic Hunter, attention turned to the idea of a two-seat radar-equipped variant of the P.1101 trainer, designated P.1114 or P.1115, according to whether an Avon or Sapphire was used. In the late 1950s, as the future project situation became increasingly desperate (the P.1127 was not funded until 1960), Fozard proposed a heavily-modified twin-Orpheus business jet derivative of the Hunter, the P.1128, seating up to six passengers. However, this would have been a relatively expensive aircraft, with economics ruined by its heavy structure.

At the stage that this writer became involved in future projects (around 1958), the company's attitude was still that new roles would have to be found for the Hunter, if we were to get rid of the used aircraft that were coming back to Dunsfold. One possibility later investigated was that the Two-Seater could be transformed into a four-seat military liaison aircraft, retaining the same external lines, but replacing the Avon with two General Electric J85s, thus eliminating the need for ejection seats.

A further investigation concerned the possible

One of many supersonic fighter projects, the P.1090 was designed by John Fozard as a possible Hunter successor. It was to have been powered by an afterburning DH Gyron engine
(BAe)

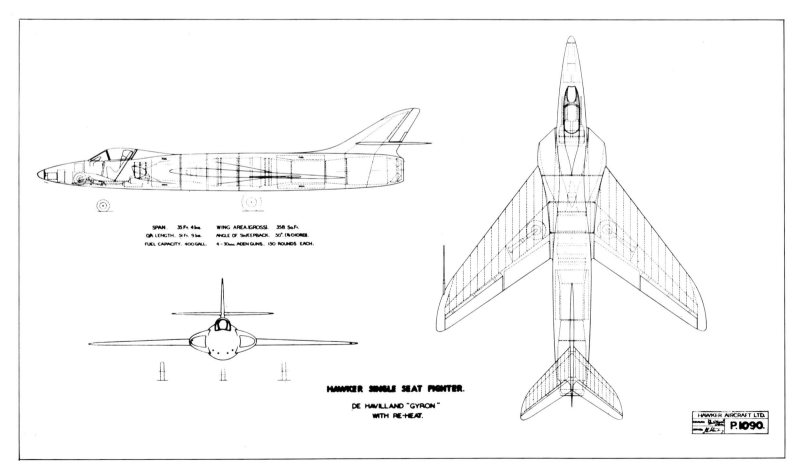

SPAN. 35 Ft. 4 In.   WING AREA.(GROSS). 358 Sq.Ft.
O/A LENGTH. 51 Ft. 9 In.   ANGLE OF SWEEPBACK. 50°. (¼ CHORD).
FUEL CAPACITY. 400 GALL.   4 - 30m.m. ADEN GUNS. 150 ROUNDS EACH.

HAWKER SINGLE SEAT FIGHTER.
DE HAVILLAND "GYRON"
WITH RE-HEAT.

HAWKER AIRCRAFT LTD.
P.1090.

use of refurbished F.4s as launch platforms for the projected Bendix 'Penny' drone, an expendable supersonic target of canard layout. In planning to introduce a supersonic target to complement the Australian (subsonic) Jindivik, the MoS had decided to use a French surface-launched, recoverable target for guided weapon trials at Aberporth. The company hoped to prove that money could be saved by air-launching a cheaper, non-recoverable drone. Unfortunately, the 'Penny' was designed to fly to a pre-programmed plan, and launch errors could not be corrected (as they could in the case of the French drone). In addition, the 'Penny' transmitted only a missile miss distance, whereas the French drone brought back cameras recording the relative path of the missile.

With a length of 20 ft (6.1 m) and a wingspan of 64 inches (1.63 m), the 'Penny' would have been the largest store ever carried on a Hunter, but it would have provided a very high target performance, reaching Mach 2.5 at 70,000 ft (21,350 m). The proposal was for the Hunter to carry two drones on adaptors on the inboard pylons, with the standard small drop tanks outboard. Performance estimates indicated that the Hunter would be able to hold for 65 minutes at 40,000 ft (12,200 m) at a radius of 125 nm (230 km).

There were no major technical problems in the use of this drone from the Hunter, but MoS felt that it was rather expensive. The Ministry also insisted on full instrumentation, not only for R&D firings and acceptance trials, but also for routine service tests. The concept was therefore abandoned.

Following the advent of the Lockheed U-2, some preliminary calculations were run on the idea of a big-wing photo-reconnaissance Hunter that would provide an altitude and range performance somewhere between the Canberra PR.9 and the U-2. This study indicated that the Hunter could be given a range approaching 4,000 nm (7,400 km), cruise-climbing from 54,000 to 61,000 ft (16,500 to 18,600 m). However, the bottom line was that the effect of the higher critical Mach Number of the Hunter derivative could not match the very low wing loading of the

The proposed P.1091 (also by Fozard) was a more modest Hunter-derivative with a simple delta wing and an afterburning Sapphire engine
(BAe)

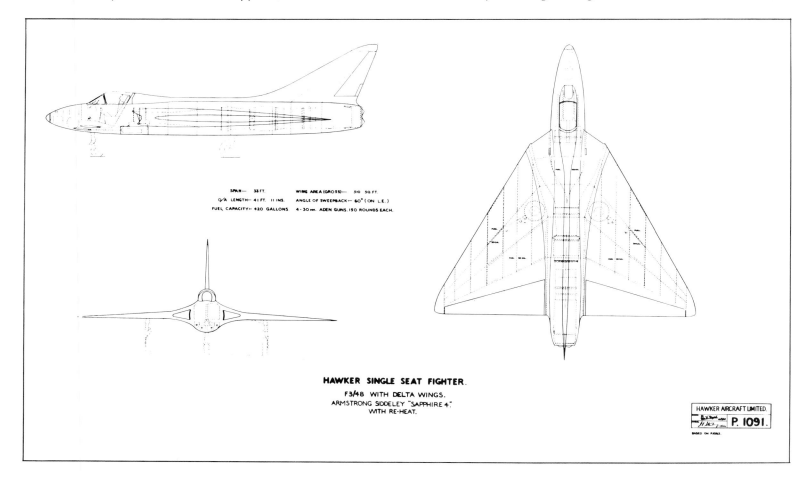

SPAN— 33 FT.   WING AREA (GROSS)—   310 SQ.FT.
O/A LENGTH— 41 FT. 11 INS.   ANGLE OF SWEEPBACK— 60° (ON L.E.)
FUEL CAPACITY— 420 GALLONS.   4 - 30 mm. ADEN GUNS. 150 ROUNDS EACH.

HAWKER SINGLE SEAT FIGHTER.
F3/48 WITH DELTA WINGS.
ARMSTRONG SIDDELEY "SAPPHIRE 4."
WITH RE-HEAT.

HAWKER AIRCRAFT LIMITED.
P. 1091.
BASED ON P.1083.

U-2 in achieving a cruise altitude that would take the aircraft above contemporary MiGs. This Hunter derivative also gave only a marginal range improvement over the Canberra. It followed that if the RAF wanted to make safe, deep penetrations of Soviet territory, the service would do far better to buy U-2s (as it had earlier operated the North American RB-45C), rather than undertake a major rehash of the Hunter.

From time to time the RAF expressed interest in being able to use Hunters from short airstrips in the Middle East. There was also interest from Switzerland, India and Peru in being able to operate Hunters from mountain airstrips. In 1960–61 an extensive study was therefore made into the possibility of improving takeoff and landing performance by various means, including rocket motors.

The starting-point for assisted take-off studies was the 'Scarab' rocket motor developed by RPE at Westcott, and fired in large numbers during tests with the Beverley transport aircraft. Whereas the traditional British 5-inch (12.7 cm) RATO motor

gave a thrust of approximately 1,100 lb (500 kg) for four seconds, the Scarab produced 3,400 lb (1,540 kg) for six seconds, corresponding to over 4.5 times the specific impulse of the earlier motor. With four Scarabs under the rear fuselage, the Hunter's takeoff roll would typically be reduced by almost 60 per cent. However, it appeared that MoS did not favour the idea of using an obsolescent rocket motor, so alternatives were sought.

Some consideration was given to the use of GW boost motors, at least as an emergency means of getting Hunters out of bombed airfields, but the safety factor on the rocket case design was judged unsuited to aircraft use. Aerojet General JATO motors are probably the most reliable in the world (hundreds of thousands have been fired in all climates), but the improvement in take-off was found to be poor. The basic reason for this was that these motors were intended primarily for use on large aircraft with long take-off times, hence they produce a small thrust of only 1,047 lb (467 kg) for a long period (14 seconds). Four of these would have reduced the Hunter's ground roll by only 30 per cent.

Hawker Aircraft was intent on developing a supersonic fighter to follow the Hunter. One of many such preliminary designs was this RA.14 or Gyron-engined P.1093, drawn by John Fozard and approved by Vivian Stanbury
(BAe)

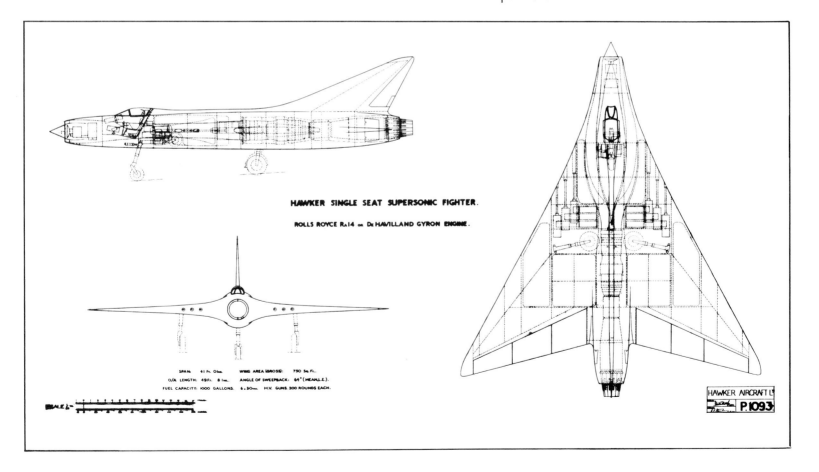

The final stage of this study was based on a reusable liquid rocket motor that de Havilland proposed to develop from a Thiokol design. We were encouraged in this by MoA advice that they were looking for an excuse to support liquid rocket development in the UK. We also studied the idea of carrying two such rockets on the gunpack to be fired forward to reduce landing ground roll, a concept pioneered on a German WW2 assault glider. The narrow jets produced may not have created too much of a FOD hazard, but there was some concern over blinding the pilot in a night landing, and the idea of carrying all that propellant in flight was less than popular. Nonetheless, proposals were made on the basis of liquid rockets, and eventually rejected due to the high R&D costs involved.

Some years later Bristol-Siddeley Engines (BSE) proposed a detachable BS.605 rocket pack derived from that used on South African Buccaneers. This was aimed specifically at the Hunter F.58, and BSE tried to interest both the Swiss and the RAF, though nothing came of the

proposal. By this stage HSA was trying to generate support for the P.1127 V/STOL aircraft, and was not out to encourage the idea of a STOL Hunter. It was clear that with rockets and arrester gears a conventional aircraft could compete with the P.1127 in most respects, though the latter had more operational flexibility in being able to land vertically. However, if STOL techniques were to be used routinely, it obviously paid to use a vectored-thrust aircraft specifically designed for such operations.

The 'CFE Hunter'

In 1964 CFE indicated to us that the RAF intended to operate the Hunter FGA.9 for a further 10 years (an underestimate), and that there was a case for improving its airfield performance, range, armament load, and navigation accuracy.

Having already failed to win interest in RATO, the obvious way to improve take-off performance in the face of an increasing gross weight was to switch to a more powerful engine. Although the

The P.1128, Fozard's concept of a six-passenger, twin-Orpheus derivative of the Hunter (BAe)

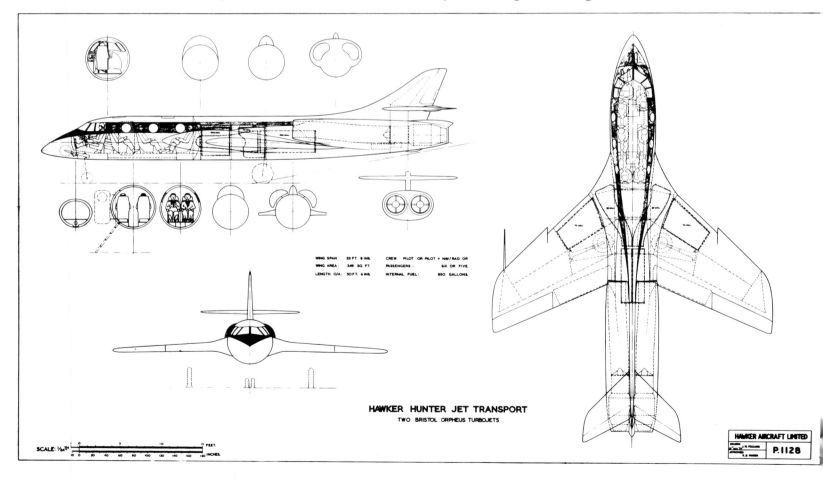

WING SPAN :   33 FT. 6 INS.   CREW :   PILOT OR PILOT + NAV/RAD. OR
WING AREA :   340 SQ. FT.   PASSENGERS :   SIX OR FIVE.
LENGTH O/A : 50 FT. 6 INS.   INTERNAL FUEL :   850 GALLONS.

HAWKER HUNTER JET TRANSPORT
TWO BRISTOL ORPHEUS TURBOJETS

SCALE: 1/24TH

HAWKER AIRCRAFT LIMITED

P.1128

R-R Spey turbofan offered some improvement in cruise fuel consumption (nothing like as much as the static test figures would suggest), it was judged that this engine's mass flow could not be accepted, and that the 'CFE Hunter' should be given a non-afterburning version of the Lightning's Avon 301, ie, a zero-staged 200-series.

One of the fundamental difficulties in the further development of the Hunter was that the intake ducts pass through two wing spars, which are difficult to modify. In the case of the Comet transport, the main spar had been 'reamed out' twice, but HAL was not keen to do this with the Hunter. The narrowest part of the duct occurs at the stub (leading edge) spar, hence the Spey would have necessitated auxiliary inlets feeding in air between this and the main spar. This information was resurrected 20 years later for the information of an American company that had innocently offered to fit the Spey in the Chilean Hunter. The Avon 301 would provide a nominal thrust of 12,650 lb (5,735 kg), and its mass flow could be accommodated by re-opening the Hunter's

suction relief doors (which by this stage had been fastened shut to prevent vibration).

To increase the aircraft's fuel capacity, it was proposed to move the front transport joint approximately two feet (61 cm) forwards, thus extending the main tanks. This was to provide an increase of around 160 Imp gal (730 litres), which could be balanced by an 80 Imp gal (365 litres) extension to the rear fuselage tanks. Modifications to provide additional fuel capacity in the wings did not appear to warrant the effort involved. Replacing the eight bag tanks with integral tanks would increase capacity by only 40 Imp gal (182 litres). Adding tanks in the outer wing structure would add only 70 Imp gal (320 litres). Inverted slipper tanks as on the Sea Vixen would have provided the necessary capacity, but only at the expense of maximum speed.

Since the aircraft was to be employed primarily in the air-ground role, there was clearly a case for replacing the standard four Aden guns with 135 rounds each by a revised gunpack configuration containing two guns with 200 rounds each. This

By 1957 HAL was desperate for a new programme. Consideration was given to this P.1124 target drone, business jets, rapid transport systems, even V/STOL! (BAe)

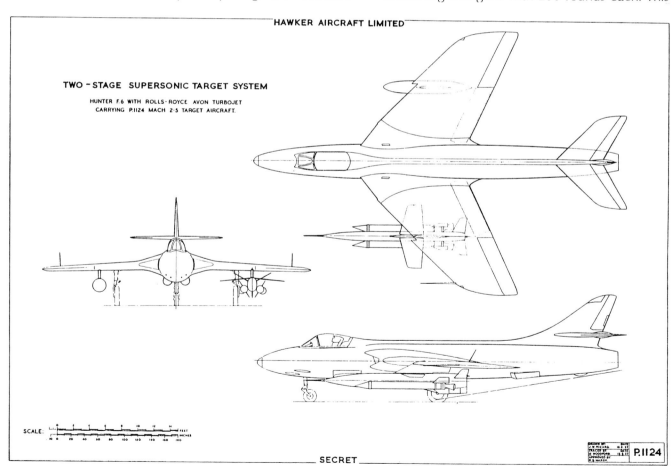

HAWKER AIRCRAFT LIMITED

TWO - STAGE SUPERSONIC TARGET SYSTEM

HUNTER F.6 WITH ROLLS-ROYCE AVON TURBOJET
CARRYING P.1124 MACH 2·5 TARGET AIRCRAFT.

SCALE:

SECRET

P.1124

would also have allowed the links to be collected within the gunpack, eliminating the drag of the blisters. Radar ranging was to be deleted as an unnecessary maintenance load (both for the avionics and the radome, which suffered from sand abrasion). The net weight saving was estimated at 670 lb (304 kg).

It was suggested that the outboard pylons should be cleared for SNEB/Matra pods, napalm tanks, and Sidewinder. The proposal to fit Sidewinder on the gunpack (which originated with Lockspeiser) was not recommended in view of CG problems and the possibility of blast or vibration from the gunpack damaging the missiles or their accessories. It was proposed to instal a dead-reckoning navigation system, based on a Kollsman TAS unit and a Sperry C-11 semi-aerobatic compass, deleting the existing compass system.

In order to make the Hunter operable from short, rough airfields, it was proposed to replace the 10.5 ft (3.2 m) parachute with one of 13.5 ft (4.1 m) diameter, as on G-APUX, and to fit an emergency 1.5 G hook, as on the Mk 8 and 11. Low pressure tyres of 150 psi (10.5 kg/cm²), as tested on G-APUX, were to be fitted in place of the usual 200 psi (14 kg/cm²) tyres. To have gone to lower pressures would have necessitated modifying the main leg, the fairing doors, and the noseleg fork.

Allowing for the deletion of 200 lb (91 kg) of existing ballast, it was hoped to achieve a net decrease of 300 lb (140 kg) in basic weight. However, the extra 2,000 lb (907 kg) of internal fuel would give a general increase in takeoff weights. For example, with two large tanks inboard and two napalm tanks outboard, the aircraft would weigh approximately 26,070 lb (11,825 kg).

This final Kingston study of an updated FGA.9 was formulated in March 1964. Although it may have been shown to CFE, it almost certainly went no further, if only because HSA was then intent that nothing should stand in the way of the P.1154, which was cancelled in the following year. If one were today to propose a Hunter update, it would probably follow the same lines as the 'CFE Hunter', although one might think in terms of a low-cost digital inertial nav-attack system, HUD, twin-store carriers on the outboard pylons and a new centre-line pylon, and two Aden 25 cannon. The Aden 25 increases the rate of fire from 1,200 to 1,800 rd/min, and is designed to accept the highly effective Oerlikon KBB 25 mm ammunition, which is a generation in advance of the Aden 30 mm.

Left Chile's ENAER *Caiquen II* radar warning receiver is associated with three antennas set high on the fin and one on the tail bullet of the Hunter FGA.71 (ENAER)

Below A chaff/flare scab of the ENAER *Eclipse* dispenser system is shown on the rear fuselage of Hunter FGA.71 serial 708, formerly the RNAF F.4 serial N-201 (ENAER)

Recent Developments

It is now more than 30 years since deliveries of the Hunter began, but it seems certain that the aircraft will remain in service with several air forces (including those of Singapore and Switzerland) until the turn of the century, and possibly beyond. Hunters are meanwhile appearing on the British and US civil registers, and with care such aircraft may continue flying for decades.

It is impossible for even the manufacturer to state precisely how many Hunters are still flying, which in itself is an indication of how seriously this aircraft is taken by those who know its operational capability. However, from information supplied by a variety of sources, it may be estimated that the situation on airworthy Hunters is roughly as follows:

a) Hunters have been withdrawn from service in 10 countries: Abu Dhabi, Belgium, Denmark, Jordan, Kenya, Kuwait, the Netherlands, Peru, Saudi Arabia and Sweden.

b) Hunters are still operated by 11 nations, or 12 if civil aircraft in the US are included. Approximate numbers at end-85 are shown below:

Chile 30–35	Singapore 35–40
India 100	Somalia 9
Iraq 12 (18 more in storage)	
Lebanon 5–8	Switzerland 60 (plus)
Oman 20 (10 more in storage)	Zimbabwe 17
Qatar 3	UK 70 (more in storage)

The main source for civil Hunters has been Danish Mk 51s, which became available in the late 1970s. The first US example is believed to have been E-403, which was given the temporary UK registration G-9-434, and was shipped to the US in 1976, becoming N72602. This aircraft was owned initially by Alfred Letcher, and from 1983 by 'Al' Hansen. There is also known to be An ex-Swedish Mk 50, owned at time of writing by David Tallichet, and intended for use by a new flight test company using ex-military jets. There may well be other Hunters in the US.

There are currently two airworthy ex-Danish Hunters on the British civil register. The single-

The only civil single-seat Hunter flying in the UK is G-HUNT, formerly the Danish Mk 51 E-418. It is shown here with its first owner, Spencer Flack (left) and its demonstration pilot, the late Stefan Karwowski
(Philip Boyden)

seater was formerly E-418, which was purchased from BAe by Spencer Flack and refurbished under the direction of ex-Hawker employee, Eric Hayward. On 20 March 1980 it was hauled off the 2,160-foot (660 m) runway at Elstree by the late Stefan Karwowski, who was with Adrian Gjertsen to demonstrate the aircraft at airshows on behalf of Flack. This Mk 51, registered G-HUNT, was sold to Michael Carlton in November 1981. The second civilian British Hunter is a Mk 53, formerly ET-274, and owned by Carlton. On 7 September 1983 this Two-Seater, registered G-BOOM, was used to re-enact the world speed record flight made 30 years earlier. The aircraft was flown on this occasion by Carlton with Duke as co-pilot.

Chile

The Hunter Mk 71 series has been modernized with locally-developed equipment, primarily with the aim of making it less vulnerable to missile attack. Work on countermeasures had been in progress for around eight years within the *Fuerza*

Aerea de Chile when the government-owned ENAER (*Empress Nacional de Aeronautica*) formed an electronics division at the end of 1984, taking over EW work being done by the air force. The first in-country product was a non-directional radar warning receiver (RWR) designated *Caiquen I*, of which a batch of 15 were manufactured for the Hunter and A-37. *Caiquen* was named after the wild geese that alerted ancient Rome to an impending attack.

The second phase, beginning in 1981, led to an improved model, *Caiquen II*, giving full coverage in azimuth over a wide frequency range (2–18 GHz). A Hunter began flying with this improved system at the end of 1982. Evaluation took 12 months, but then the equipment went into production for the Hunter. This system, which weighs only 17.6 lb (8 kg), is associated with three antennas mounted high on the fin (one forward- and two side-looking) and an aft-looking antenna in the tip of the tail bullet. The pilot hears a special tone, and a display on the instrument panel indicates the quadrantal bearing of the transmitter, the type of radar and its

As part of the 'Hunter-80' update programme, many Swiss F.58s and F.58As have been modified to take the Hughes AGM-65 TV-guided air-ground missile on the outboard pylon, as illustrated here on Mk 58 J-4079

operating mode. The *Caiquen II* deals with both AI and SAM radars.

Chilean Hunters have also received the ENAER *Eclipse* chaff/flare dispensing system. A Hunter can take up to four 'scabs' on the rear fuselage, each containing 16 MJU-7/B flares or 32 RR-170 chaff cartridges. The complete system weighs 159 lb (72 kg).

Singapore

As mentioned earlier, Singaporean Hunters have been updated by Lockheed Aircraft Services to carry more armament and to incorporate modern avionics. This programme is still cloaked in secrecy, but the aircraft has presumably been given a dead-reckoning navigation system and twin-store carriers on the outboard pylons and centreline. In 1978 at a local air display one FGA.74B was exhibited with Sidewinders mounted on pylons projecting ahead of the wing (probably to keep the missile clear of the main under-carriage) and with two 1,000 lb (454 kg) bombs on the centreline station.

Switzerland

In recent years various Swiss companies have been involved in the 'Hunter-80' programme to refurbish and upgrade the aircraft. Modifications include the installation of RWRs and chaff/flare dispensers, and provisions for 28 rather than 16 Hispano rockets, and the Hughes AGM-65B Maverick TV-guided air-surface missile. The Hunter has also been flown with the Northrop ALQ-171(V) jammer pod. Press reports indicate that the Hunter T.68s of Staffel 24 have a dedicated ECM role.

The Northrop ALQ-171(V) electronics countermeasures pod, fitted on the outboard pylon of Swiss Hunter F.58A J-4104, which was originally built as an F.4 (serial XF947) with a 100-Series Avon (Northrop Corp)

Chapter 12

Hunters At War

The Hunter has been operated by the air arms of no less than 21 nations, and it is therefore hardly surprising that it has been involved in a large number of conflicts around the world. Its operational use began in 1956 with the deployment of the Sapphire-engined F.5 to Cyprus to provide air cover for attacks on Egypt around the disputed Suez Canal Zone. Today Hunters are probably still being used by Iraq (some reports say in chemical warfare) in the war with Iran. Lebanese Hunters have been used against militia forces around Beirut. At time of writing, Zimbabwe Hunters are being used over the border against the rebel forces of the Mozambique National Resistance.

The following outline of the Hunter's operational use looks first at its service in the RAF, then at its use by overseas nations in alphabetical order.

Royal Air Force

The deployment of Hunters to Cyprus in October 1956 served little useful purpose, other than to emphasize the need for larger drop tanks to improve endurance. The aircraft used were F.5s of Nos 1 and 34 Sqn, then based at Tangmere. They were ferried to Akrotiri to provide fighter escort for RAF and FAA attacks on targets in the Canal Zone, following Egypt's nationalization of the Suez Canal and the Anglo-French 'Operation Musketeer' to regain control. As was undoubtedly expected, at a radius of around 270 nm (500 km), when allowance was made for combat fuel, the Hunter with two small tanks had an extremely limited time on station. The aircraft's role was therefore quickly changed to providing air defence for Cyprus against possible Egyptian attacks. Fortunately, although Egypt already had some useful Soviet equipment (including the MiG-17), daylight attacks on facilities around the Canal do not appear to have met air opposition, and there were no retaliatory strikes against bases in Cyprus.

Kuwait

Hunters of the RAF were again deployed from their normal peacetime bases in July 1961, when the Ruler of Kuwait requested British assistance to deter a threatened attack from Iraq. Iraq's prime minister (Gen Kassim) had laid claim to Kuwait on June 25th, and in July troops and armour were moved south from Baghdad toward the Kuwaiti border.

Britain's intervention is of some historical interest, as it illustrates the nation's ability in the early 1960s to project power to a remote location (in this case to protect oil supplies), despite the problems of overflight restrictions. The units involved were Nos 8 and 208 Sqn, based at Khormaksar (Aden) and Embakasi (Nairobi) respectively. These units had been flying the FGA.9 since 1960.

The legal background to Iraq's claim was that under the old Ottoman Empire Kuwait had been part of the Iraqi province of Basra. Whatever the rights and wrongs of the situation, the British assessment was that an attack might be made on Kuwait on July 14th, Iraq's National Day.

In anticipation of a request for assistance, the Hunters of Nos 8 and 208 Sqn were moved up to Bahrain on June 30th. Over-flying Saudi Arabia was not permitted, hence the flight from Aden represented around 1,300 nm (2,400 km). The Kenya-based squadron also had the 1,000 nm (1,850 km) flight from Nairobi to Aden before embarking on this main stage. However, the

reinforcement operation was completed in the course of the day, and by nightfall two squadrons of Hunters were dispersed around the airfield at Bahrain, only 225 nm (415 km) from Kuwait.

One Canberra squadron was moved from Germany to Sharjah, two Shackletons were repositioned from Aden to Bahrain, and V-bombers were flown from the UK to Malta. Fortuitously, the commando carrier HMS *Bulwark* was at Karachi and heading for the Persian Gulf. The bad news was that neither Turkey nor Saudi Arabia would allow overflights to Kuwait from the UK and Cyprus, so a long logistics chain had to be established via El Adem (Libya), Nairobi and Aden.

On July 1st Royal Marines from *Bulwark* were landed by helicopter at Kuwait New Airfield, and No 8 Sqn flew in from Bahrain, where they were soon joined by No 208 Sqn. The plan was to leave the old civil airport as a logistics airhead for the Beverley and Valetta tactical transports of AFME, while Bahrain acted as the main terminal for the RAF's Britannias and the RRAF's Canadair DC-4Ms and leased Argonauts. Troops began to be airlifted

Hunter FGA.9 XG298/E of No 43 Sqn at Khormaksar with locally-supplied ground transport and security forces. This aircraft was first flown as an F.6 on 29 November 1956 by Duncan Simpson. After serving with No 4 Sqn it was converted to an FGA.9 and handed back to the RAF in October 1961. In late 1967 it was transferred to the Royal Jordanian Air Force (serial 826) (MoD)

into Kuwait to reinforce the Commandos, and by July 9th the buildup had been completed, with 5,691 British servicemen on the ground in Kuwait.

One of the principal problems in achieving satisfactory air defence for Kuwait was that the country had no radar. Fortunately, the radar on *Bulwark* gave a range of about 80 nm (150 km), and the carrier was able to stand in close to shore during daylight hours. The Type SC787 transportable radar was available from Bahrain and was flown to Kuwait, but was not fully operational until July 18th, and lacked a height-finding capability. However, on the 9th the carrier HMS *Victorious* had arrived from the Far East with Sea Vixen all-weather fighters and a much more effective radar.

Operating conditions were appalling, with ground temperatures around 120°F (49°C), high humidity and sandstorms, which gave a ground level visibility of around 400 yards (370 m). One Hunter spun into the ground, evidently due to pilot disorientation. The limited radar coverage available implied the use of cockpit readiness, but with cockpit temperatures on the ground often exceeding 140°F (60°C) this was out of the question. Instead, some Hunters were held at 15-minute readiness, with the pilots in a crewroom close to their aircraft, and an air conditioning unit holding temperatures in this room down to a more bearable 112°F (44,5°C).

The prompt reaction of the British forces undoubtedly deterred any move by Iraq, and by July 20th it was judged that the peak risk period had passed. Withdrawal began, with No 208 Sqn pulling back to Bahrain, while No 8 Sqn remained at Kuwait New, along with the Type 787 radar. *Bulwark* sailed for the Far East, but *Victorious* remained in the Gulf until the end of the month, when she was replaced by HMS *Centaur*.

Not one shot had been fired in anger, but the reinforcement of Kuwait had proved to be *'perhaps the most comprehensive realistic and valuable movement exercise ever carried out by the three British services'* (in the words of Air Chief Marshal Sir David Lee). If Iraq had invaded, there can be little doubt that the Hunters of the RAF's two most experienced ground attack squadrons would have created havoc among Iraqi tanks and armoured vehicles.

Radfan Operations

With Kenya heading rapidly toward independence (a situation finally achieved in December 1963), it was clearly necessary to phase out the use of Nairobi as an RAF base, and it was therefore decided to move No 208 Sqn's base to Aden, where the unit joined No 8 Sqn to form the Khormaksar Wing. Early in 1962 these aircraft were involved (together with some Shackletons) in an operation reminiscent of pre-war 'policing' in Iraq, when dissident villages in the Western Aden Protectorate first received warning leaflets, than 1,000 lb (454 kg) bombs and 20 lb (9 kg) fragmentation weapons.

In September 1962 an Egyptian-inspired revolution took place in the Yemen, and the new leaders called on the indigenous inhabitants of Aden and the Protectorate to rebel against British rule. Some Yemeni aircraft crossed the border and attacked villages in the Protectorate with rockets. Hunters from both squadrons began dawn-to-dusk patrols along the border, and the incursions ceased.

However, the Yemenis worked to transform the various tribes of the Radfan area into effective dissidents, and in December 1963 growing unrest in Aden culminated in a grenade attack at Khormaksar against the High Commissioner. A punitive expedition ('*Operation Nutcracker*') with three battalions of troops was therefore mounted in the Radfan early in 1964, supported by a sustained air effort.

At this stage the RAF had three Hunter squadrons permanently based at Khormaksar, viz, Nos 8, 43, and 208 Sqn, plus a four-aircraft flight (No 1417 Flt) of FR.10s. These aircraft were used initially to provide cannon fire against tribesmen firing on sections of troops and artillery guncrews landed by helicopter. The helicopters were known to the Arab soldiers as '*the father of grasshoppers*' (Wessex) and '*the father of two fans*' (Belvedere). The expedition was successful, but when the ground forces found it impractical to garrison the Radfan, dissident morale rose, and there was a resurgence of aircraft incursions from the Yemen.

In retaliation, on 28 March 1964 eight Hunters attacked the fort at Harib, just across the border into the Yemen. As usual, leaflet warning was given before the Hunters went in with bombs and rockets, the leaflets showing up clearly in the photographs taken by the FR.10 of the destruction of this stone-built fort.

This action deterred further air penetrations from the Yemen, but dissidence on the ground continued, and it was judged that air action would be more effective than further large-scale effort on the ground. It was nonetheless decided to land at night an SAS section, using Scout helicopters, so that the SAS could mark out a DZ for 120 men of the 3rd Parachute Regiment. However, the SAS came under strong small arms fire at daybreak, and they called for close air support.

This was provided throughout the day by Hunters of Nos 43 And 208 Sqn, which flew 18 sorties, and fired 127 rockets and 7,131 rounds of 30 mm. It was the start of an action that went on for 30 hours, with Hunters straffing rebel positions as close as 150 yards (140 m) from the paratroops, and ended with British forces firmly established in the heart of insurgent territory, with only two men killed and 10 wounded.

In the following period of consolidation, Hunters maintained pressure on designated areas by day, while Shackletons took over the task by night. In the fighting for a succession of dissident-held wadis, the Hunters provided invaluable fire support, their excellent manoeuvrability and heavy built-in armament making them ideally suited to the task.

By mid-1964 the combined efforts of the British forces had broken the back of rebel resistance, and the insurgency continued only at a much lower level. During the period 30 April to 30 June 1964, Hunter FGA.9s had flown 527 sorties, while FR.10s had flown a further 115. Armament expenditure for the FGA.9s amounted to 176,092 rounds of 30 mm and 2,598 rockets, while the FR.10s fired 7,808 rounds of 30 mm.

In the period from 1964 to 1967 (when Britain left Aden), the Hunters were primarily concerned with border patrols to deter penetrations by Egyptian-flown MiGs. These defensive operations included use of the 1,800 yard (1,650 m) strip at Beihan. The Radfan tribes were sueing for peace, but terrorism within Aden was on the increase.

It became standard procedure to keep a pair of Hunters overhead whenever an RAF or Army Air Corps (AAC) aircraft was on the ground at one of the up-country airstrips. In withdrawing the FGA.9s, the plan was to form a fighter/ground attack wing at Muharraq (Bahrain), while retaining No 43 Sqn at Khormaksar until the final stage of withdrawal, when the unit's Hunters were to be divided between Nos 8 and 208 Sqn, or returned to the UK.

Meanwhile No 1417 Flight was to be disbanded, and its tasks taken over by No 8 Sqn. The last Hunter ground attack sorties were flown on 9 November 1967, and the last Hunters (the FR.10s of No 1417 Flight) flew out to join No 8 Sqn at Muharraq on the 28th, the day before the last British troops left Aden.

Confrontation

The 1960s also saw RAF Hunters active in the Far East with No 20 Sqn, although in this case relatively few shots were fired. The squadron, which had been disbanded in Germany early in 1961, was reformed at Tengah (Singapore) in September of that year with FGA.9s. From Tengah the unit was to reinforce other RAF bases in the Far East, including Kai Tak (Hong Kong), which was home for No 28 Sqn. In 1962 No 20 Sqn spent six months in Thailand. However, its principal deployment was in the context of the 'Con-frontation' with Indonesia, which lasted from late 1962 to 1966. This affair arose out of an Indonesian reaction against the formation of Malaysia on 16 September 1963, the essence of the argument being that Indonesia's President Soekarno wanted Borneo as part of his own nation.

Confrontation began with an Indonesian-backed rebellion in Brunei and Sarawak. There followed a rapid buildup of British and Gurkha troops from Singapore, and simulated attacks by Hunters and Canberras (from Labuan) on villages that the rebels had occupied. By early 1963 the initial revolt had been crushed, but there remained the threat of Indonesian insurgents crossing the border from Kalimantan to raid villages in Sarawak and Sabah (which was shortly to become Eastern Malaysia).

From September 1963 Britain and Indonesia were virtually in a state of undeclared war. Most of the British community was evacuated from Djakarta, and RAF overflights of Indonesia were forbidden, although Indonesian Air Force B-25 Mitchells and P-51 Mustangs made a number of incursions into Malaysian airspace. In much the same way that a Total Exclusion Zone was formed around the Falklands in 1982, an Air Defence Identification Zone (ADIZ) was formed to protect Sarawak and Sabah. To enforce the ADIZ, four Hunters and two Firestreak-armed Javelins were positioned at Labuan (off the coast near Brunei), and a similar force was established At Kuching, near the Western tip of Sarawak. To make it clear that Britain was in earnest, the normal rules of engagement were modified to allow RAF pilots to destroy Indonesian aircraft over the ADIZ without obtaining prior permission from the ground.

Strikes against guerilla camps over the Kalimantan border were ruled out, hence the RAF's main role was to provide all forms of support (troop movement and supply, photo-reconnaissance, etc) for the ground forces opposing infiltration, using fixed- and rotary-wing transports and Canberras, while the Hunters deterred large-scale air incursions.

From mid-1964 the guerillas were supplemented by regular Indonesian troops, and it became necessary to provide infantry bases with both artillery and air support. In August around 100 Indonesian regulars were landed at three points in Johore in Western Malaysia, and in the following month these men were augmented by paratroops dropped from a C-130 Hercules. This widening of the conflict emphasized the potential air threat to RAF bases on Singapore Island and the RAAF base at Butterworth. The Hunters of No 20 Sqn, Javelins of No 60 Sqn, and the RAAF F-86s were accordingly placed on alert. The Hunters also made 14 sorties against the Indonesian paratroops on Johore, each aircraft firing 16 3-inch (76 mm) rockets and a full load of 30 mm. However, landings continued in Western Malaysia, and the Hunters were called upon to make further strikes.

Air defences for Singapore and the Malaysian Peninsula were strengthened by the arrival of eight more Javelins, the installation of 20 mm AAA, a Bloodhound SAM squadron, radar-equipped RN Gannets from HMS *Victorious* to provide an AEW capability, and the County-class cruiser HMS *Kent* to fill an important radar gap. A number of Victors were flown in to provide a deterrent capability.

In Eastern Malaysia in 1964–65 there were hit-and-run attacks by Indonesian aircraft, but the Hunters and Javelins at Labuan and Kuching were unable to make intercepts. On one occasion a Javelin passed a C-130 on a reciprocal heading in a narrow valley, but by the time the RAF aircraft had turned round the Hercules was back across the border.

In September 1965 there was a coup in Indonesia and President Soekarno fell from office. In August 1966 Malaysia and Indonesia signed a peace treaty. Activity across the border then ran down, and the RAF fighters were withdrawn to Tengah.

Although the RAF Hunters and Javelins had shot down no Indonesian aircraft, they had provided a useful deterrent against more serious attacks on Malaysia. An Indonesian commander confessed afterwards that the aircraft they had feared most was the Hunter. Indonesia then had Tu-16s and old B-25s for offensive operations, and MiG-17s, -19s and -21s for air defence.

The MiG-17 could have been used in hit-and-run strikes, and this would have presented the Hunter with a difficult target. Generally similar to the Hunter in performance, the MiG-17 has an afterburner, hence the best tactic may have been to run it out of fuel. It was also believed that the MiG-17 could not perform rolling pullouts without flicking over, so the Hunter would have played it in the vertical, changing direction during the pullout. There is a story that a Hunter met a MiG-17 on the Indonesian side of the border, but that the MiG flicked into the ground before a shot could be fired. Officially, the incident never occurred, because Hunters did not cross the border.

Chile

The Hunter FGA.71s of the *Fuerza Aerea de Chile* (FACH) were actively involved in the overthrow of President Allende in 1973. Reports at the time indicated that on September 11th 20 bombs were dropped on the 150-year old presidential palace,

The Hunter FGA.9s of No 20 Sqn (exemplified here by XJ683/F) played an important role in Confrontation with Indonesia. Normally based at Tengah (Singapore), flights were moved to forward to carry out defensive patrols from Labuan and Kuching. Hunters from Tengah carried out rocket and cannon attacks against Indonesian paratroops who had landed in Western Malaysia (MoD)

known as *La Moneda* (The Mint), causing it to go up in flames. In reality the palace was rocketed with great precision, and is still in use today.

India

Hunter F.56s of the Indian Air Force have been used operationally on at least four occasions: during the invasion of the old Portuguese colony of Goa in 1961, during the border fighting with China in late 1962, and in the clashes with Pakistan in September 1965 and December 1971.

In the 1965 Indo-Pakistan conflict the Hunters were employed both for air defence and ground attack, the latter role taking the form of strikes on airfields and tactical interdiction with guns and rockets. That war lasted three weeks, and it included the well-known incident at Sarghoda airfield in Pakistan, in which Sqn Ldr Alam of the PAF (and CO of an F-86F squadron) got behind a section of four Hunters and destroyed all four in as many minutes. The IAF pilots had only just begun their tactical training, they all broke in the same direction, and Alam was using API ammunition, which set fire to all four. As another PAF officer has commented to this writer, it was sheer lunacy to send untrained pilots over the principal PAF fighter base in broad daylight.

According to the PAF, in that war Sabres destroyed nine Hunters for the loss of six aircraft. Since all but two of the clashes took place at low level, since the PAF had Sidewinders, and since the IAF Hunter pilots had been trained only for ground attack, this assessment may well have been correct.

It is also interesting that, when Alam tried to turn with a Hunter at 20,000 ft (6,100 m), his Sabre flicked at around 6.5G. There was only one clash between Hunters and Starfighters, a pair of F-104s intercepting two intruding Hunters at 25,000 ft (7,800 m) over Lahore. One Hunter appears to have stalled and dropped out of the fight, while the other turned so tightly that the F-104 was unable to fire. The F-104 then used afterburner to disengage.

The 1971 conflict arose from the secession of East Pakistan, which became Bangladesh. On this occasion the fighting lasted only two weeks, but was more widespread, with considerable activity in the east. The PAF aircraft encountered by Hunters included the Shenyang F-6 (MiG-19) and the Mirage III. The Hunters appear to have been used primarily against ground targets such as troops, vehicle concentrations, artillery positions,

headquarters railway stations, radar installations, and oil refineries. According to PAF sources, six Hunters were lost to F-86s, four to Mirages, three to MiG-19s, and four to ground fire. Reports indicate that IAF Hunters claimed only two Sabres and one MiG-19, which presumably reflects the role in which they were employed.

Iraq

Hunters of the FGA.59 series have taken part in a number of major conflicts, and it seems likely that they have also been used on occasion against Kurdish dissidents. There were unconfirmed reports that, when Iraq entered the Soviet fold, two Hunter pilots defected to Egypt, after destroying a large number of MiGs on the ground.

In the 'Six-Day War' with Israel in June 1967, the Israelis struck at Habbaniyah, destroying five Hunters and 10 other aircraft on the ground. The Iraqi Air Force played little part in the war, although Hunters did patrol the border.

In the 'Yom Kippur War' of October 1973 the FGA.59s flew top cover for Su-7s carrying out ground attacks, and were frequently involved in air combat with A-4s and Super Mystères.

Iraqi Hunters are also believed to have taken part in the war with Iran, which started in 1980. One published photograph purports to show the Hunter being used in a gas attack, with chemicals streaming from tanks on the inboard pylons. This picture was almost certainly taken in a UK exercise simulating gas attacks on forward troops.

Jordan

Though traditionally regarded as the most professional of Arab air forces, the Royal Jordanian Air Force lost most of its Hunters in the Israelis' pre-emptive strike on Mafraq in June 1967, after the country's early warning radar had been taken out. The remnants were withdrawn to Iraq, pending cessation of hostilities. Three replacements were donated by Saudi Arabia, and further Hunters were purchased from HSA. These aircraft were delivered between 1968 and 1971, and were later augmented by Hunters from Abu Dhabi. Late in 1975 Jordan gave most of its Hunters to Oman, and appears to have returned the remainder to Abu Dhabi.

Lebanon

Reports suggest that a small number of Lebanese Hunters may have been destroyed by Israeli incursions, but no accurate records appear to exist. The Israeli invasion of the Lebanon in 1982 led to a chaotic situation in the country, with rival armed factions struggling for power. In September 1983 it was reported that three Hunters were operating from a stretch of road near Byblos (north of Beirut) and attacking Druze forces in the hills with cannon fire and 68 mm rockets. On the 16th one Hunter diverted to Akrotiri, after suffering damage from ground fire.

Netherlands

The first deployment of Hunters to the Far East occurred in August 1960, when 24 F.4s of the RNAF were shipped in the carrier *Karel Doorman* to strengthen the country's forces in Dutch New Guinea, which was faced with the prospect of invasion from Indonesia. The Hunters were based for a time at Biak and Mokmer, but in 1962 the Netherlands bowed to the inevitable and ceded the territory to Indonesia.

Oman

The Sultanate of Oman is a particularly important state in the Persian Gulf, since it not only has substantial oil reserves, but is also strategically located at the entrance to the Gulf, where it could control the Straits of Hormuz. It is therefore British Government policy to safeguard the independence of Oman, which means protecting it against the Communist-backed PDRY (People's Democratic Republic of Yemen, often referred to simply as South Yemen). Dhofar is the most westerly province of Oman, and is thus situated next to the PDRY, but contains only 50,000 people, around 10 per cent of the population of Oman.

It may well be that the seeds of revolution in Oman were sowed by the previous Sultan (Said bin Taimur), in failing to use his oil revenues to improve the country, providing education, medical and communication facilities. Insurgency began with a minor rebellion in 1962, and by 1970 the Sultan's power in the Dhofar was restricted to the Salalah area. In July of that year Said bin Tamur was replaced by Sultan Qaboos, who announced plans to develop the country and to regain control of Dhofar. In 1973 the Shah agreed to provide an Imperial Iranian Battle Group of 1,500 men, supported by C-130s operating into Thumrayt and Manston. Further aid was forthcoming from King Hussein, who visited Thumrait in April 1975 in his Boeing 707 'Jordan One' to inspect his Special Forces battalion and engineer squadron. At that stage the only ground attack assets available were eight BAC Strikemasters, based at Salalah on the coast, and armed only with 500 lb (227 kg) bombs, 80 mm Hispano SURA rockets, and 7.62 mm machine guns.

In July 1975 the Sultan of Oman's Air Force (SOAF) acquired a batch of Hunters from Jordan, 15 of which were used to form No 6 Sqn at Thrumrayt. There was a general shortage of manpower and spares, so the remaining aircraft (together with some FGA.57s from Kuwait and some ex-RAF FGA.9s) were placed in storage as attrition replacements and a basis for cannibalization. The Hunters were mainly flown by RAF pilots loaned to SOAF, but there were also mercenary pilots from Britain, New Zealand, and Jordan. The mercenaries were paid a modest £26 per day.

Insurgents had been coming across the border from South Yemen for some time, and on August 19th a Strikemaster was badly damaged by an SA-7 man-portable missile. This aircraft was returned to Manston with severe damage, especially to the elevators. Two weeks later another Strikemaster was hit and broke in two, but the pilot escaped by parachute.

In view of the escalating insurgency, it was decided to carry out strikes across the border to neutralize the enemy's military capability, and discredit the PFLO (Popular Front for the Liberation of Oman). Far from being simple desert bedouin, the enemy had a full range of Soviet equipment up to the 130 mm field gun, and some of them had been trained in Russia. For anti-aircraft use they had the self-propelled four-barrel ZSU-23-4 automatic cannon, and (from 1975) the SA-7. For their attacks the Hunters used Pakistani 1,025 lb (500 kg) bombs, the 80 mm Hispano SURA rocket, and 30 mm Aden for strafing.

The action began just after 0700 hr on October 17th, with an attack by Hunters and a shore bombardment by ships of the Imperial Iranian Navy. Further air strikes were flown at 1100 hr and at dusk. The RAF pilots were not allowed to take part in offensive missions, so these were carried out by the mercenaries: Nigel Charles and Barry Stott from the UK, Stefan Karwowski from New Zealand, and Mohammed Ferarj from Jordan.

The Hunter squadron decided that the best tactic was to transit at 15,000 ft (4,600 m), since they believed the SA-7 was effective only up to 10,000 ft (3,000 m), attack throttled back for minimum aural and IR signature in a 60° dive, release bombs at 2,500 ft (760 m), and recover in a 7G spiral up to 10,000 ft (3,000 m), since they believed that a 4G aircraft was the maximum that the SA-7 could accommodate. The Hispano rockets were fired at a slant range of 4,000 ft (1,200 m). Below 10,000 ft (3,000 m) the Hunters maintained 480 knots (890 km/hr), again to defeat the SA-7.

In the course of the action a number of SOAF Strikemasters and helicopters were shot down, and a Hunter flown by Ferarj had an SA-7 strike on the jetpipe, but limped back and crash-landed at Salalah. Another Hunter had a wing 'creased' by a 57 mm round, and was judged not worth repairing. One Hunter took two 40 mm strikes on the front windscreen. All these hits occurred when the aircraft was making a second pass, so this practice was eliminated as far as possible. In addition (as recounted later) one Hunter on a reconnaissance mission had the engine stop, possibly due to a 14.7 mm strike, and the pilot had to be lifted out of the sea by a Bell 'Huey'.

The SA-7 was seen as a very serious threat. If the pilot was high enough, he would see the white smoke produced on firing and a smoke trail as it climbed toward his aircraft. The missile quickly

winds up to Mach 2, hence prompt action was necessary, although only a small percentage of SA-7s appear to have 'acquired' their targets successfully. The SOAF Hunter tactic was to break toward the missile, throttled back. A total of 23 of these missiles were fired in Dhofar, but only three hit their targets.

Another factor in the virtual immunity of the Hunters to ground fire was that no R/T was used by No 6 Sqn from start-up to first pass. In contrast, the indications were that the enemy knew the Strikemasters were coming. It may be added that the Iranian aircraft participated only later in the operation. One F-4 was shot down while patrolling the border at 360 knots (670 km/hr), presumably by machine gun fire.

The conflict continued until December, with the Hunters attacking a wide variety of targets. Karwowski's missions included a bombing attack on a storage cave in a cliff on the shoreline, but his most frightening moment was in attacking an airfield 80 nm (150 km) south. He could see AAA firing by the dust-clouds thrown up around the

Rhodesian Air Force Hunters played a vital role in counter-insurgency operations during the 1970s, mainly using a 1,000 lb (454 kg) blast bomb. This particular aircraft, serial 1038, was not one of the 12 supplied by Britain in 1963. The fact that it had blast deflectors suggests it was some export version of the F.6

guns, but he was flat-out only two or three feet (0.6–0.9 m) off the ground, and the tracer was passing above the aircraft, since it was below the maximum depression angle of the flak.

Aside from ground attack missions, they also flew as decoys for reconnaissance aircraft, the decoy positioned 1,000 yd (900 m) ahead and on the other side of the target, with airbrake out and at full throttle, to attract the enemy's attention. Karwowski, who was awarded the Sultan's Bravery Medal for his many ground attack missions against heavy opposition, survived the Dohfar War, only to die in a Pitts Special crash in New Zealand in April 1985.

Faster Than The Average Huey

A somewhat more light-hearted episode occurred in the middle of the conflict, with what became known as 'The Great Champagne Race'. There was a good relationship between the Hunter and Huey (Bell 205) squadrons of the SOAF, which was just as well, because the Hunter pilots relied on the helicopters to save them if they were forced down. However, one particularly relaxing evening in the mess led to an argument as to which aircraft was faster bar-to-bar over the 27 nm (50 km) from Thumrayt to Salalah. In the heat of the moment, each squadron backed its own aircraft to the tune of 20 crates of champagne. In the cold light of day the rules of the contest were worked out. Each pilot would be in flying gear, and was allowed one 'helper' and a vehicle at either end. The engines would be running, the Huey outside the mess and the Hunter at the end of the runway, 2,500 yards (2,300 m) away across the *bundu*.

Aside from the fact that it was suspected the Hunter pilot omitted to strap in (he just wound the hood and the throttle forwards), this might have been a perfectly straightforward contest. However, someone on the rotary-wing side had the bright idea to radio Salalah that there was an unidentified aircraft in the area, that it could be hostile, and on no account was it to be allowed to land. The Iranians accordingly manned the AAA, and the Hunter was forbidden to approach the airfield. Ignoring the risk of being shot down by his own flak, the pilot landed, jumped in the waiting Land Rover, and was pursued back to the mess by another Land Rover full of Iranian soldiers intent on arresting him. There was a potentially dangerous situation at the finishing post, with men milling around waving SLRs and 9 mm Brownings.

However, it eventually cooled down and the Hunter was declared the winner, though not without some complaints from the Huey squadron.

The sequel came next day, when the CO of the Hunter Squadron was obliged to eject two miles (3.2 km) off the enemy coastline at Hauf. The story goes that no sooner was he in the water than a Huey appeared, equipped with a loud-hailer, from which he heard the message: *'If you want to be picked up, you buy half the champagne!'*

Rhodesia

In terms of sorties flown and ordnance expended, there is little doubt that the COIN war in Rhodesia (1972–79) was the largest-scale action in which the Hunter has yet taken part. The government of Ian Smith had made a unilateral declaration of independence (UDI) in November 1965, but it was only in late 1972 that a major insurgency broke out. The insurgent forces were known as the Patriotic Front (PF), combining Mugabe's Chinese-backed ZANLA and Nkomo's Soviet-backed ZIPRA. The ZANLA forces were supported from bases in Mozambique and Tanzania, and those of ZIPRA from Angola, Botswana, and Zambia.

The Rhodesian Air Force (RhAF) consisted of eight squadrons, equipped with Hunters, Vampires, light transports, Cessna 337s with armament provisions, Canberras, SF.260s, Alouette IIIs, and Bell 205s.

The 12 Hunter FGA.9s supplied in 1963 formed No 1 Sqn, with the motto *'Speed and Courage'*. They were based in the centre of the country, at Gwelo (now renamed Gweru). The Hunters used 30 mm cannon and 68 mm SNEB rockets to good effect, but it was found that the standard British 1,000 lb (454 kg) GP bomb tended to bury itself in the ground and simply throw dirt upward in a narrow cone. Some special weapons were developed to overcome this problem, the Hunters mainly using the 1,000 lb (454 kg) blast weapon termed the Golf bomb. This was approximately 5 ft (1.52 m) long and 18 inches (45.7 cm) in diameter. The filling was Amatol, which the RhAF referred to as 'Anfo'. In the tradition of US 'daisy-cutters', the Golf bomb had a three-foot (0.9 m) rod projecting from the nose to ensure detonation above the ground. The standard attack procedure was to release two bombs simultaneously in a 60° dive, one being retarded by drag plates so that there was a slight separation in impact time and position. Blast kills were achieved out to 100–165 ft

(30–50 m) with some fragmentation kills further out.

Toward the end of the fighting the Rhodesians developed a flèchette bomb holding 4,600 darts, rather like nails with plastic tails. Dropped in a low level pass at 450 knots (835 km/hr), the darts covered an ellipse 350 ft (110 m) long and 100 ft (30 m) wide. Intended for use in night attacks on insurgent camps for maximum psychological effect, they were in fact used only twice. On one of these occasions a strike was made on a group of 26 ZANLA insurgents, of whom 16 were killed.

For air defence the insurgents had automatic weapons of 7.62, 12.7 and 14.5 mm, and later the SA-7 missile. This appeared first in the defence of bases in Zambia and Mozambique, which also had three-barrel 20 mm flak and some 23 mm. These external bases had radar, but the RhAF was never clear whether this was used solely for warning of attacks, or for gun-laying. The first in-country use of the SA-7 came on 3 September 1978, when a ZIPRA unit shot down an Air Rhodesia Viscount taking off from Kariba. On 12 February 1979 the same insurgents shot down a second Viscount with an SA-7.

There were two principal means by which the RhAF could kill insurgents: by attacking their small encampments within Rhodesia, and by making major strikes against larger camps over the border. In both types of attack, aerial reconnaissance played a vital role, groups of insurgents being located primarily from photographs, usually taken from low-level Hunters or Canberras at altitude. Additional information was obtained by searching and interrogating captured insurgents, many of whom had kept diaries.

In-country strikes were generally based on information supplied by radio from observation posts (OPs), giving a description of the target and its location to within 660 ft (200 m). Pilots navigated by compass and stopwatch using quarter-million scale maps and instructions from the OP relating target position to prominent ground features. This procedure worked well, aside from in forested areas in the south, which lacked such features.

The first aircraft at the target would be a Cessna 337, approaching low, and popping up to mark it with smoke. Other Cessnas would drop 82 lb (37 kg) blast bombs, while the Alouettes would orbit the target, firing their 20 mm GIAT M.621 cannon. Alternatively, if the insurgents were in a good defensive position, the Cessna would act as FAC,

and the attack would be carried out by Hunters and Canberras. Bell 205s would then land 'stop-lines' of 12-man sections of troops, supplemented by more distant stop-lines of paratroops dropped from C-47s.

These 'Fire-Force' actions were effective, but results on a large scale could be achieved only by cross-border raids, known as 'externals'. These also provided the opportunity to capture guerilla leaders, equipment, and documents. To give some indication of the scale of such operations, some 300 guerillas were killed in a raid into Mozambique in August 1974, and 1,200 in a similar raid in November 1977. The biggest single result was 1,500 killed in a raid into Zambia in response to the destruction of the civil Viscount in September 1978. The most distant 'external' took place on 26 February 1979 on a ZIPRA base in Angola, some 540 nm (1,000 km) from the Rhodesian border.

In these 'externals' warning of attack was minimized by the Hunters approaching at 20,000 ft (6,100 m) and descending quietly to make dive attacks with Golf bombs. As a second wave, Canberras would approach at low level with fragmentation bombs. The Rhodesians developed their own fragmentation weapon, known as the Alpha bomb. Constructed of two concentric spheres, separated by rubber balls, the Alpha bomb would provide a wide coverage through the use of large numbers, and achieved effectiveness by exploding at 6–12 ft (1.8–3.65 m) above the ground. Up to 300 Alpha bombs could be carried in six dispensers within the Canberra bomb-bay.

For deep penetrations and 'externals' in bad visibility, the Canberras went in first to take advantage of their better navigation aids. For strikes on Zambian camps, Hunters were also used to provide fighter escort against Zambian AF MiG-19s, but in fact no air opposition was encountered.

It was originally anticipated that the SA-7 would be a major threat to air operations, but a cross-border raid into Mozambique resulted in the capture of a number of SA-7 launch units and operating manuals. These manuals quoted a maximum target speed of 420 knots (780 km/hr), and warned that the missile was prone to home on to the sun or brightly-illuminated clouds.

The information obtained in this operation allowed defensive measures to be developed for all the aircraft used against the insurgents. In the case of the Hunter, the plan was to stay above the missile's critical target speed, or to stay out of range, or above 15,000 ft (4,600 m). If an SA-7 was fired against a Hunter, the pilot had to pull 6G–7G, which put it in a turn that the missile could not follow. Slower aircraft relied on extremely low flying and IR-suppression, including the use of special paints.

In the course of the war, around a dozen aircraft were lost due to ground fire, and only two of these were shot down by the SA-7 (both slow-flying AL-60FS aircraft). Only two Hunters were shot down, one due to small arms and the other due to 30 mm AAA.

In the eyes of the RhAF, they were winning the war against the insurgents, but there was no defence against external economic measures. The Lancaster House Agreement was signed in London on 21 December 1979, leading to a cease-fire seven days later. Elections in the following February led to a coalition government under Mugabe, and formal independence on 17 April 1980. Some 30,000 insurgents handed in their weapons.

Saudi Arabia

Sporadic fighting broke out between Saudi Arabia and the Yemen in 1962. Egypt (then under President Nasser) provided Il-28 light bombers and MiG-17s to the revolutionary government of North Yemen, and these aircraft began to intrude into Saudi airspace, sometimes flown by Soviet crews.

There began to be occasional bombing and strafing attacks on Saudi villages close to the border. The Royal Saudi Air Force therefore decided to buy a batch of Lightnings and Thunderbird SAMs, with four single-seat Hunter F.6s and two T.7s as an interim measure.

The supply of British fighters began in 1966, the Hunters being flown to Riyadh airfield, near the Saudi capital. They were then moved down to Taif for tactical training, prior to establishing No 6 Sqn at Khamis-Mushayt in the south-west of the country, close to the Yemeni border. Servicing was performed by Airwork Services, the main problem being spares shortages. Khamis is 47 nm (87 km) from the border, and has a runway length of almost 10,000 ft (3,000 m), but is 6,600 ft (2,000 m) above sea level, and at 90° to the prevailing wind.

The first Lightnings arrived in August 1967. The Hunters and Lightnings appear to have fulfilled their main purpose, in that attacks on Saudi villages stopped as soon as these aircraft arrived at Khamis, although occasional intrusions continued. The 'Magic Carpet' Operation, in which British personnel provided a stop-gap air defence system for Saudi Arabia, terminated at the end of March 1968. The Hunters were subsequently maintained by Pakistan Air Force engineers, assisted by Airwork, until these aircraft were donated to Jordan in 1969.

Chapter 13

The Final Analysis

The Hawker Hunter is one of the best-looking, most useful and popular combat aircraft ever built, and as such it represents a milestone in fighter development. In practical terms, its principal features have been its heavy firepower, immensely strong structure, and its operational flexibility, allowing it to be deployed to overseas theatres in both the ground attack and air defence roles. Even today, almost 40 years after the P.1067 first flew, a Hunter simply updated with four Aden 25 cannon would still be a fearsome adversary. Singapore has demonstrated the Hunter's continuing value in the ground attack role.

From a designer's viewpoint, the Hunter was the classic example of a Hawker fighter. It was an aeroplane over which countless hours had been spent in refining its lines until there emerged a shape that chiefs of air staff would instantly fall in love with. Aerodynamically, it was streets ahead of the simple Sabre, the Hunter's careful integration of fuselage, wings and intakes maximizing isobar sweep and thus delaying the drag rise.

Where the F-86 excelled was its systems, especially its flying tail. Longitudinal control was one of the Hunter's major shortcomings. Even when it acquired an electrically-activated follow-up tailplane, longitudinal control was poor at high Mach No. The other principal fault was that the Hunter was catastrophically short of internal fuel, though this was the direct result of the RAF's *'straight up, straight down'* interception philosophy of the 1950s. One cannot criticize the Hunter in this respect without mentioning the stupidity and ignorance of the OR Branch, who evidently dreamed that it was possible to combine the endurance of a Sabre with the climb performance of a stripped Venom.

The airbrake affair, which delayed the Hunter's entry into service, was never really satisfactorily resolved. The final airbrake configuration could not be used in landing, and in effectiveness was poor in comparison with that of the preceding Meteor. In rear view the Hunter was certainly inferior to the Sabre, though this difference reflected their design roles as much as anything else. The Sabre pilot risked being shot in the back; the Hunter pilot was more at risk from a Tu-16 disintegrating immediately in front of him, at least as far as the planners were concerned.

The Hunter's vertical tail was almost certainly on the small side, and directional stability in turbulence was poor, although a yaw damper brought a little improvement. The airframe was far heavier than it should have been, although some of this extra weight paid off in terms of an outstanding fatigue life.

One striking facet of the Hunter is the vast difference in design philosophy between it and the Hawk trainer, which emerged from the same stable 23 years later. The Hunter began life with no fuel in the wing, whereas the Hawk has around half its fuel in integral wing tanks. The Hunter fighter started out with no provisions for external loads, while the Hawk trainer from the outset had five hardpoints, each designed for a 1,000 lb (454 kg) bomb. Kingston did not learn as much as it should have done from marketing the Hunter, but at least we had learned about operational flexibility.

The Hunter's switch to the ground attack role brought more problems, although it was in these duties that the aircraft was to excel. The Hunter's inboard pylons were set too close to the main undercarriage to permit the use of twin-store carriers. The outer pylons were set too far out, in a high-drag region that gave very little range improvement from the carriage of drop tanks, and too great a pitching moment on bomb release to permit a wide speed range in this form of attack. As the aircraft's armament capacity grew, the Hunter's cockpit became a chaotic mess, with switches added wherever there was space, and variations in armament panel layout.

Many of those connected with the Hunter programme regretted that various developments were never funded, either because the RAF regarded the aircraft from 1960 as 'an old workhorse with only two years left', or because HSA pushed the V/STOL concept at the expense of the Hunter. Many regretted that a supersonic thin-wing Hunter was never built. Neville Duke regrets that the Two-Seater did not have tandem seating. Many feel it was a mistake that RAF Hunters never had Sidewinder. The later 'Charlie' Cray would doubtless shake his head over the fact that only the Singaporeans have centreline stores. This writer will always regret that we never stretched the aircraft at the front transport joint to give it the internal fuel capacity it deserved, revised the gunpack to two guns with enlarged shell-boxes, and installed the Avon 301. In the context of 'the Hunters that never were', it is worth recording that quite late in the day we were talking of re-opening the Hunter line. On this writer's recollections, the idea was to keep the F-5E out of Switzerland until we had a Harrier worth buying.

This writer discussed the Hunter on many occasions with 'Bill' Bedford, who was CTP at Dunsfold from 1956 to 1967, and is probably better qualified than anyone else to comment from a pilot's viewpoint on the Hunter that actually got built. He felt that essentially it had the right combination of wing loading and thrust/weight ratio, making it exhilarating to fly. Bedford approved of its 'beautiful lines and thoroughbred character'. In his view, it was 'a friendly aeroplane: it didn't want to spin'.

On the subject of longitudinal control, Bedford admitted that some pilots felt it 'a bit light, especially the Mk 6 at high IAS'. 'At high Mach, the rate of G application left a lot to be desired'. 'The flaps provided a useful lift and drag at combat speeds, but at really high speeds the nose-down trim was certainly excessive: above Mach 0.9 it couldn't be held'.

In Bedford's view, the aircraft needed a slab tail and duplicated hydraulics. The facility for manual reversion, which might have been useful in war, meant that pilots had to train to fly both in 'power' and 'manual', which was an undesirable complication. Directionally, 'perhaps it needed a little stiffening up'. Turning to relatively minor points, Bedford criticised the slow rate of undercarriage retraction, and the fact that the control column grip obscured the compass.

In ground attack, Bedford rated the Hunter much higher than the contemporary 'lead-sled' F-84F. In air combat, he felt that the Hunter was good for its generation. 'It was forgiving, but in a low-speed scissors it could diverge into a partial spin, though it came out when the pilot relaxed the controls'. He also recalled a competitive sortie flown from Gutersloh by the Hunter and F-100. In contrast to the Hunter's self-contained starting system, the F-100 had a huge external starter, so its engine had to be wound up in advance. The signal was given, and the Hunter had already disappeared into the 2,000 ft (600 m) cloudbase while the F-100 was still on the runway, though the situation was reversed at 38,000 ft (11,600 m).

The Hunter certainly had its faults, but in its heyday there was no other aircraft to rival its combination of good looks, firepower, operational flexibility, sheer strength, and safe fatigue life. For Hawker Aircraft the Hunter was the end of the line, but in its ultimate fighter the company had produced an aircraft that will long be remembered as one of the most beautiful designs of all time, and as the favourite mount of many hundreds of fighter pilots around the world.

Abbreviations

AAA	anti-aircraft artillery
AAC	Army Air Corps
A&AEE	Aeroplane and Armament Experimental Establishment
ADF	automatic direction finding (radio compass)
AEW	airborne early warning
AFB	air force base
AFDS	Air Fighting Development Squadron
AFME	Air Forces, Middle East
AI	air interception (radar)
AJ	axial-flow jet engine (R-R)
AOA	angle of attack
API	armour-piercing/incendiary
ATAF	Allied Tactical Air Forces
AWA	Armstrong Whitworth Aircraft
BAC	British Aircraft Corporation
BAe	British Aerospace
BAF	Belgian Air Force
BTH	British Thomson-Houston
C(A)	Controller (Air)
CFE	Central Fighter Establishment
CG	centre of gravity
CO	commanding officer
COIN	counter-insurgency
CTP	chief test pilot
DArm	Director of Armaments
DFLS	Day Fighter Leader School
DGTD(A)	Director General of Technical Development (Air)
DME	distance measuring equipment
DO	design office, or drawing office
DR	dead reckoning
DWP	Defence White Paper
DZ	dropping zone
EAS	equivalent airspeed
ECM	electronic countermeasures
ECU	engine change unit
ETPS	Empire Test Pilots' School
EW	electronic warfare
FAA	Fleet Air Arm
FAC	forward air control(ler)
FACH	*Fuerza Aerea de Chile*
Flak	*Flugabwehrkanone* (AAA)
FOD	foreign object damage
FRADU	Fleet Requirements and Air Direction Unit

GA	general arrangement
GCA	ground-controlled approach
GE	General Electric
GGS	gyro gunsight
GP	general purpose
GW	guided weapon
HAL	Hawker Aircraft Ltd
HSA	Hawker Siddeley Aviation
HUD	head-up display
IAF	Indian Air Force
IAS	indicated airspeed
ICAO	International Civil Aviation Organization
IFF	identification, friend or foe
IMN	indicated Mach No
IPN	iso-propyl nitrate
ITP	instruction to proceed
JATO	jet-assisted take-off
MDAP	Mutual Defence Aid Programme
MEWSG	Maritime Electronic Warfare Support Group
MoD	Ministry of Defence
Mod	modification
MoS	Ministry of Supply
MSA	Mutual Security Agency
MU	Maintenance Unit
NAS	Naval Air Station
NPL	National Physical Laboratory (Teddington)
OCU	Operational Conversion Unit
OP	observation post
OR	operational requirement
ORP	operational readiness platform
PAF	Pakistan Air Force
PF	Patriotic Front
PFCU	powered flying control unit
PFLO	Popular Front for the Liberation of Oman
PIO	pilot-induced oscillation
PR	public relations
PRO	Public Record Office
psi	pounds/square inch
P&W	Pratt & Whitney
QGH	course to airfield

RAE	Royal Aircraft Establishment
RAF	Royal Air Force
RARDE	Royal Armament Research & Development Establishment
RATO	rocket-assisted take-off
RCL	recoilless
R&D	research and development
RhAF	Rhodesian Air Force
RLM	*Reichsluftministerium*
RNAF	Royal Netherlands Air Force
RP	rocket projectile
RPE	Rocket Propulsion Establishment
rpm	revolutions per minute
R-R	Rolls-Royce
RRAF	Royal Rhodesian Air Force
R/T	radio telephone
RWR	radar warning receiver
SAM	surface-air missile
SBAC	Society of British Aerospace Companies Ltd
sfc	specific fuel consumption
SLR	self-loading rifle
SOAF	Sultan of Oman's Air Force
TAS	true airspeed
t/c	thickness/chord ratio
TET	turbine entry temperature
TI	trial installation
TMN	true Mach No
TWU	Tactical Weapons Unit
UHF	ultra high frequency
USAAF	United States Army Air Force
VHF	very high frequency
V/STOL	vertical or short take-off and landing

Appendix 1: MoS Form 2110 Data

Hunter type		F.1	F.2	F.3	F.4	F.6
Powerplant		RA.7	Sa.6	RA.7R	RA.7	RA.28
Maximum thrust	(lb)	7,500	8,000	9,500	7,500	10,000
	(kg)	3,400	3,628	4,310	3,400	4,535
Clean TOW	(lb)	16,350	16,300	17,850	17,000	17,400
	(kg)	7,415	7,392	8,095	7,710	7,891
Internal fuel	(Imp gal)	330	310	400	410	390
	(litres)	1,500	1,410	1,818	1,863	1,773
Maximum speed*	(knots)	524	527	542	522	527
	(km/hr)	971	977	1,004	967	976
Rate of climb*	(ft/min)	1,150	1,600	2,800	1,000	1,700
	(m/sec)	5.84	8.13	14.23	5.08	8.64
1,000 ft/min	(ft)	45,900	47,800	50,700	45,000	47,500
(5.08 m/sec) height	(m)	14,000	14,575	15,455	13,720	14,480
Time to 45,000 ft (13,700 m)	(min)	11.65	9.3	5.7	12.5	7.1
Take-off to 50 ft	(ft)	4,900	5,450	4,550	5,100	3,900
(15 m)	(m)	1,495	1,660	1,387	1,555	1,189
Landing from 50 ft	(ft)	5,800	5,800	5,800	5,800	5,800
(15 m)	(m)	1,770	1,770	1,770	1,770	1,770

* at 45,000 ft (13,700 m)

Specification

Hawker Hunter FGA Mk9

Type: single-seat ground attack aircraft with secondary air-air capability

Powerplant: one 10,150 lb (4,603 kg) Rolls-Royce Avon Mk 207 non-afterburning turbojet

Dimensions: span 33 ft 8 in (10.27 m); length 45 ft 10.5 in (13.99 m); height 13 ft 4 in (4.06 m); wing area 349 ft² (32.43 m²); wing thickness/chord ratio 8.5 per cent (constant); sweep 40° at quarter-chord line; aspect ratio 3.33

Design load factor: +7.5G

Weights:

basic	14,530 lb (6,590 kg)
internal fuel	3,081 lb (1,397 kg)
ammunition	582 lb (264 kg)
clean gross	18,373 lb (8,332 kg)
maximum gross	24,422 lb (11,076 kg) ferry configuration

Armament: four 30 mm Aden cannon with 135 rounds per gun, in an easily removable package. The aircraft is normally flown with two 230 Imp gal (1,045 litre) combat tanks on the inboard pylons and two Matra batteries of 68 mm SNEB rockets (19 per pod) outboard

Performance: (in standard atmospheric conditions)

maximum level speed	Mach 0.92 at sea level Mach 0.945 at 36,080 f (11,000 m)

maximum sea level rate of climb 16,500 ft/min (84 m/sec)

service ceiling 47,000 ft (14,330 m)

take-off ground roll (clean) 1,950 ft (600 m)

landing roll (with parachute) 2,200 ft (670 m)

HI-LO-HI radius of action 545 nm (1,000 km) for strafing, or 385 nm (715 km) with eight three-inch (76 mm) RPs.

Appendix 2: Hunter Weights

Aircraft Type	Basic Weight	Clean Gross
F.1	12,648 lb (5,736 kg)	16,145 lb (7,322 kg)
F.4	13,250 lb (6,009 kg)	17,265 lb (7,830 kg)
F.6	14,122 lb (6,405 kg)	17,910 lb (8,122 kg)
T.7	13,497 lb (6,121 kg)	17,225 lb (7,812 kg)
T.8	13,482 lb (6,114 kg)	17,210 lb (7,805 kg)
FGA.9	14,572 lb (6,609 kg)	18,360 lb (8,327 kg)
FR.10	15,346 lb* (6,960 kg)*	24,415 lb (11,072 kg)
GA.11 (pre-Mod 228)	12,767 lb (5,790 kg)	16,145 lb (7,322 kg)
GA.11 (post-Mod 228)	13,322 lb (6,042 kg)	16,700 lb (7,574 kg)
PR.11	13,292 lb (6,028 kg)	16,670 lb (7,560 kg)
Mk 12	14,462 lb (6,559 kg)	17,840 lb (8,091 kg)
T.66	14,663 lb (6,650 kg)	18,365 lb (8,329 kg)

Notes: * indicates that the company's records give the FR.10 with two 230 Imp gal (1,045 litre) and two 100 Imp gal (455 litre) drop tanks.

Ballast was carried as follows: 200 lb (91 kg) in FGA.9, 433 lb (196 kg) in pre-Mod 228 GA.11, 852 lb (386 kg) in post-Mod 228 GA.11, and 727 lb (330 kg) in PR.11.

Note also that there are inevitably minor inconsistencies in the figures quoted for Hunter weights, since:

a) aircraft weight varied with modification standard

b) there are differences over usable fuel volume

c) fuel weight was based on a density varying between 7.7 and 8.0 lb/Imp gal (0.77–0.80 kg/litre).

d) the ammunition weight was initially 676 lb (307 kg), based on 150 rounds per gun. It was later found that the feed performed more reliably if each gun was limited to 135 rounds, reducing ammunition weight to 608 lb (276 kg).

Appendix 3: Weight Breakdown for Hunter F.6

		lb	kg
Structure:	Mainplane	2,807	(1,273)
	Fuselage	1,640	(744)
	Tail	524	(238)
	Undercarriage	850	(385)
	Total:	5,820	(2,640)
Powerplant:	Engine	2,860	(1,297)
	Mounting	50	(23)
	Jetpipe	206	(93)
	Accessories	380	(172)
	Fuel tanks	475	(215)
	Fuel system	376	(171)
	Total:	4,350	(1,971)
Services:	Flying controls	280	(127)
	Hydraulics, Pneumatics	320	(145)
	Seat, misc.	350	(159)
	Total:	950	(431)
Armament:		1,900	(862)
Operational equipment:	Electrics	710	(322)
	Instruments	104	(47)
	Oxygen	50	(23)
	Avionics	324	(147)
	Fire precautions	109	(49)
	Misc military load	94	(43)
	Total:	1,391	(631)
BASIC WEIGHT		14,416	(6,535)
Pilot		180	(82)
Fuel		3,000	(1,361)
Contingency		54	(24)
CLEAN TAKE-OFF WEIGHT		17,650	(8,002)

Appendix 4: Hunter Service in the Royal Air Force

RAF Sqn	Hunter Mk	Service Dates	Replacing/ Replaced By	Airfields Used
No 1	F.5	Sept 55–June 58	Meteor F.8/	Tangmere, Akrotiri, Stradishall
	F.6	July 58–June 60	Harrier GR.1	Waterbeach
	FGA.9	Mar 60–July 69		West Raynham
No 2	FR.10	Mar 61–Mar 71	Swift FR.5/ Phantom FGR.2	Jever Gutersloh
No 3	F.4	May 56–June 57	Sabre F.1, F.2/ Javelin FAW.4	Geilenkirchen
No 4	F.4	July 55–Feb 57	Sabre F.4/	Jever
	F.6	Feb 57–Dec 60	Harrier GR.1	Gutersloh
	FR.10	Jan 61–May 70		West Raynham
	FGA.9	Sept 69–Mar 70		
No 8	FGA.9	Jan 60–Dec 71	Venom FB.4 +	Khormaksar
	FR.10	Apr 61–May 63	Meteor FR.10/ (disbanded)	Muharraq Sharjah
No 14	F.4	May 55–Dec 62	Venom FB.1/	Oldenburg
	F.6	Apr 57–Dec 62	Canberra B(I).8	Ahlhorn Gutersloh
No 19	F.6	Oct 56–Nov 62	Meteor F.8/ Lightning F.2	Church Fenton Leconfield
No 20	F.4	Nov 55–Oct 57	Sabre F.2, F.4/	Oldenburg
	F.6	Aug 57–Dec 60	(disbanded)	Gutersloh
	FGA.9	Aug 61–Feb 70		Tengah
No 26	F.4	June 55–Sept 57	Sabre F.1, F.4/	Oldenburg
	F.6	June 58–Dec 60	(disbanded)	Gutersloh
No 28	FGA.9	May 62–Jan 67	Venom FB.4/ (disbanded)	Kai Tak
Mo 34	F.5	Feb 56–Jan 58	Meteor F.8/ (disbanded)	Tangmere

No 41	F.5	Aug 55–Jan 58	Meteor F.8/ Javelin FAW.4	Biggin Hill
No 43	F.1 F.4 F.6 FGA.9	Aug 54–Aug 56 Mar 56–Dec 56 Dec 56–1960 1960–Oct 67	Meteor F.8/ Phantom FG.1	Leuchars Nicosia Khormaksar
No 45	FGA.9	Aug 72–June 76	Reformed 1972/ (disbanded)	West Raynham Wittering
No 54	F.1 F.4 F.6 FGA.9	Mar 55–Oct 55 Sept 55–Jan 57 Jan 57–Mar 60 Mar 60–Sept 69	Meteor F.8/ Phantom FGR.2	Odiham Stradishall Waterbeach West Raynham
No 56	F.5 F.6	May 55–Nov 58 Nov 58–Jan 61	Swift F.1, F.2/ Lightning F.1A	Waterbeach Wattisham Nicosia
No 58	FGA.9	Aug 73–June 76	Reformed 1973/ (disbanded)	Wittering
No 63	F.6	1956–Oct 58	Meteor F.8/ (disbanded)	Waterbeach
No 65	F.6	Dec 56–Mar 61	Meteor F.8/ (disbanded)	Duxford
No 66	F.4 F.6	Mar 56–Oct 56 Oct 56–Sept 60	Sabre F.4/ (disbanded)	Linton-on-Ouse Acklington
No 67	F.4	Jan 56–Apr 57	Sabre F.1/ (disbanded)	Bruggen
No 71	F.4	Apr 56–Apr 57	Sabre F.1, F.4 (disbanded)	Bruggen
No 74	F.4 F.6	Mar 57–Jan 58 Nov 57–Nov 60	Meteor F.8 Lightning F.1	Horsham St Faith Coltishall
No 79	FR.10	Dec 60–Dec 60	Swift FR.5/ (renumbered No 4)	Gutersloh
No 92	F.4 F.6	Apr 56–May 57 Feb 57–Apr 63	Sabre F.4 Lightning F.2	Linton-on-Ouse Middleton St George Thornaby Leconfield

No 93	F.4	Jan 56–Feb 58	Sabre F.4	Jever
	F.6	Feb 58–Dec 60	(disbanded)	
No 98	F.4	Mar 55–July 57	Venom FB.1/	Jever
			(disbanded)	
No 111	F.4	Jan 55–Nov 56	Meteor F.8/	North Weald
	F.6	Nov 56–Apr 61	Lightning F.1A	Wattisham
No 112	F.4	Apr 56–May 57	Sabre F.4/	Bruggen
			(disbanded)	
No 118	F.4	Mar 55–July 57	Venom FB.1/	Jever
			(disbanded)	
No 130	F.4	Apr 56–May 57	Sabre F.4/	Bruggen
			(disbanded)	
No 208	F.5	Jan 58–Feb 58	Meteor FR.9/	Tangmere
	F.6	Jan 58–Mar 59	(disbanded)	Nicosia
				Eastleigh (Kenya)
	FGA.9	Mar 60–Sept 71		Stradishall
				Khormaksar
				Muharraq
No 222	F.1	Dec 54–Aug 56	Meteor F.8	Leuchars
	F.4	Aug 56–Nov 57	(disbanded)	
No 234	F.4	May 56–July 57	Sabre F.4	Geilenkirchen
			(disbanded)	
No 245	F.4	Mar 57–June 57	Meteor F.8/	Stradishall
			(disbAnded)	
No 247	F.1	June 55–July 55	Meteor F.8/	Odiham
	F.4	July 55–Mar 57	(disbanded)	
	F.6	Mar 57–Dec 57		
No 257	F.2	Sept 54–Mar 57	Meteor F.8/	Wattisham
	F.5	July 55–Mar 57	(disbanded)	
No 263	F.2	Feb 55–Oct 55	Meteor F.8	Wattisham
	F.5	Apr 55–Oct 57	(renumbered No 1)	Wymeswold
	F.6	Oct 57–July 58		Stradishall

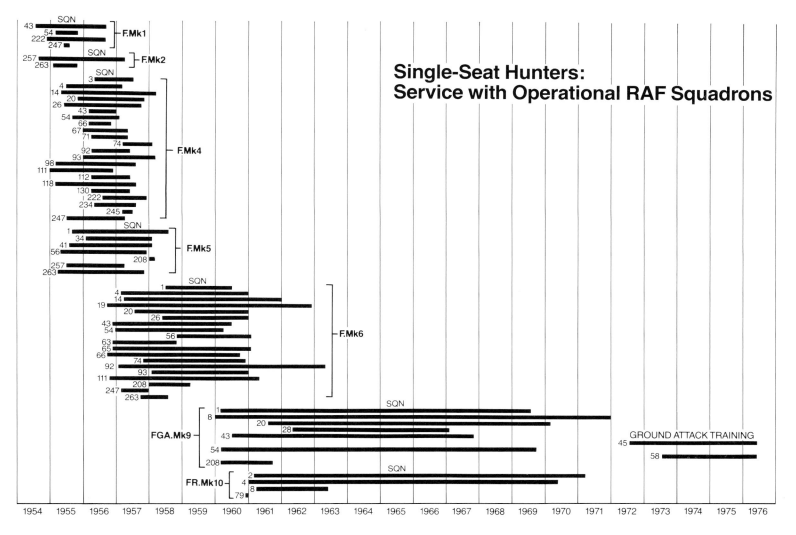

Single-Seat Hunters:
Service with Operational RAF Squadrons

Appendix 5: Notes on Hunter Production

Kingston: a total of 946 new-build Hunters were constructed at Kingston, of which 621 were for UK services and 325 were exports. In addition there were six prototypes (two F.1s, one F.2, one F.6, and two T.7s).

Peak annual production rate was 230 aircraft in 1956. Highest monthly rate was 19.2 aircraft, also achieved in 1956. Total UK quarterly rate peaked at 90 aircraft in the second quarter of 1955.

Blackpool: a total of 299 new-build Hunters were constructed at Blackpool, consisting of 26 F.1s, 177 F.4s and 96 Mk 50s.

Coventry: a total of 278 aircraft were constructed by AWA at Baginton, consisting of 45 F.2s, 105 F.5s and 128 F.6s.

Licence production: Belgium built 112 F.4s and 144 F.6s, and the Netherlands built 96 F.4s and 93 F.6s. These figures for the F.4 appear to include one aircraft for either country that was first built at Kingston.

The above figures give a total of 1,972 new-build Hunters, including the six prototypes. In addition there were 574 'conversions', of which 512 remained single-seaters, and 62 became Two-Seaters. At the bottom of the learning-curve, a new Hunter represented approximately 30,000 man-hours of work for the aircraft manufacturer.

Appendix 6: High Mach No Dives

The Hunter first went through the 'sound barrier' in June 1952, but it was to be another five years before its highest dive speed was achieved. In 1957 a series of high Mach No dives were made as part of a programme to check elevator strength, using three Mk 6s: XE587, XE588 and XF378. In the fastest of these dives the Mach meter showed a sudden jump in IMN from around 1.20 to 1.35. It was assumed that the jump was caused by the wingtip-mounted pitot-static head passing through the shock wave produced at the wing leading edge root. Further analysis (by Trevor Jordan) indicated that a speed of approximately 1.25 ·TMN had been attained. It is believed that the fastest dive was made by Hugh Merewether on 12 July 1957 in XE587. Merewether had previously zoomed the P.1109A to 55,000 ft (16,770 m) in May 1956, and was later to fly Hunter F.6 XF374 nonstop 1,609 nm (2,980 km) to El Adem in October 1958, hence it is probably true to say that he has flown the Hunter faster, higher and further than any other pilot.

Appendix 7: Rolls-Royce Avon Designations

In view of the possible confusion over the system of designations for Avon engines, the following notes have kindly been provided by Alec Harvey-Bailey on behalf of Rolls-Royce.
1. The basic design had a 12-stage axial-flow compressor, variable whirl on the inlet guide vanes, compressor bleed valves, and straight-through flame-tubes feeding a two-stage turbine.

The basic Hunter engine was the Mk 104 rated at 7,200 lb (3,265 kg) thrust at 7,950 rpm. The Mk 107 and Mk 113 had a similar rating but were mechanical variants, the latter having uprated turbine blade materials. The Mk 113–19 was the same engine operated by the Belgian Air Force.

The Mk 115 and its variants were RA.21s rated at 7,815 lb (3,545 kg) thrust at 7,950 rpm. The Mk 119 was an RA.7, but fitted with the gun-firing modifications. The Mk 120 and variants were RA.21s with gun-firing modifications. The Mk 121 was an RA.21 re-matched to 7,425 lb (3,367 lb) thrust at 8,100 rpm. The Mk 122 was similar, but with minor mechanical changes. The Mk 23, 23S, 24 and 24S were all RA.21s for the Swedish Air Force, the latter two having gun-firing modificatons. The Mk 25 and 25S were re-matched RA.21s with various mechanical modifications.

The Mk 110 with RA.7R rating introduced reheat for the record attempts.
2. The 200-series featured a 15-stage compressor, variable inlet whirl, bleed valves, and tubo-annular flame-tubes feeding a two-stage turbine. Engines for the Hunter started with the Mk 203 with an RA.28 rating of 9,950 lb (4,510 kg) thrust at 8,000 rpm. The Mk 207 was a high modification standard of the 203; the Mk 207C was for the Royal Jordanian Air Force.

Appendix 8: Hunter production by location

	Kingston	Baginton	Blackpool	Schipol	Gosselies		
Prototypes	6					Two F.1s, one F.2, one F.6, one T.7, one T.66	6
Hunter F.1	113		26				139
F.2		45					45
F.3						*1st Prototype Conv.	
F.4	190		177	111	95		573
F.5		105					105
F.6	255	128		144	93		620
T.7	45						45
(Holland) T.7	20						20
T.8	10						10
(Sweden) F.50	24		96				120
(Denmark) F.51	30						30
(Denmark) T.53	2						2
(India) F.56	145						145
(Swiss) F.58	88						88
(India) T.66	22						22
(Jordan) T.66B	2						2
	952	278	299	255	188		1,972

Index

Bold numbers denote illustrations